THE VIOLENCE MYTHOS

SUNY Series, The Margins of Literature
Mihai I. Spariosu

THE VIOLENCE MYTHOS

BARBARA WHITMER

State University of New York Press

AKM7591

Cover artwork: Andy Warhol, American 1930–1987. *Elvis I and II,* 1964. Left panel: silkscreen on acrylic. Right panel: silkscreen on aluminum. Art Gallery of Ontario, Toronto. Gift from the Women's Committee Fund, 1966.

Cover production: Charles Martin

Published by
State University of New York Press, Albany

For information, address State University of New York Press, State University Plaza, Albany, N.Y. 12246

Production by M. R. Mulholland
Marketing by Bernadette LaManna

Library of Congress Cataloging-in-Publication Data

Whitmer, Barbara, 1959–
    The violence mythos / Barbara Whitmer.
        p.   cm. — (SUNY series, the margins of literature)
    Includes bibliographical references and index.
    ISBN 0-7914-3517-2 (hc : alk. paper). — ISBN 0-7914-3518-0 (pb : alk. paper)
    1. Violence—History.   2. Violence in popular culture.
3. Violence—Psychological aspects.   I. Title.   II. Series.
HM283.W55   1997
303.6'09—dc21   96-51554
                                                                                     CIP

10 9 8 7 6 5 4 3 2 1

FOR MOM AND DAD

CONTENTS

ILLUSTRATIONS

PREFACE

The following investigation of violence from the perspectives of cultural history, cultural understanding, and interdependence in Western culture arises from my interests in human community, cultural values, and the beauty and connectedness of life. Growing up on a farm gave me an appreciation of human dependency on nature and vulnerability in the midst of its unpredictability. The rhythms of the seasons resonated in growth cycles of planting, cultivating, harvesting, and resting; mating, birth, growth, and death; and the quiet protracted time of taming, trust, and responsibility with animals. These cycles were enhanced by the sacred stories of the interconnectedness of life of the native Americans who were our neighbors.

Violence disrupts the connectedness of life. I experienced violence on the native American reservation where I went to school, where friends committed suicide or were beaten and lain unconscious on railroad tracks, left as dismembered remains. A friend's mother sometimes felt too "ill" to leave the house; her "illness" was husband battery. And there was a child, sodomized at barely six, who years later when affectionately asked to quiet down, would hug the wall and chant to himself, "I hate myself, I hate myself." University friends, so bright and yet so inclined to self-sabotage, struggled with the skeletons of incest. In Guatemala, I saw how nations struggling with the vultures of poverty and domestic terrorism continued to cultivate an endurance born of village values and tradition, similar to life on the reservation. Racism simply changed color and became more subtle in academic discrimination when I moved to the American South. The absence of ghettos in a sizeable Canadian city left me wondering how a border between countries with comparable standards of living could make such a difference.

There were continuities such as the recurrent reports in the media of the discovery of yet another woman's body. This cross-cultural phenomenon is now called "femicide," due to the high numbers of women killed by husbands or boyfriends. It appears to be a tragic result of cultural role changes in intimate relationships between men and women that increasingly rely upon the quality of emotional involvement instead of traditional dependency on a hero figure.

These varied, blatant enactments of violent behavior, inflicting pain and injury on another, and their discrete discriminatory cousins seemed to be the tip of an iceberg of a more comprehensive cultural acceptance and endorsement of violence as permissible behavior, with acceptance legitimated by beliefs entrenched by centuries of reinforcement.

Versed as I was in the "isms" of colonialism, classism, racism, sexism, speciesism, the insights offered by these discourses seemed insufficient. The remedies proposed by isms opponents seemed simply to switch places in a dynamic of victimizer-victim or depicted such beatific communality as to deny the rough edges of everyday life. These answers failed to go beyond the dynamic altogether, and, while condemning violence, retained an acceptance of the unfortunate inevitability of violence in their critiques. They failed to come to a more satisfactory understanding of violence from probing deeper than the apparent opposing differences in conflict.

To try to understand these cultural phenomena, I researched violence from an interdisciplinary perspective, and unacknowledged consistencies became apparent in the assumptions of the authors. The assumption of violence as innate and natural in a metanarrative of a violence mythos in Western culture included a mind/body split. A firm believer that self and cultural understanding come from our experiences, I began looking for clues as to what kind of experience would lead to such a split, that could then be externalized in dualistic cultural beliefs and attitudes that normalized violence. I found the answer in posttraumatic stress disorder, not surprisingly the psychoneurological result of violent traumatic experience.

The discourses of our self and cultural understandings are not transparent. Our participation in these discourses provides opportunities both for reinforcing habitual thought and action and for disclosing and replacing assumptions by creating new meanings and actions. Hence, our conventional understandings of violence are questioned to bring unreflected influences to awareness and to open possibilities for change.

Acknowledgments

The journey has been more than a thousand miles since I took the first step over a dozen years ago. It would not have been possible without the support and contributions of many colleagues and friends. Thank you to State University of New York Press and Joseph Natoli of Michigan State University for making this information publicly accessible. Gratitude is extended to the Art Gallery of Ontario for granting me the privilege of association with two of the most extraordinary artists of my lifetime, Andy Warhol and Elvis Presley; I am honored. I would like to thank Ron Perrin and Bill Chalupka of the University of Montana for their critical contributions to the text, and for their passion and commitment to intellectual exploration and integrity. Thank you to James P. Buchanan for his phenomenological exactitude. Gratitude is extended to Paul Gooch, Thomas McIntire, and Roger Hutchinson for their astute fairness and open-mindedness in seeing the project through its tumultuous seven years of research at the University of Toronto. James DiCenso and Rebecca Comay at the University of Toronto contributed painstaking content revisions and editorial readings of the text. Thank you to Richard Zaner at Vanderbilt University for cultivating my seedling "there's something more happening here" of violence. Gratitude is extended to Ray L. Hart of the University of Montana for inititating me to the profound richness of the religious imagination. For their intellectual encouragement, provocation, and rigor during my time at Vanderbilt University, I thank Sallie McFague, Charles Scott, and Alasdair MacIntyre. Thank you to Wendy Cukier for the opportunity to research and interview interactive multimedia executives in the emerging digital economy. Much appreciation is extended to Regina Grzywaczewska and Joy Walsh for their repeated technical assistance, and to Education Wife Assault for their research resources. Thank you to Julius Koerus for allowing me to include an excerpt from his 1945 unpublished manuscript, "To the West."

Thank you to my family, especially Clint Whitmer and Rita Whitmer for their creative contributions; and Patsy Hollingbery; Boone A. Whitmer; and my mother, Marilee Calk Whitmer, for their support and understanding during the convolutions of the research and discovery process. For the courage to continue to tell the truth as I saw it, I thank my deceased father, Boone W. Whitmer. Many friends provided support, comic relief, debate, and inspiration, including Tammy teWinkel, Elizabeth Campeau, Bonnie Zimmerman, Cynthia Reimers, Pat Cross Chamberlin, Gail Williams Cluff, Greg Fraser, Beverly Harrison, Russell Owen, Patty Jung, Phil and Laurie Barker, Maria Schiavone, Virginia Mak, Megan Williams, Caroline Davidson, Jane Tweeddale, Catherine and Bill Nelson, Blair Nonnecke, R. J. Cannon, Irvin Wolkoff, Dominic Richens, and Jacqueline Isaac. Thank you also to those previously or presently affiliated with the Dynamic Graphics Project at the University of Toronto: Kevin Schleuter, Michael Bonnell, Tom Milligan, Tracy Narine, Ron Baecker, Eugene Fiume, Marilyn Mantei, Andrew Clement, Hiroshi Ishii, Gordon Kurtenbach, Tim Brecht, George Drettakis, Chris DiGiano, the late-too-young (thanks for the midnight Jack Benny sessions when we were both laboring at the lab) Gary Hardock, Greg Chwelos and Mim Curtis, Garry Beirne and Anne Serazin, George Fitzmaurice, Paul Kabbash, and William Hunt, who provided technical and financial support as well as wit, empathy, raucous laughter, spontaneity, and wings. Thank you all, *ex animo.*

INTRODUCTION

What is *mythos*? Mythos is a pattern of beliefs that articulates, often symbolically, the prevalent attitudes in a culture. It is more than a single myth, which only tells one narrative or story.[1] Mythos is a collection of beliefs; a cultural mindset; the framework that expresses a pattern of beliefs, attitudes, behaviors, discourses, and practices in a society. *The violence mythos* is a collection of beliefs that articulates attitudes in Western culture about violence. Violence is defined as injurious or destructive discourse or action of one person or group toward another. The violence mythos includes the war hero myth, the victimizer/victim dynamic of exploitation, the mind/body dualism, the cowboy myth, the myth of competitive individualism, the theory of innate violence, the myth of male aggression, the military-industrial complex, technological determinism (especially destructive technology), the subordination of women, the myth of the superiority of rationality over emotion and creativity, and the myth of the elite human species. The violence mythos contains these shattered traces of trauma in the Western cultural imagination.

The relationship between human and community is expressed in a particular way in the violence mythos. At the core of the violence mythos is the belief that humans are innately violent and hence require external community structures to control them. The cultural system is then able to legitimate, rationalize, and use violence against "violent humans" as a means of social control. The cultural system thus becomes a self-reinforcing, self-perpetuating structure of using "violence to prevent violence."[2] The culture is able to subsume violence and destructive conflict under the rubris of cultural security and the protection of its citizens against themselves, in the name of cultural survival.

If one assumes a death instinct, an aggressive impulse, or innate violence, this dynamic of violence appears to be part of a repetitive "natural" order. If one questions innate violence and its requisite social control, then the legitimation of violence becomes suspect as a socially constructed justification for specific cultural values in a violence mythos.

If the assumptions underlying violence change, if it is redefined, then the assumptions underlying methods of deterrence and control also change. The systematic application of deterrence and social control relies upon a uniform definition of those who are controlled, that is, innately violent humans and all of the subgroups culturally stereotyped by degrees of violence according to sex, race, creed. If one changes the definition that shows humans *not* to be innately violent, then deterrence and social control are delegitimated and can no longer be applied in the same/Same systematic manner. The focus of deterrence and social control is shifted from violence as cause to violence as symptom. It does not mean the methods are destroyed; it means they are appropriately altered to address the issues behind the symptom.

Systemic applications of deterrence and social control include the obvious agents of social regulation and intervention, like the judicial, military, and civilian police systems. These are necessary structures in any culture, to maintain appropriate boundaries, to protect and enable the life that is a culture. However, the intricacies of social interaction hold within them powerful regulatory systems for social behavior and attitudes that act as the invisible arms of the laws of the land, both written and unwritten. Some of these invisible constraints are insidious, such as racism and sexism. These attitudes create confusing gaps in social reality between perceptions/proclamations of social beliefs as public knowledge articulated in written laws, that is, equality and the criminality of assault, and their contradictory practices/behaviors enacted through unwritten social norms, that is, racial discrimination and female assault.

Hence, systemic social control refers to a complex of social phenomena and the explicit and implicit applications of control to social/ human behavior within a culture. The violence mythos is a symbolic constellation of visible and invisible forms of social control in relation to violence, and their effects and the assumptions behind them as articulated in a pattern of cultural beliefs, attitudes, and behaviors.

The most recent cultural shift philosophically from the modern to postmodern and economically from the industrial to information eras has served as a watershed to place our attitudes about violence in perspective with, for instance, attitudes about women. In tandem with the shift from the industrial to information era, from centralized to decentralized production, over the past thirty years feminism has had a tremendous impact on our attitudes about women and men, decentralizing traditionally male-centered power. The public voice achieved by so many millions of women was not possible before the feminist movement. It has created a permanent shift in the dynamics of social relationships. Philosophically our ideas about women have changed. Questioning patriarchy allowed postmodernism to rattle the

rafters of almost every arché of institutions and legitimation of rationality. Yet our ideas about violence have changed so little, it has made
violence nearly immune to the postmodern probe, even accepted and
legitimated by it.

Within the discussion of the transition from centralization to
decentralization, there is a lacuna in cultural discourse about violence.
The Foucauldian observation that though Freudian psychoanalytic
theory discusses the repression of sexuality in society, simultaneously
sexuality is ubiquitously represented in advertising, film, and media is
helpful here. Although violence is condemned, at the same time it is
represented ubiquitously, in the media, the news, sports, entertainment, advertising, as conflict resolution, with a plethora of inadequate
measures for damage control in an age of the victimizer/victim and
an addiction to violence.

Looking for a language for the lacuna, my research hermeneutic
of discovery and development moves in five dimensions of cultural
discourse. Moving within the personal and the cultural spheres, this
process includes (1) the testimonial discourse of social participants; (2)
the language of somatic interchange between social participants; (3)
the interpretive structures or theories of individual and cultural discourse; (4) the prescriptive symbolic discourses of myth and ideology;
and (5) the historical tradition or paradigm of these discourses. The
last of these, the historical context, provides the grounds for continuity and the opening for change in reinterpreting tradition in new experience. Together, these five dimensions form the interpretive
infrastructure for beliefs, attitudes, and behaviors in cultural discourse.

Humans respond to and creatively initiate change in their environment. We constantly update our inner understanding and develop
neurologically, psychologically, emotionally, and experientially in the
processes of interaction with others and the world. We externalize and
negotiate our understandings to form collective understandings. Hence,
change and new values may influence self-understanding, behavior,
attitudes, social interaction, social theory, legitimation of authoritative
beliefs, and cultural tradition.

In this text, violence is investigated from a selection of texts that
represent the five different dimensions of the discourse infrastructure.
They will be interwoven throughout the text, with some discourses,
such as testimony and theory, juxtaposed to show the contrast between actual experience and abstract explanations of these experiences.
The discrepancies show how dominant beliefs intentionally or unin-
tentionally obscure and rationalize certain attitudes and behaviors.
They show the gap between the walk and the talk and what consti-

tutes the gap between them. Violence and social behavior are resignified in a reinterpretation of experience that reveals a consistent pattern of dynamics in Western culture, that of transgenerational trauma transference and its externalization in cultural attitudes and beliefs of innate violence legitimated in the violence mythos. Violence is the symptom; trauma is the problem. The latent tradition of holism and organicism is reappropriated in the trust triad of self, other, and world. This includes the integration of the somatic processes of respect, trust, and responsibility in a shift to an interdependent description of human community.

The violence mythos is a matrix of cultural discourse that influences institutions, symbolic discourse, beliefs, attitudes, and social practices. The violence mythos is based upon control as exploitive force, dualism, hierarchy, detachment, and the mind/body split, all abstracted elements of trauma experience and symbolized in a hero mythology. In contrast, the interdependent mythos matrix contains complex social processes that generate trust, reliability, freedom, consistency, continuity, and flexibility in somatic interchanges.

Violence is associated with beliefs grounded in social discourse and practices that have arisen from maladaptions to trauma, such as the equation of anger and violence. Cultural discourse can be opened to more accurate and sophisticated articulations of emotion and guides to ethical action based upon respect and trust. This resituates violence from innate trait to acquired behavior. Separating violence from anger means understanding anger as emotion and violence as learned behavior and one possible way to express anger.

The historical context of violence proceeds through an archeology of discourses, followed by cultural understandings of violence in theoretical discourses, and finally alternative discourses. We will work our way backward to see what possible historical influences may inform the discourses of violence in more recent periods.

In Western culture, the context and understanding of the person and community has shifted over time. The contemporary cultural shift is one from the centrality and homogeneity of mass values in supply-driven industrialism to the decentered plurality and particularity of individual and multicultural values in a consumer-driven information economy. Our global culture is multidimensional; we can talk about the radical encounter between the creationist religions of Judaism, Christianity, and Islam with the Asian religions of Hinduism, Buddhism, Confucianism, Taoism, and Shintō; the political shift from nationalism to global regionalism; the social shift from the paternal nuclear family to single-parent or same-sex-partner families.

In conjunction with industrialism, the modern, scientific/industrial vision saw the world as a binary division between spirit and matter. An emphasis on the natural sciences created an understanding of the material world as a machine governed by quantitative laws.[3] The cultural shift to the postmodern is a transition to holism and nonhierarchical participatory relationships in an age of creation/communication and complexity management in worldwide dialogue.[4] The industrial ethic of control by domination centralized authority and knowledge in institutions. The information ethic of postindustrial countries has diversified accessibility of customizable information to a plurality of decision makers.

From a political perspective, those discriminated against and traumatized by centralized control in classism, racism, sexism, and speciesism have made themselves visible and audible, gaining a place in public awareness. For instance, Judith Lewis Herman identifies three ongoing political movements since the nineteenth century associated with resolving psychological trauma. These are the establishment of secular democracy, the abolition of war, and the liberation of women.[5] However, this cacophony of voices of difference seems to be a disharmonious aggravation and threat to those whom status and privilege or the promise thereof, have provided a buffer. These conflicting interests make themselves visible in backlashes of extremism and resistance to change, using resentments and nostalgia to fuel insecurities and protectionism. For those working to relieve injustice and suffering, the gains of recognition are mixed with the hostility of those who fear losing the benefits of position. Western culture has primarily resolved such conflicts through violence or force. The cessation of the predilection to use violence for conflict resolution, for understanding difference, is part of the shift from the violence mythos to the interdependent mythos.

The critique of the violence mythos displaces both the mind/body dualism and the reification of social reality as a natural ordering of laws of the universe. This reification was forged in the era of the mechanical concept of the universe and extended to the economics of the industrial revolution. Mechanical scientific laws were described by scientists motivated by an attempt to "think God's thoughts after him"[6] and were paralleled in the economic laws of supply and demand with Adam Smith's market mechanism of the invisible hand. The British "came to regard the international division of labor and free exchange of commodities as part of providential dispensation."[7] Aided by the idealist assumption of a universal rationality, individuals as mass consumers were considered motivated by presupposed needs, wants, and desires in a homogenous capacity for self-interest.

This was the rule of the Same, the rule of mass production and consumption. The mechanical social stasis and fascination with techno-scientific progress and profit were critiqued in the nineteenth and early twentieth centuries by Karl Marx, Friederich Nietzsche, and Sigmund Freud, the masters of suspicion. They indicated that all was not as progressive as it appeared, that the invisible hand may be underhanded, and that all was not well in the industrial era. In the twentieth century, members of the Frankfurt School characterized monopoly capitalism as an administration of instrumental rationality.[8] For L. S. Stavrianos, the awakening from the mass somnambulance in the free market system by colonial peoples since 1914 was due to mounting internal contradictions and conflicts within monopoly capitalism.[9]

In this context of the social critique of industrialism, Freud situated internal contradictions and conflicts in the individual at the turn of the twentieth century in his novel concept of an unconscious part of the mind, which influences conscious thought. This introduced the idea that the human mind was not transparent to itself, that it could not be certain of pure knowledge and objectivity of the external world because it could be informed by internal influences that were not part of conscious reflected thought. Previously, the philosophical conditions for a shared reality had been grounded in the concept of a common pure realm of thought, where you and I understand each other because we can share the same pure understanding of a thing in the world in our pure capacities for understanding. The unconscious subverted this idea.

There was a turn to language where words were signs of things, as the basis of a shared reality and understanding. Here I can talk about my interpretation of a thing from my experience, and you can as well. We do not have the same experience of a thing, for that is not physically possible because you and I are in different bodies. We do share language, the capacity to signify, through exacting words, ingrained social protocols, an opera aria, the flow of a brushstroke, the private language of lovers. We share the capacity to communicate our different experiences of reality. We do not share the same experience, nor the same reality. We share the capacity to express somatic language. These expressions are discourses that enhance our similar understandings of our perceived realities. This is the linguistic turn toward the particularity of symbolic language and praxis that constitutes a shared human reality in the sphere of human discourse and action.[10]

The concept of mass consumers with universal presupposed interests represented in the one-size-fits-all marketplace changed. It became a plurality of consumers who could no longer assume that everyone was the same as them, and so needed to obtain information about and from the other in order to interact with the other. Similarly, producers needed to make products for consumers who had their own particular histories which shaped their needs, interests, and wants. Satisfaction and interaction thus rely less upon the equation between "mass" interest and "mass" product than upon the information that informs the decision making which shapes a person's interest and the information which permits the customization of a product to fit that particular interest. In contrast to the labor and raw-material-resource-intensive industrial economy, information and its distribution becomes its own product and the basis for other products.

This is part of the transition from modern to postmodern thought in a nutshell and is not meant to be exhaustive. However, what has not made the transition is the idea that like a capacity for pure thought, humans have a capacity for pure violence, or rather, that violence was innate to humans. Freud articulated this as an aggressive impulse. This assumption is left over from the model of the self-interested consumer, where violence would be like one more presupposed "interest" constitutive of humans, that we are born with, and need the right "market" to express this innate aggression and regulate it with an "invisible hand" of social prohibition. This is the basis of a cathartic theory of aggression.

Akin to the doubtful transparency of the conscious mind, the imperviousness of violence as an independent human motivation is as doubtful. To make the transition from violence as part of the modern cookie-cutter typology of humans, talk about violence in this book is placed in the context of history, signification, and experiences in a postmodern socially constructed reality.

We can discuss the forms of consensus agreements around the meaning and definition of violence. Individual and collective values and interests that focus upon violence enter first into the use of symbolic language, an act of conversation with diverse participants. The conversation that ensues *is* a collective. Those who are not part of the conversation are by virtue of their absence silent partners. A lesson of deconstruction attempts to recognize the marginalization of the silent by instantiating plurality and otherness.

A form of consensus, head counting, results in the formation of cultural discourse and action as values, morals, beliefs, knowledge, and institutions. These are conscious agreements about how participants conduct themselves in relation to other participants, and agreements about what to do if these agreements or rules are not followed. These agreements are usually made public knowledge as laws, judicial and legislative. There are other agreements made as a result of public consciousness raising, such as the feminist movement, where grass-roots changes in women's attitudes toward empowering themselves slowly influenced changes in social norms and laws.

There are also agreements that are a result of one's upbringing or tradition, religious or otherwise, which influence a person not necessarily through conscious consent, but through repetition and reinforcement in childhood and socialization and are enforced through social acceptance or ostracism. These may or may not be questioned and altered in adulthood. This type of consensus becomes an indirect acquiescence to particular agreements or assumptions as conventions through a willingness to engage in a given social practice.[11]

For example, in a liberal society, persons who "bargain in good faith" may not be aware of the assumptions behind the practices of a market economy. Through their participation, they have acted out a faith in the "interest-conscious individual, the moral autonomy of the will, the sanctity of contract, and the importance of utilitarian motives."[12] While persons may bring all sorts of attitudes to the bargaining process, what is not brought to negotiations is the set of ideas and norms which make up bargaining itself.[13]

Human forms of social order are a result of historical creative human interaction with parameters of acceptability and unacceptability, and tolerance and intolerance. Hence, the parameters of acceptability and tolerance that include violence also include historically created definitions of and assumptions about violence in that society. It is these definitions of violence and their attendant direct and indirect assumptions which are explicated in this text. It is my belief that to gain insight into that which is most unacceptable or intolerable for a society reflects more completely on the makeup of that which does not accept or tolerate. In mirroring the medusa, the golden opportunity for constructive critique and possible change arises.

The nature of human language reflects "the adequacy of its grammatical, lexical, or 'cultural' resources to the expression of complex philosophical, scientific, political, or moral ideas."[14] The use of language in speech and writing is the actualization of discourse as communication between participants. In this respect, "language is itself the process by which private experience is made public."[15] It is dynamic in at once representing and creating an understanding of human experience. Through discourse, the private experiences and public understandings of violence may become evident.

The five dimensions of discourse are interwoven in lexical and somatic language. Testimony relies upon available cultural symbols to orient a set of beliefs to order new experience and hence understand oneself. Analysis requires standards for the shared understanding of common experiences, and also the language of several testimonies to articulate a common understanding of experiences. Theory is a distillation and ordering of the varied understandings of analysis from which similar elements may be extracted. As well, cultural symbols rely upon the testimony of social participants to the symbols' validity of meaning in order to retain their authoritative influence within a society. At the same time, language itself is inherently symbolic in its mediative stance as metaphors describing what is experienced and to be understood by the human mind. The design of the paradigm includes facets of the other four forms of discourse, which taken together become an authoritative belief system and a cohesive element of a culture.

These discourses may be used to examine the institutions of a culture, as an infrastructure of discourses. Institutions are understood as loci of communication, information, and praxis with a defined set of goals and a degree of power accorded through social acceptance. Tracing the content of testimony, analysis, theory, symbol, and paradigm, we can begin to see the influences that shape collective institutions.

For instance, the events in the personal life of sixteenth-century Italian astronomer and physicist Galileo Galilei involved him in a struggle for freedom of thought, which became integral to his scientific and philosophical convictions, or testimony. These convictions were articulated in the analysis and discourse of science as support for the Copernican theory which asserted the motion of the earth and the stability of the sun and appeared to contradict the religious discourse of the Bible and the teachings of the Catholic church. His individual convictions thus entered the larger realm of collective symbolism and cultural discourse, and posed a challenge and an alternative to the dominant cultural paradigm of universal monotheism and the Christian understanding of the cosmos during his time. As a cultural participant, Galileo's understanding was derived from his experience of the heliocentric symbolic discourse of his culture and modified by his experience of questioning this discourse, which gave him a unique understanding of the symbolic discourse of his culture as geocentric. The difference between his individual understanding and the collective cultural understanding legitimated by the church became extreme to the point where the church silenced his alternative voice, deeming his scientific thought heresy and subsequently marginalized the Copernican challenge to the Catholic world view in cultural discourse. Since the sixteenth century, there has slowly been sufficient acceptance of Galileo's views within the culture to motivate the Catholic church to rescind its ban of his views.[16]

Galileo's story indicates the dynamic of cultural change at the intersection of different types of discourse at work. Galileo's discourse was the voice of a possible imaginative alternative to the legitimated collection of authoritative beliefs of the Catholic biblical doctrine of creation. This dynamic was played out in later centuries, through the cultural discourse of the acceptance and nonacceptance of the claims of competing authoritative sets of beliefs held by cultural participants.

The story of violence is told within a discourse infrastructure. This is done through the firsthand testimony of victims and perpetrators of violence; the analysis of violence by specialists; theories of individual and cultural violence derived from analysis; the examination of the symbolic significance of myths of violence; and the paradigms of innate and acquired violence. Together, these categories and their comprehension as a complex whole constitute a critique of the violence mythos.

The five dimensions of discourse for violence will be used to varying degrees throughout the text. They are meant to be heuristic devices to show the influences of the different dimensions of discourse upon each other. When we communicate, we communicate our own ideas and experiences, other people's ideas and experiences, modes of organizing and understanding ideas and experiences, the cultural associations and significance of ideas and experiences, and the cultural integration of all of these into an infrastructure of identity to guide collective understanding and behavior. These modes of communication are the dimensions of discourse used throughout the text. I warn the reader that there are some graphic descriptions of experiences of violence in this text. I include them as evidence of the silenced torture suffered by so many in the violence mythos that renders victims invisible within the rationalizations of legitimate and innate violence.

As an example of a discourse infrastructure, consider the military as an institution of war. The military is organized patterns of discourse, practices, and beliefs for the purposes of destroying and killing, whether legitimated as offensive or defensive deployment. There is an immense amount of cultural resources and decisions and trillions of dollars that support this infrastructure over decades. There are organizations for war manufacturing, production, and technology. There are sophisticated systems for transportation and communication. There are computerized intelligence operations of reconnaissance and surveillance. There is detailed strategical, logistical, and tactical planning. Food, uniforms, barracks, and compounds must be grown, sewn, and built for training and combat. Weapons and ammunition are made from tons of metal ore that must be mined and smelted. There are aircraft, bombs, gunboats, carriers. There are millions of human beings who are conscripted or volunteer for the school of war in training, command, and rank advancement, as well as medical care for the mutilated.

All of this relies upon a cultural belief that war is an effective means to conflict resolution. This belief relies upon propaganda and public relations to justify and legitimate war. As Van Creveld reminds us, "On both the individual and collective levels, war is . . . primarily an affair of the heart" that relies upon the cultural belief in honor, duty, courage, loyalty and resoluteness.[17] These attributes glorify the predominantly male war hero with the cultural belief that might is right and that killing, mutilation, self-sacrifice, and foreshortened death are admirable and to be emulated as masculine. As well, it prioritizes war and those who partake in it over the wrenching loss of loved ones felt by those "outside" the "legitimate" war zone, usually women and children. Immense amounts of resources are applied to the adminis-tration of foreign policy and domestic preparedness for war at any time. As observed by Ursula Franklin, tax funds must be allocated over decades to pay for war, and hence "generates the need for a credible long-term enemy" to justify the public outlay of funds.[18] The core of the violence mythos, the belief in innate violence, creates this permanent enemy, regardless of nationality. In this illustration of the military as a discourse infrastructure, we can see the varied, deep, and costly influence of cultural beliefs, communication, and interactions rationalized for the purposes of legitimated violence within the vio-lence mythos.

The belief in the innateness of violence to human beings seems to indicate a collapse in the distinction between anger the emotion and violence the behavior, which has led to an equation between anger and violence such that anger has been perceived both to be violent and to have violence as its "natural" means of expression. The result of this misnomer of "violent anger" is the location of violence within the human being and to position control of violence in external collec-tive authority. This is "legitimate violence" because it rationalizes control of "illegitimate" violence as socially acceptable.

The collapse in the distinction between anger and violence may be associated with a cultural distinction which separates the mind from the body. This mind/body split identifies disapassionate ratio-nality with the mind, distinct from emotion, feelings, and bodily in-voluntary functions identified with the body. The mind also has been valued as a constructive element of order and civilization while the body has been devalued as a destructive element of chaos and nature.

In Western history, this mind/body split has been articulated in gender terms, where the mind as superior has been associated with being male and the body as inferior has been associated with being female. In associating mind with divinity, the male has been seen as the image of the male transcendent ego or God, while woman has been seen as the image of lower, material nature.[19] Although both are seen as "mixed natures," the male is deemed "higher," and the female is deemed "lower." Thus, "gender becomes a primary symbol for the dualism of transcendence and immanence, spirit and matter."[20] Further, the appropriation of gender dualism is manifested in the distinction between biology and culture. This distinction depicted the "biological necessity, to which both men and women submitted and adapted, and culturally constructed customs and institutions, which forced women into subordinate roles."[21]

Foucauldian discourse analysis may be used to expand on the construction of customs and institutions around the mind/body dualism and women's subordination. According to Foucault, there exists an "economy" of intersecting discourses with intrinsic technologies, necessities of operation, tactics employed, and the effects of power which underlie them and what they transmit.[22] This economy of discourses, and not their representations, is what determines the essential features of their definition. Thus, in the sense of a "marketplace" of disourses, it is not the products, or representations, that are produced which shape these discourses. Rather, it is the techniques of social categorization, valuation, and implementation involved in social production which construct the representations of social thought. Hence, the representation of the woman as wife and caretaker arises from social categories and values of woman as inferior to man, excluded from participation in community interests because she is perceived as irrational, subordinate, sexual object, and reproducer of the species. Thus, a history, or recorded and interpreted past, of the mind/body dualism, women's subordination, the superiority of strength and inferiority of vulnerability, and violence would be written first from the perspective of a "history of discourses."[23]

Although the prototype of the mind/body dualism and its symbol of gender division and women's subordination are important for the analysis of violence, what is more important than these representations of gender are the discourses that formed them as cultural constructs. The claim is that the cultural preoccupation with the development of the dualistic paradigm of universal hierarchical gender constitution of human beings inclusive of assumptions of innate violence has overshadowed alternative discourses for a paradigm of interdependency. Interdependency includes assumptions of gender-equal integrity of emotion that is distinct from behavior, where multivalent articulations of emotion are distinguished from the articulations of acquired violence in cultural discourse, as well as assumptions that depict the valuation of trust relationships.

Under the dualistic prototype, man (characteristically white man) and woman are both embodied, where man had the capacity to transcend his body through mind or rationality, but woman supposedly did not. The lower valuation of the body, and hence emotion and anger, would mean that anger would be associated with the biological necessity of the body, yet controllable by the male mind. However, because of the "deficiency" of rationality, emotion is seen as completely uncontrollable in the woman. This view becomes a justification for abuse of women as men's means to control them, as they supposedly cannot control themselves. Thus, the outbreak of disorder or chaos in a society under male authority would mean that forces other than the rational male mind are at work, because otherwise, the analogically divine mind of rational man would prevail. Such *irrationality* would need to be ascribed to the ungodly, the faulty and the lesser body, in short, what was other than rational man.

As violence is by definition destructive and chaotic, instances of violence would then need to be attributed to something other than the divine, other than the mind, and hence include the biological necessity of the body. And because acts of violence have been predominantly accompanied by the emotion of anger, a causality between anger and violence could be established. This would be particularly acute in the war experience.

In the war experience of combat, a phenomenon called "purposeful distanciation," discussed in chapter 1, occurs in the trauma of life-threatening events to oneself and one's comrades. In purposeful distanciation, the traumatized persons distance themselves emotionally from the event and the circumstances of the event. This distancing works to numb the pain, loss, and damage done to the self and to the other. Extreme rage often results, as one has little or no control over the events and is helpless to prevent an event from happening or amend what has happened. The loss of control and emotional pain must be countered in restoring trust with another in order for the person to reintegrate oneself in the world and function without disorientation. When restoration does not occur, the mind becomes split from the body, emotions are repressed, and consequently circumstances requiring emotional connection are avoided. This means the intimacy of friendship, with feelings of tenderness, trust, and vulnerability associated with relationships, is avoided or denied. Positive feelings are replaced by distancing, using anger and rage as defense mechanisms to prevent further pain and hurt. Circumstances similar to the traumatic event are sought out in an attempt to regain control over the trauma. The substitution of distancing anger for intimate affection, to prevent destruction to the self, thus becomes externalized as a potentially destructive reaction to the perceived cause of the injury or further threat of injury. Thus, the situation is less one of inflicting injury than it is attempting to prevent or stop injury to oneself or to loved ones.

Because these painful emotions and the chaotic situation in which they occur are associated with the body (if I did not have a body I would not feel this pain), the body becomes distanced, objectified, either to be manipulated, instrumentalized, or ignored in self-perception. This objectification is used to truncate emotional associations in oneself or for the other, especially in the trauma of war or sexual abuse, to cope with the possibility of killing or being killed.

The rationalization of purposeful distanciation thus results in a mind/body split. For woman, this would mean the denial of anger at almost any cost, as its direct expression would simply mean a cultural affirmation of her "irrationality," and hence would necessitate its internalization as self-hatred (I cannot prevent or destroy the external cause of the pain and the injury, so I must destroy myself to prevent further pain and injury to myself) and contribute to woman's subordination through an inability to express a need for change in her circumstances, signified by anger. Gerda Lerner declares Freud's statement that for women "anatomy is destiny" is "wrong because it is ahistorical and reads the distant past into the present without making allowances for changes over time. Worse, this statement has been read as a prescription for present and future: not only is anatomy destiny for women, but it *should* be. What Freud should have said is that for women anatomy *once was* destiny. . . What once was, no longer is so, and no longer must be or should it be so."[24]

For men to retain the illusion of control, the mind would need to rationalize violence as acceptable male behavior by deeming it "natural" and by sublimating it as a quasi-virtue in physical strength and make it innately intentional as aggression. But because violence would seem an inescapable, at best tolerable, given for a society, the problem would be simply one of collectively controlling it and, if possible, making it work for the social order. Thus, the individual could be made the cause of violence, with collective tolerance of violence against the "irrationals," that is, those other than men, such as women and their children. The collective restraint of the violent but rational male individual and appropriation of individual violence for the collective could then be used to legitimate certain types of violence (e.g., war, police brutality, incarceration, violence against "irrationals") in the name of protecting the collective from the individual.

Such an ideology of violence, or set of ideas and concepts which elaborate an authoritative belief about violence as innate, would have within it a definition of men as violent with legitimated acceptable collective (hero) and tolerable private (perpetrator) modes of expression, with those other than men (victims) constrained by collective force, physically and in the form of cultural constraint in customs and institutions.

Thus, the expression of "violent anger" by males would become accepted as a natural and unalterable behavior and would be allowed expression because of the legitimate valuation of males in society. Expression of "violent anger" by women and others, as devalued members of society, would be illegitimate, not permissable, and hence internalized as hatred of oneself and others like oneself.

If anger became accepted as simply an emotion signifying the need for a change in circumstances and relationship, with broader possibilities for expression than simply violent behavior, perhaps male violence against women and others would become intolerable and unacceptable, and women and marginalized others would be accepted as legitimate in their expressions of anger and the need for change.

As the home of vulnerability to pain, loss, and injury, the devaluation of the body as instrument for the mind has consequences for how technology is perceived. Technology has been touted as antihuman and dehumanizing, particularly in the works of Jacques Ellul.[25] In contrast, Marshall McLuhan views technology as an extension of human perceptual senses.[26] From the perspective of the mind/body dualism, the body that is seen as an instrument of the mind has the extensions of the body, or technology, as instruments as well. Thus, technology is not antihuman, but antimind in a paradigm that legitimates only half of what is human in affirming mind and rejecting the body/technology. Technology would be devalued as is the body, particularly in its success at obtaining control of the environment, as it would enter into competition with the function of the mind. In such a threat to a hierarchy of human constitution, if technology became too successful, it could be rejected and set in opposition to mind to protect the domain of rationality, as well as named the irrational scapegoat for the failures of rationality. In such an instance, it is not technology that ought to be condemned as the culprit, but the web of rationalizations that defend bodyless rationalism. A valuation of the body reverses this view and allows the human to be constituted as an integration of reflective instrumentality and perceptual awareness. Thus, technology becomes appropriately an augmentation of the creativity, responsibility, and embodiment of human beings.

The discussion of violence takes place in three parts. Part 1 positions the question of violence within the discourses of innate and acquired violence in a context of systemic cultural legitimation and history, to show how they are supported or marginalized culturally, and hence become part of a culture's authoritative beliefs. Part 2 describes the valuation of violence in the assumptions within theoretical works. These analyses are not intended as reductions of the authors' work to one core assumption, but rather to show how culturally the misidentification of trauma reenactment as innate violence influences their work through cultural assumptions that inform the discourses used to articulate their theories. Part 3 describes the interdependent mythos as a restorative paradigm to trauma in the violence mythos, utilizing insights gained from the previous chapters. The process of establishing trust, attachment, and collective reconnection is extended to include technology.

It may be that our culture has been inculcated with an erroneous fear of "violence" of the other and ourselves that disallows three important objectives for the future. First, we are able to become accountable for and change behavior in relationships previously apportioned to the individual as unalterable, natural, given, and unchangeable, particularly male violence. Second, the use of violence for conflict resolution or simply getting what one wants can be seen as a choice and not an inevitability of the expression of anger, rage, or desire. And third, technology may be removed from the stereotype of instrumental invasion and destruction and developed as an instrument of creativity and collective connection.

In this manner, we may be able to perceive the human being in the global environment in relationships of somatic interchange, that has among other beliefs, a particular collection of beliefs and habits called "the violence mythos." These beliefs may be subject to change through alternative action and belief in the trust process of relationships. This places violence in the perspective of a chosen, not a given, behavior for the expression of anger and the use of technologies to selectively enhance our relationships with the world.

PART I

VIOLENCE IN CULTURAL DISCOURSE

FIGURE 1

Lone Cowboy

Photographer: Clinton C. Whitmer

FIGURE 2

Oil Fire Smoke Clouds from the Persian Gulf War, Oman, January 1991

Photographer: Clinton C. Whitmer

1

The Violence Question: What *Is* It?

What is essential is invisible to the eye.[1] There are two invisibilities this work seeks to understand; the first is the context of embodied friendship, and the second is the context of desensitization that erodes this friendship. Taken to a cultural level, this desensitization can have devastating effects on the unity and integrity of social interactions. Hence, an interrogation of desensitization to violence in Western culture is explored within the context of a revaluation of relationships.

The pattern of acceptability and sanction of violence expressed through the discourses of symbols, institutions, beliefs, attitudes, and social practices within Western culture is *the violence mythos*. Violence refers to injury or destruction of body or of relationship by one person or group toward another. This work addresses two primary assumptions about violence: one, that violence is innate, or inherent to humans, and two, that violence is acquired by behavior. The cultural transmission of the belief that violence is innate as natural, through tradition and authoritative beliefs, contributes directly to violence being sanctioned and accepted within Western culture and exported to the larger global community.

Culture and Interpretation

Culture may be defined in three different ways according to Northrop Frye.[2] First, there is culture as lifestyle, the ways in which a society carries out its everyday social rituals. This includes its protocols for eating, drinking, and clothing itself. One illustration is the Chinese mode of communal dining and use of chopsticks contrasted with the North American individuated serving style and use of utensils. Second, there is culture as a "shared heritage of historical memories and customs, carried out mainly through a common language."[3] And third, there are the creative expressions of a society, which take shape through architecture, music, sciences, scholarship, and applied arts.

In the following text, the ways in which persons in a society relate, in the protocols of trusting and nontrusting behavior, are developed. The focal facet of culture examined here is that of the shared memories, customs, and language, or traditions, of a society. In this respect, what is under question is the serious cultural "story" of violence for a society. To this end, the language of scholarship presented expresses the thought of neurobiologists, sociologists, and psychologists, as well as psychoanalysts, theologians, linguists, philosophers, futurists, and technologists.

Consider for a moment that in most societies, there are two types of stories that crystallize. First, at the center of a culture is a nexus of "serious" stories that are claimed to have happened, but that is not as important as their status as stories that are "particularly urgent for the community to know,"[4] such as the hero myth. Their structure is not different from other stories, but they serve a different social function. The second type of story is less serious and becomes a folk tale. The more serious stories "become the cultural possession of a specific society: they form the verbal nucleus of a shared tradition."[5]

Frye's analysis is close to José Miguez Bonino's appropriation of Paul Ricoeur's model of the three layers of human construction in a civilization.[6] First is the level of "tools," "instruments," or technologies humans devise to fulfill their purposes. This information is cumulative and transmissible from one civilization to another. The second layer corresponds to the "ethos" of a civilization. The ethos includes the habits, attitudes, and relations that make up how the culture works. A change in ethos affects the institutions which support and embody the ethos. The third layer includes the "core" of a civilization, its self-understanding of its origin and destiny expressed in symbolic terms. Without this core, the civilization would have no unity or integrity.[7]

Thus, we are not looking for a causal relationship between the story of violence and violent behavior in society, but a prescriptive one. Rather, as a story that is urgent for a community to know at its core, the story of violence would inform the heritage and unity of the community and its language through a shared tradition of a common understanding, embodied in institutions and transmitted through knowledge and practice, of violence. Thus, the means to investigate the cultural understanding of violence becomes a form of the following question: What is the possible correlation between the symbolic interpretations or cultural expressions of violence and the acceptance of violent behavior in a society? Humans are educable creatures that negotiate their understanding and boundaries. They are inculcated with the beliefs of a culture that allow them to survive in that culture or alter that culture if need be. What possible systems of signs, metanarrative, and paradigm would organize authoritative beliefs about violence that rationalize, legitimate, and give meaning to behavior as violent or not? This investigation is significant for more than the two obvious reasons of (1) political legitimation of aggression and (2) abusive relationships between men and women. The former is ably characterized by Edward Herman and Noam Chomsky in their description of the propaganda model of the mass media to align itself with state policy and censor dissent.[8] The latter is an ongoing task in feminist scholarship.[9] More fully, the story of violence, from a perspective of marginality, needs to be examined for what it excludes, rather than what it includes. In other words, what is not being said when the story of violence is told? What is the absent presence in the discourse of violence? It seems that the discourse of the embodied fullness of human attachment and emotional and creative life is silenced, through limiting anger to a one-dimensional equation with violent behavior that destroys relationships. Such cultural censorship restricts the meaning of being human by disallowing anger as a sign of a need for change, through devaluing and making dangerous this emotion and the attachment wherein this emotion is aroused. Hence, implicitly, change is labeled as an undesirable violent phenomenon, and so is attachment.

When the literature on anger is reviewed, it appears that anger signifies change as *difference*, not as *threat*, and that humans respond to difference in their environment, rather than to a *higher risk* in their environment. Our culture has chosen to interpret change as threat instead of difference. This is not the fault of emotion or anger, but of our traditional interpretation of change and new experiences. It may be the case that change and stability in Western culture have been characterized by a violent dynamic of exploitation modeled on mistrust and trauma.

To examine these issues, I will attempt a manageable exploration of the discourses concerning anger and violence, primarily through the discourses of innate violence and acquired violence. Thus, through the examination of some of the history and linguistic products of culture, it may be possible to come to a closer understanding of the shared memories and traditions of a cultural understanding of the story of violence.

Definitions of Violence

Robert McAfee Brown gives an expanded definition of violence as a violation of personhood, in the sense of an infringement, denial, abuse, or disregard of another physically or otherwise.[10] To address personhood is to give an inclusive description of violence as more than just the body or the soul. It recognizes acts that depersonalize as acts of violence.[11] Personal and institutional overt physical destructive behavior against another would be considered acts of violence. There is covert personal violence which does psychological damage to another, and institutional covert violence where social structures violate the personhood of groups of persons, for instance, substandard living conditions in a ghetto.[12] Thus, for McAfee Brown, the problem is structural violence,[13] and its remedy is genuine reconciliation of antagonisms. McAfee Brown warns that being on the side of justice may make some people unhappy, especially those who benefit from existing structures, but that "the task of subversion, the task of engaging in deep-seated social challenge, is the only true route to genuine reconciliation, in which the true sources of conflict have been exposed and overcome."[14]

McAfee Brown seems to propose a shift in thinking about violence as originating in the individual (body or soul) to violence as a result of harmful relationship (injustice) between persons. This shift is helpful in articulating the social complexity of violent behavior and its remedy. However, it does not address the issue of why someone would commit injustice, a question which the binary dualism of body and soul attempted to address. It is not enough to sideline the discussion of violence as internal in the body/soul dualism and then shift to a discussion of violence as external and structural. Persons are part of and contribute to the production of the structure. Without a revised anthropology of intentionality which replaces the body/soul dualism, McAfee Brown's project is incomplete. Without an understanding of the motivation to commit injustice, one may be attempting simply to fix a wheel when it is the axle that requires replacement.

Such an anthropology of intentionality is part of Ricoeur's hermeneutics of suspicion. An indirect route, or detour, to the story of violence is taken in a hermeneutic of suspicion and retrieval as a demythologization and delegitimation of symbolic discourses in culture. The meaning of symbolic discourse undergoes a type of archeology, or reflection upon the past as history or tradition, from which a type of teleology or retrieval of meaning from this past is appropriated in the form of new meaning. This methodology of hermeneutic phenomenology was developed by Paul Ricoeur and elaborated in *Freud and Philosophy: An Essay on Interpretation*, a work discussed in more detail in chapter 4.

Ricoeur's methodology is part of the tradition of the work of the so-called masters of suspicion, namely Marxist critique of ideology, Nietzchean geneology, and Freudian psychoanalysis which decenters the ahistoricity of idealist concepts and locates and the self as social, historical, and linguistic.[15] The task of the self for Ricoeur is to find meaning in the expression of experience in relation with another. The open-ended hermeneutic principle is a mediation where the self goes out of itself in expression and returns to itself in the appropriation of linguistic meaning.[16] This is Ricoeur's hermeneutic of distanciation which describes mediation or the relation between self and other.[17]

Another concept of hermeneutical mediation is developed in regard to texts by Hans-Georg Gadamer. For Gadamer, understanding texts cannot be limited by the original intentions of the writer, nor by the assumptions and expectations of the reader. The meaning of the text goes beyond the limit of understanding both of author and of reader, detaches itself, and makes "itself free for new relationships."[18] Gadamer's open-ended hermeneutic of associative understanding is teamed with Ricoeur's hermeneutic of suspicion and retrieval to interpret cultural texts and open them to possible new meanings in cultural understanding. Inclusive of an acknowledgment of Ricoeur's own assumptions about violence, the aim is to discern an interpretation of possible meanings of intersubjective assumptions of social discourse and practice regarding violence.

Human environments are partly symbolic structures that stretch from the remote world of the "once was" through the imperatives of the "now" to the imaginative possibilities of the "might be." "All of these times co-exist in the 'present,' which consists not only of buildings, roads, rules, values and institutions but also of nostalgia, hope, despair, memories, deprivation and desire."[19] In this respect, a person who becomes "conscious," no matter on how rudimentary a level, "awakens" in a context of meanings. Persons thus discover themselves as active agents both of "the interpretation of meanings and of their practical organization in the everyday world."[20] "Even if 'interpreted' is to mean the wholesale acceptance by the person of someone else's interpretations, this too, is an interpretive act. In other words, meanings should be viewed not as introjected objects but as available patterns of values, norms and rules. These patterns provide fields of pressure and opportunity for the negotiation of motives, projects, constraints, and legitimations among persons and groups."[21]

The person becomes an agent in the attempt to make sense of oneself and one's actions in a human environment. The person "produces" and "consumes" interpretations, legitimations, and delegitimations, some of which are articulated in the form of deeds as indirect acceptance of intersubjective assumptions. This all occurs in a human symbolic environment.[22]

The exploration of the question What is the association between the symbolic interpretations or cultural expressions of violence and the acceptance of violent behavior in society? includes both direct and indirect acceptance of assumptions about violence. On the one hand, there is an exploration of conscious cultural products in the form of scholarly texts. On the other hand, there is the exploration of symbolic interpretations of violence in myths and historical norms and values. This is the context of indirect intersubjective assumptions which persons enact in interpreting what is perceived as violence. Thus, the story of violence will be formulated in these two modes of cultural interpretation.

Innate and Acquired Violence

The discourses of violence follow primarily two paths, that of innate violence and that of acquired violence. An argument over whether what is perceived as aggression is innate or acquired is succinctly encapsulated in the 1968 article "'Innate Depravity,' or Original Sin Revisited" by Ashley Montagu.[23] Montagu mounts a feisty reply to Robert Ardrey's claim that human beings are "killers" by nature because australopithecines used tools as weapons to bash the skulls of baboons. He responds that the myth of humans as ferocious "wild animals" is "one of Western man's supreme rationalizations" that serves to explain the origins of human aggressiveness and deny responsibility for it because it is supposedly "innate."[24]

According to Montagu, early hominization was characterized by nonviolence in the development of cooperative activities. This included the social process of hunting itself, the invention of speech, and the development of food-getting tools. Primitive humans hunted not for pleasure, to satisfy "predatory instincts," but for food, to satisfy the hunters' hunger and the hunger of their dependents. Hunting served bodily and social survival needs.

For Montagu, the appeal of Ardrey's argument is the spurious psychological gratification in finding "father confessors" to relieve some of the "burdensome load of guilt" humans bear by shifting responsibility for violent behavior to "natural inheritance" and "innate aggressiveness." The triteness of the argument is reflected in the nineteenth-century proposition that ontogeny recapitulates phylogeny (since proven erroneous),[25] in Herbert Spencer's doctrine of "social Darwinism," as the survival of the fittest and struggle for existence. Phylogeny, or the developmental history of the species, was thought to provide the initial biological repertoire for natural selection in the developmental history of the individual, or ontogeny. As innate or a natural given, aggression as a species trait would necessarily be an unavoidable part of each individual's genetic makeup. The implications of this position were expressed by General von Bernhardi in 1912 when he used the concept of 'biologically necessary aggression' to justify war. "War is a biological necessity... it is as necessary as the struggle of the elements of Nature ... it gives a biologically just decision, since its decisions rest on the very nature of things."[26]

However, the understanding of violence as natural and biologically necessary is an interpretation of emotionally charged symbols, such as war (the close association between anger, fear, and violent behavior) that may have as their cognitive evaluation, or reason for the violent behavior, the belief that violence is innate. War may be legitimated or sanctioned by social authority as acceptable when waged against an "aggressor" who is expressing "uncontrollable violent behavior" that can be stopped only in kind. Or war may be waged on grounds that it is irrepressible not to aggress against another, in that it is within the biological makeup of humans to want to wage war against another. There is a circle of violence that is legitimated and reinforced by the belief, or cognitive evaluation, that violence is a necessary expression of anger construed as aggression, or an impulse to dominate or destroy that is innate as an undauntable "will to power."

The belief that anger is violent involves a category mistake between anger the emotion and violence the behavior. How anger is expressed depends upon the social values and beliefs through which the meaning of the emotion and the behavior that expresses it are interpreted. The expression of anger is dependent upon social expectations for behavior, and the permissability of that behavior. The interpretation and the expression of emotion is socialized. On this view, there is no direct line of causality from impulse to behavior which would constitute reactional motivation. Rather, motivation is a complex of prioritizing emotional arousal, reflective evaluations, symbolic significance, authoritative beliefs, and socially mediated behavior.

In developing a working vocabulary for the discourse of violence, a general definition of aggressive acts is behavior that results in personal injury and physical destruction.[27] Social violence has been defined as assault upon an individual or his/her property solely or primarily because of that person's membership in a social category.[28] These definitions portray violence as acts that cause physical damage, are intentional, and have direct effects. Other kinds of destructive or coercive acts may be considered the use of types of force that prevent the normal free action or movement or inhibit persons through the threat of violence. Verbal threats have been considered nonviolent yet aggressive as attempts to destroy a person's reputation or undermine their relationships with other people. Violence committed against women and children includes verbal and physical abuse.[29]

There are three components to ascertain an act as aggressive. First, some action which may or may not be coercive is observed. Second, an intent to do harm is inferred. Third, the action is judged to be antinormative. The actor in this situation probably will be blamed, disapproved of, or possibly punished.[30] In this setting, a behavior is observed, a motive is inferred, and a moral judgment is made. In order to make a more specific distinction between violence and aggression, we may distinguish between the *behavior* of "violence" and "socially destructive acts," and the *motive* of "aggression."[31] As well, the distinction needs to be made between the intent of aggression and the emotion of anger, where the perceived willful intent of an act of aggression may be a conditioned defense mechanism to aversive events activated by anger to prevent or cease injury or pain, as in the case of posttraumatic stress disorder.

Social Prohibition

The argument for "innate aggression" seeks to justify violent behavior and suggests social prohibition as a means to control aggressive individuals. The argument for phylogenetic and hence ontogenetic aggression is reflected in Freud's theory of instincts and the need to control them by social means. This argument is developed more fully in chapter 4.

In Freud's injunction against the individual, clarification between "particular ideal demands" of the individual and what is "civilized in general" for the collective reveals the need to regulate social relationships.

Without such regulation, relationships would be subject to the arbitrary will of the individual: that is to say, the physically stronger man would decide them in the sense of his own interests and instinctual impulses . . . Human life is commonly only made possible when a majority comes together which is stronger than any separate individual and which remains united against all separate individuals. The power of this community is then set up as 'right' in opposition to the power of the individual, which is condemned as 'brute force' . . . The final outcome should be a rule of law to which all . . . have contributed by a sacrifice of their instincts, and which leaves no one . . . at the mercy of brute force.[32]

Freud claims the "truth behind all this" is that "men are not gentle creatures who want to be loved."[33] Rather, they have a "powerful share of aggressiveness" in which their neighbor becomes for them not only a potential helper or sexual object, but someone who tries to "satisfy their aggressiveness on him," in terms of sexual exploitation, economic exploitation, seizing his or her possessions, humiliation, pain, torture and intent "to kill him." For Freud, civilization and its means of prohibition through socialization and institutions are the necessary regulation of otherwise uncontrollable natural individual aggression.

Anatol Rapoport suggests that it was the trauma of World War I that inspired Freud's idea of aggression. "The faith in 'progress,' in steady maturation of civilization with its commitment to civility and its abhorrence of savagery, was shattered by four years of senseless carnage. The outbreak was consistent with the idea of a dormant destruction drive suddenly released."[34] Thus, Freud articulates a phylogeny of violence, of innate aggression, and hostility in humans, particularly in men. As we shall see, it is Western culture's fundamental lack of understanding of trauma for the self, other, and collective that has given rise to interpretations of violence as innate and a vacuity of resources to heal from and prevent trauma.

Humanist psychologist Abraham Maslow tempered the aggressive drive from injurious to assertive aggression as "righteous indignation," "passion for justice," or "healthy self-affirmation."[35] Thus, a different name was given for the same drive to aggress. Even traits deemed life affirming were reduced to a more fundamental violence. Indeed, the giving of a different name to what appears as the same violent aggression is thus arguably the inhibition or transformation of an urge to aggress into an acceptable form, a disguise for the primal urge itself.[36]

Konrad Lorenz's work, *On Aggression*, follows Freudian instinct theory. For Lorenz, what compels reasonable humans to behave unreasonably are the laws that prevail in "phylogenetically adapted instinctive behavior" derived from the study of the instincts of animals.[37] Montagu counters Lorenz's ambiguous anthropomorphism by saying that with the exception of "instinctoid reactions in infants due to sudden withdrawals of support and to sudden loud noises, the human being is entirely instinctless."[38] If all instincts are characterized by "spontaneity" and humans are genetically programmed for aggression then "the aggression drive" becomes very dangerous.

According to Montagu, Lorenz claims that "hostile neighboring hordes" were the target of "phylogenetically programmed aggression" that needed to be controlled by "responsible morality." Montagu insists there is no evidence of hostility between neighboring hordes of early humans. Montagu repudiates Lorenz by declaring that evidence shows that learning and experience influence the development of aggression in the history *both* of the individual and of the group. Modifications in the development of the individual influence modifications in the species group. For instance, by not rewarding and showing aggression to be unrewarded behavior, with the Hopi and Zuni Indians, aggression is minimal or nonexistent.[39]

Trophic Theory

To take the discussion about a biological basis for aggression even further, the perspective of neurobiology may be include here. The influence of learning and experience, or appropriate adaptive responsiveness to uncertain circumstances, on individual and group development is reflected in trophic theory. Changes in the circumstances of the external environment are coordinated with changes in internal neural development. The neural and somatic development of the individual is interdependent with the environment or context in which development occurs.

Within the body, the connections between neurons and the cells they ennervate (target cells), or more simply, the nervous system of the body, are interdependent, not determinate. Patterns of neural connections are sustained in maturity by *ongoing* interactions with target cells. The fact that experimental perturbation can alter patterns of connections in maturity demonstrates a persistent potential for change. The primary purpose of neural adjustment is thought to be to encode experience. However, change in the neural system is necessary for another reason: the body, as well as the external environment, changes continually. In order to monitor a body that is changing both in size and in form, the nervous system must also change.[40]

Changes in the neural system are not identical for members of the same species. Studies performed to assess normal variability in the human brain show substantial differences in the arrangement of the same functions between individuals. Thus, the size and arrangement of the nervous system is not identical among different individuals of the same species.[41]

Conventionally, studies concerned with understanding how behavior is modified by experience and learning have focused on how neural activity affects anatomically stable circuits. This is the "hardwired" view of neural connections. Here, the neural connections in the nervous system are fixed, and "tell" the body how to respond to stimuli. On this view, the mind rules the body. However, it may be plausible that for certain kinds of learning, that is, changes in behavior that develop slowly and last a long time, experience may be encoded by altering the arrangement of neural connections themselves.[42] The mind itself becomes formed through information from the body and hence is part of the body.

Neural connections in the mature nervous system are actively *maintained*.[43] In the course of development and mature maintenance, new neural branches and synapses are constructed apparently concurrent with the removal of some pre-existing ones. Target cells compete by elaborating trophic signals, to which neurons are "selectively sensitive" and elicit the alteration of neural connectivity through adapting to the changing needs of the target cell.

This fluctuating rearrangement of neural connection does not reflect an "abstract Darwinian principle," but rather reflects adjustments of neuronal branches and their connections required by changes in somatic development and maintenance.[44] The evidence of neural development and the continual plasticity of neural connections for individual responses and adaptation to internal and external changes show that the view that ontogeny recapitulates phylogeny is erroneous.[45] The space is opened for a discourse of aggressive behavior as a biologically *acquired* characteristic of human functioning as a result of learned or adaptive behavior that is maintained as socially appropriate behavior in the face of uncertain or changing circumstances.

To return to Montagu, because of the highly developed capacity for learning in human beings, the human must learn to be human through culture. The "*acquired* deplorabilities" of innate depravity, programmed aggressiveness, "the beast" and wild animal as ferocious killers are human-made constructs to make aggression easier to understand and to accept. For Montagu, these are merely diversions from the real sources of aggression, namely false contradictory values by which humans in a disorderly world attempt to live.[46] As we shall see, one such value contradiction is the demand for vulnerable humans to be invulnerable heroes.

In order to investigate what might be false and contradictory values about violence, we need to shift from discourse about phylognetic innate violent impulses to discourse about acquired aggressive behavior. What is involved in the acquisition of aggression? How do we learn to be aggressive?

Symbol and Belief

The human as neurobiological organism continually adapts to changes in the environment. The interpretation of adaptation or experience also involves cognitive and affective systems that are interrelated with an organism's neurochemical system. The selective inclusion and exclusion of certain information from processing differentiates between acceptable and unacceptable information for cognition according to the developmental needs of the person within a specific environmental situation.

Experience is stored cognitively by representations of experience or symbols. Symbols are the codification, naming, and labeling of experience (thoughts, emotions, desires, cognitively mediated responses) in memory representations which serve as models for potential behavior. We preserve our interpretations of experiences in symbolic associations. "It is difficult to explain the overwhelming hold symbols possess over us unless they were learnt in association with powerful emotional experiences."[47]

Symbolic representation that defines experience is central to the formation of estimations of reality, or beliefs, through awareness and judgment. Beliefs and evaluations about violence vary according to time, place, and setting. Beliefs and evaluations are included in cognitive schemas or patterns of thought by which a person organizes and interprets experience.[48]

Beliefs as estimations of reality are formulated by symbolic representation and the selective principle of judgement, or authority, and the neurochemical and affective systems of awareness. Beliefs are tied to evaluations, or appraisals of desirable consequences that potentially direct behavior. The capacity to discern between acceptable and unacceptable information for integration into a cognitive schema is the decision of authority that labels or names information.

The process of naming or languaging includes a history of selecting and creating words to interpret changed circumstances to allow for adjustment and adaptability to internal/external events. This is the individual's history of development or linguistic ontogenesis. Thus, naming, or the metaphoric nature of language, is a dual process of openness to the unlimited aspect of changing reality and the establishment of a delimited selection or valuation of information that is incorporated into a cognitive schema of beliefs (which may be integrated into conscious beliefs or given "selective inattention" and stored on an unconscious level).

Language is already social, as it embodies agreed upon signs by which participants understand each other. Thus, the question of *who* or *what* it is that signifies, or *what* is signified, is of less import than the acknowledgment *that* a sign signifies. Thus, naming or signification as metaphor and symbol is intrinsically relational or social as communication.

Symbols are loci of the historical selection of names, or imaginative representations between experience and reality that may derive from direct experience or vicarious learning. Vicarious or observational learning can occur by viewing the behavior of others and its consequences for them. The information acquisition process is foreshortened through observational learning. This acquired knowledge is the acquisition of external authority, as having acceptably obtained what is sought, as implied in observing another's cognitive schema and conduct, or its symbolic representation, and choosing it as appropriate behavior.

Behavior is conditioned by cognitive appraisal, the modes of response learned from direct or vicarious experience for coping with the world. It is also conditioned by their relative effectiveness in a matrix of social relations and expectations of social acceptability, tolerance, or social cost. The self as relational is situated in a symbolic linguistic context of social motives for interpersonal conduct rather than motivated by intrapsychic factors, such as instincts, brain centers, or so-called aggressive energy that influence what we label aggressive motivation and violent behavior.

The cognitive schemas of belief—including value judgments, personal history, and expectations of anticipated consequences—situate the self as socially motivated within a cultural context of acceptable and unacceptable behavior. Social motivation is directed by the acceptance of the authority implied within the models and symbols that prevail in a culture, through cultural discourse with the power to give names to behavior and the power to delimit the parameters of acceptable and unacceptable behavioral diversity in a society. Now that the self has been contextualized as a socially motivated self, the topic of aggression will be discussed within this model.

Acquired Aggression

Research conducted with animals has revealed subcortical structures (nerve centers below the cerebral cortex of the brain), primarily the hypothalamus and limbic system, that act as neurophysiological mechanisms to mediate aggressive behavior *and* that are selectively activated and controlled by the central processing of environmental stimulation.[49] Social learning factors affect the kinds of responses that are likely to be activated by stimulating the same neural structure.

Hypothalamic stimulation of a dominant monkey in a colony prompted him to attack subordinate males but not the females with whom he was on friendly terms. In contrast, hypothalamic stimulation elicited submissiveness in a monkey when she occupied a low hierarchical position, but increased aggressiveness toward subordinates as her social rank was elevated by changing the membership of the colony. Thus, electrical stimulation of the same anatomical site produced markedly different behavior under different social conditions.[50]

Aggression for most animals is ritualized into displays of threat, submission, and appeasement, from which human beings are exempt.[51] However, humans do not solve conflict through ritual display. The apparent lack of innate inhibitions in humans leaves the regulation of conflict to the sanction of authority and social custom.[52] The social environment of humans, not extrapolations from animal behavior, needs to be the focus of inquiries into human aggression.

The debate between innate and acquired aggression was brought to a focus in the early 1970s in *Violence and the Brain,* which advocated mandatory social testing for "thresholds of violence." Those who did not pass the test would be identified and prevented from causing "harm" to society. One of the prevention techniques was psychosurgery, or what was more commonly known as "lobotomy," as characterized in Ken Kesey's novel *One Flew Over the Cuckoo's Nest.*

In *Violence and the Brain,* an organic view of mental dysfunction was expressed clearly in terms of the "hardwired" brain as an organ of behavior. "Any act or state of being (i.e., behavior or thought) is a reflection of some particular mode of organization of the complex circuits of the brain."[53] Individual violence was a symptom of a disturbance in the brain mechanisms that control violent behavior. A disturbance could be due to brain disease, both genetic and acquired (a blow to the head).

Those persons showing symptoms of disturbances or dyscontrol could be prone to violent acts or have a "low threshold for violence."[54] In view of such possibilities, the authors claimed it was "necessary" to identify those persons with malfunctioning brains so that they could be treated and thus their violence could be "prevented."[55] The identification and regulation of the violent individual echoes the claim that "the prerequisite of all civilized communal life is that people learn to properly control their impulses."[56]

The proposal to prevent violence by way of regulation of individual behavior brought a rash of rebuttals. Some critics claimed psychiatry had become a political force by disguising social conflict as "illness" and justified coercion as "treatment."

Others argued that the claim that violence issues from an individual's brain is dubious because of "the essentially social [or anti-social] nature of violent assaultive actions."[57] Violence refers to a "behavioral transaction in which one person exerts upon another person [or thing] an action considered [by the recipient or others] to be injurious and unwarranted."[58] Violent action occurs in a social context of interaction and naming where the "violent" actor is one participant. Therefore, the context, including the person or thing to which the act is directed, is "also an expression of the functioning brain of the person who commits the action . . . [therefore], the action in question . . . involves more than the 'expression' of a particular brain."[59] Violence cannot be reduced to a property or a process located solely in a particular individual. There is no *a priori* basis to localize a cause of the violent behavior within the brain of someone "who is identified [by someone else] as expressing 'abnormal aggressive behavior.' "[60]

A disorder described as an entity (impulse) "located" in the individual is rather a relation with something which "locates" and evaluates the behavior/body of the person in a social context. It is clear that the "power to diagnose—to give names to—problematic behavior" is one facet of the power to delimit, or to "define the limits of allowable behavioral diversity in a society."[61] Such power to label and enforce definitions is a "touchstone of social control." In this sense, the "violent individual" is not a discrete biological entity, but a historical social construction of definitions of violence that delimit behavior.[62]

If we consider that there is socially mediated violent behavior, then a different slant is given to how we perceive the phenomenon of violence as war and those who participate in it. To develop this thought further, from the perspective of learned aggression, fighting is a learned behavior based on the principle of reinforcement.[63] Defensive fighting can be stimulated from pain of attack, but "aggression in the strict sense of an unprovoked attack can only be produced by training."[64]

S. L. A. Marshall, appointed chief historian for World War II and later a general in the Korean War, interviewed hundreds of infantry companies in the central Pacific and European theatres. The results showed that no more than 15 percent of the soldiers had fired at the enemy. Only one-quarter of an infantry could be expected to strike a blow in an engagement with the enemy unless compelled by overwhelming circumstance. This one-quarter included well-trained and campaign-seasoned troops: "I mean that 75 percent will not fire or will not persist in firing against the enemy and his works. These men may face the danger but they will not fight."[65] Marshall describes an unwillingness to kill, not a fear of being killed, during a war to which nearly everyone was ideologically committed. He includes psychiatric studies of combat fatigue that found that

> fear of killing, rather than fear of being killed, was the most common cause of battle failure in the individual . . . It is therefore reasonable to believe that the average and normally healthy individual—the man who can endure the mental and physical stresses of combat—still has such an inner and usually unrealized resistance toward killing a fellow man that he will not of his own volition take life if it is possible to turn away from that responsibility.[66]

The account of Lee Childress, a sergeant of the 206th Assault Helicopter Company at Phu Loi, Vietnam, from June 1967 to May 1968, offers a similar perspective and questions the moral validity of authoritatively sanctioned war in the discourse of profanity that accompanies conflict and combat: "The first time you were under fire, you thought, 'How the fuck can they do this to me? If only I could talk to the cocksuckers firing at me, we'd get along, everything would be all right.' I just had the overwhelming feeling that if I could talk to these people, that they really are the same as I am, that it's not us that are doing it, it's some other system and we're just pawns in this fucking thing, throwing the shit at each other."[67]

That "there is no such thing as an instinct for fighting" supports the claim that aggressive behavior is learned behavior. On this view, aggression produced by training implies that the "motivation for fighting is increased by success; frustration leads to aggression, and all so-called physiological causes can be traced to external stimulation."[68]

The role of learning in aggression contains a distinction between two concepts, acquisition and habit. The *acquisition* of fighting behavior depends upon biochemical factors. The *habit* of fighting depends upon previous learning, or a history of fighting. Inherited aggressive motor patterns may be a part of an organism's behavioral constitution, but whether or not and how they are expressed depends upon learning. This is supported by evidence that "attack behavior in humans occurs no earlier than talking and walking."[69]

Instinct theorists accept the idea that the urge or instinct to aggress arises spontaneously, resulting in hostile behavior. However, an inborn drive of this kind has yet to be found.[70] Yet, drive theorists accept the idea that aroused aggressive drive presumably remains active until discharged by some form of aggression.[71] Here, aggression is a result of frustration, which replaces instinct as the activating source. The two theories are very similar. The commonness of frustration would be explained as persons having excess aggressive energy needing to be discharged.

Knud Larsen includes Lorenz among the drive theorists who support such "hydraulic myths." The logic is as follows: technological achievements have progressed faster than innate inhibitions, and persons thus have less opportunity to work off excess energy. Humans must have an outlet, or an opportunity for the "discharge of aggressive energy" or catharsis, by means of sports and other competitive activities. The assumption is that after the discharge, lower levels of aggression will occur because lower levels of aggressive energy will remain. Larsen notes that this assumption overlooks the possibility that instead of decreasing aggressive behavior, competitive activities may actually strengthen a habit of aggression.[72]

Indeed, studies of violent television viewing found that violent television encourages aggression and that aggressive persons are more attracted to violent programs.[73] This runs counter to the "catharsis theory of media violence." Research designed to test the catharsis theory shows an opposite effect: "Ventilation and vicarious participation, rather than serving to work off aggression, tends to increase it."[74] Further, for persons with a tendency to behave aggressively, different sources of emotional arousal can heighten their aggression.[75] Thus, if violent behavior is learned, then exposure to violent events, activities, or symbolic models would serve to teach violent behavior and reinforce such behavior as well.

Frustration-aggression, or drive theory, has lost its explanatory value in light of evidence that frustration has varied effects on behavior; "aggression does not require frustration."[76] Frustration or anger arousal is a "facilitative, rather than a necessary, condition for aggression." Frustration subsumes too wide a variety of conditions—physical assault, deprivation, defeat, harassment to insults.

The apparent build-up of "aggressive energy" is due to a lowered response threshold. A low level of stimulation will produce a response because of a person's lack of stimulation tolerance. The lowering of the response threshold may change as a function of alterations in a person's physiological status. There may be a pain threshold below which level stimuli may not elicit attack, whereas pain exceeding this minimum intensity may elicit hostile behavior.[77] A hypoglycemic patient may experience mounting feelings of irritability and hostility that will be eliminated with the intake of a glass of orange juice without the hostile feelings being expressed. "There is no aggressive energy which continues to accumulate, and there is no *necessity* for the expression of hostility."[78]

The attempt to equate biological aggression with a lack of serotonin is another example of this lowering of the response threshold. It is a convenient explanation of violence proposed in a time of widespread social violence and disruptive global multicultural migration, similar to the "violence threshold" theory put forward by Mark and Ervin in 1970, in the context of conflict and social upheaval caused by the civil rights movement, anti-establishment protests against the Vietnam war, and the cold war.

Social Learning Theory

In contrast to frustration-aggression theory, in social learning theory, "aversive stimulation produces a general state of emotional arousal that can facilitate any number of responses."[79] Stimulation by something a person does not like will create an emotional arousal that may have a variety of responses. The resulting behavior depends upon "how the source of arousal is cognitively appraised, the modes of response learned for coping with stress, and their relative effectiveness."[80]

The source of the aversion is sifted through value judgments, personal history, and expectations of anticipated consequences. Some people may respond to aversive situations by seeking help and support, others by withdrawal, others by increased achievement efforts, others by self-anesthetization with drugs and alcohol, and still others by constructive problem solving. The comparative strengths of the emotional arousal of anger and fear in circumstances of distress and their associated action tendencies, or responses, depends upon situational conditions and prior learning.[81]

To elaborate upon the context of emotional arousal, sensations, including painful ones, logically must be felt. The "object" of distress is the overall threatening situation and the expectation of pain: "If a person insists that they felt pain, we cannot contradict them. Ultimately only [the person] can tell us whether [he/she] was in pain or not."[82]

Alice Miller makes a distinction between emotion that is *experienced* and emotion that is warded off as unacceptable and denied its proper identification and integration into a person's repertoire of feeling. For instance, "hatred is a normal human *feeling*, and feeling has never killed anyone."[83] For Miller, an appropriate emotional response to the abuse of children, rape of women, and torture of the innocent is anger and hatred. "It is not *experienced* hatred that leads to acts of violence."[84] Rather, for Miller it is hatred that is denied and placed under the name of ideology that leads to violence where it can be legitimated as acceptable. Miller argues for the validation and expression of these very real yet conventionally unacceptable feelings of anger and hatred instead of more insidious consequences resulting from their denial. The connection between violence and legitimation is important and will be discussed in the next chapter.

One theory describes emotion as a physiological reaction that includes the cognitive activity of labeling, or identifying an emotion as a certain sort according to appropriate knowledge of the circumstances.[85] Emotion entails physiological sensation and its assessment in a particular situation. "Dispositional" emotions may not require a detectable feeling at the moment, as when we say, "I've loved her for years" or "I've been afraid he'd do that." It is important to keep in mind that the theory requires a causal analysis. Emotions here are "feels" that are unanalyzable and cannot be made up of desires, behaviors, the awareness of objects, and so on.

John Dewey has argued for a behavioral interpretation of emotion.[86] Emotional behavior is not caused by a pre-existent emotion. The behavior is determined by the situation and can be explained by referring to actions that were formerly and continue to be useful in coping with the situation. Emotions have three components: (1) intellectual, or the idea of the object of emotion, (2) a "feel," and (3) a disposition for behavior. Emotion thus is interwoven with a person's individual history and behavioral tendencies.

Emotions are not simply an "inner" feeling, like a headache. They also have an "outer" reference, to some situation, person, object, or state of affairs.[87] In evaluative theories of emotion, emotions are "intentional" in that they are directed toward objects in the world. They are more than mere "feels" about the world; they are ways of being aware of things in the world.

In cognitive theories of emotion, emotions logically presuppose both evaluative and factual beliefs, and each type of emotion has a typical set of beliefs.[88] The words that describe emotion form part of the vocabulary of evaluation for appraisal and criticism. To say one is angry at one's sister is to make a negative evaluation of one's sister. It is an indirect value judgement that presupposes factual beliefs about the emotional context.

The advantage of cognitive theory is that an analysis of the rationality of emotions is possible. Our emotions may be "irrational" or inappropriate to the actual situation. It is "reason" and not emotion that should be charged with irrationality. Emotions are in part "cognitive" and "evaluative" phenomena that presuppose rationality in a psychological sense—the ability to use concepts and have reasons for what one does or feels. Whether those reasons are good reasons is another matter.[89] Hence, emotions have physiological and cognitive components which are situation dependent for their expression. Let us now turn to emotional arousal and behavioral response in the context of social learning theory.

There are two broad classes of motivators to behavior in social learning theory.[90] First, there are the biologically based motivators, where behavior is mainly a result of the experience of painful effects of internal and external sources of aversive stimulation. Second, there are cognitively based motivators. The capacity to represent future consequences in thought allows individuals to generate current motivators of behavior. The outcome expectations may be material (physically painful or consummatory), sensory (enjoyable, novel, or unpleasant) or social (positive and negative evaluative reactions). Cognitive motivation may also take the form of self-motivation that operates through goal setting and self-evaluations.

Some aggressive acts are motivated by painful stimulation. Most situations that lead people to aggress—such as insults, verbal challenges or unjust treatment—"gain this activating capacity through learning experiences."[91] People learn to dislike or to attack certain people either through direct unpleasant encounters with them, or "on the basis of symbolic and vicarious experiences that conjure up hatreds."[92] Because of the regularities in events in the environment, "antecedent cues come to signify future events and the outcomes particular actions are likely to produce. Such uniformities create expectations about what leads to what."[93] Thus, these uniformities in the environment have parallels in the patterning of behavior and expectations in the individual.

In the example of the monkey colony, stimulation of the hypothalamus (the neural locus for mediation of aggressive behavior) brought about distinctly different behavior under different social conditions. How neurophysiological systems operate internally is conditioned by external stimuli such that they can be socially activated for different types of action. "Biological systems are roused in humans by provocative external events and by ideational activation."[94] According to the social learning view, persons are biologically endowed with neurophysiological mechanisms (hypothalamus and limbic system) that enable them to behave aggressively, but the arousal of these mechanisms depends upon "appropriate stimulation and is subject to cognitive control."

Isolated Boys Wounded Heroes

People are not born with preformed patternings of aggressive behavior. They must learn them.[95] New modes of behavior are the outcome of a combination of biological endowment and experience. The argument that males are aggressive due to an excess of testosterone was tested in an experiment by Leslie Rogers at the University of New England in Australia.[96] In this study, female rat pups were given testosterone in the first five days after birth. As adults, their behavior was more like that of male rats with a high level of aggressiveness. However, the behavior of female maternal rats showed that they lick the anal/genital region of male pups more frequently than they do that of female pups. The mothers know which pups are male. The question arose whether it was the licking or the testosterone itself that caused aggressive behavior. To test this, the researchers used a brush to simulate what mother rats normally do to male pups by artificially stimulating female pups in the anal/genital region. The artificially stimulated females as adults also exhibited "masculine" aggressive behavior. An external environmental stimulus changed behavior in a similar way to a hormone.

Social conditioning influences expectations and behavior in the interchange between caregiver and child. The primary role of the face in early childhood development is prior to language in the communication between parent and child.[97] Memory in young children is highly visual, sensory, and iconic.[98] This is the "unmistakable language of somatic interchange" between child and caregiver that establishes the first fundamental understanding of the world as basic trust or basic mistrust.[99] Basic trust is established if the give-and-take between caregiver and child is successfully somatically negotiated. The child obtains a unity between the inner and the outer worlds as a basic wholeness and interrelated goodness in the relation between self, other, and community (world). If this interchange is not successfully negotiated, the child experiences basic mistrust, with rage, fantasies of domination, or destruction of the sources of pleasure and provision that may be relived as an adult.

The somatic interchange of the child relies upon the facial cues of the caregiver to process appropriate emotional responses with behavior and expectations. There is evidence that for at least five emotional categories (happiness, anger, surprise, sadness, disgust) there are facial behaviors specific to each emotion and that these relationships are invariant across cultures. Cultural differences in facial behaviors and emotion are ascribed to the circumstances that evoke an emotion, the action consequences of an emotion, and display rules governing the management of facial behavior in particular settings, as well as attitudes about emotion.

One study investigated the emotional characteristics children associated to each sex. Boys and girls were individually presented with two identical cartoon animal images.[100] Only the facial expressions of the characters were different. One face was angry and unsmiling, and the other face was smiling and pleasant. The children were asked which image was the daddy and which was the mommy. Consistently, the children chose the angry face as the "daddy" image and the smiling face as the "mommy" image. At an early age, these children had already developed prototypical emotional characterizations and expectations for each sex.

These emotional expectations for each sex are reflected in the somatic interchanges between caregivers and infants. As boys, men have shared patterns of conditioning in the process of becoming men.[101] The deliberate "toughening up" of boys generally begins immediately after birth. A number of cases concerning human contact and infant boys show infant boys in America receive fewer demonstrative acts of affection from their mothers than infant girls and are touched less.[102]

This can affect neurological development. Tactile stimulation is an important factor in stimulating the growth of nerve tissues and their protective coatings. The neural pathways of the brain are still being formed in the first sixteen months of life. The dramatic difference in verbal dexterity between boys and girls may be due to how infants are initiated to language and the degree of stimulation they receive.[103]

Boys are touched less and talked to less frequently than girls. Boys are weaned earlier than girls and are deprived of the natural tranquilizers and immune-system support of the mother's milk as well as the comfort of the breast.[104] They lag between four to six weeks in their development behind girls: they crawl, sit, and speak later and tend to cry more in infancy.

One implication of the lack of nurturing contact is that men are more uneasy with touching than women. As well, boys are more likely to be held facing outward, toward the world and other people. Girls are held close, and inward, toward security, warmth, and the comfort of the parent.[105] In the somatic language of distancing, the communal attitude becomes apparent, as boys are not expected to need the same degree of nurturance, safety, intimacy, love, and support to which girls are entitled.

Girls are encouraged to stay close to the mother, restricted, nurtured, and protected, while boys are pushed to become more independent. Girls are more likely to get a positive response when crying for help than boys. If a child has a minor injury, parents are quicker to comfort girls than boys. These types of gender disparaties in caregiving have been criticized accurately as making girls more dependent.

For the boys, the negative effect of this conditioning is that they become independent to the point of isolation.[106] "Boys are *pushed* into assertive, aggressive, and nondependent behavior. They are also more restricted, especially by the father, to traditionally heroic, male-gender-specific toys."[107] It also means they do not want to do anything that might make them appear unmanly or like girls. "To become *unmen* is to essentially risk nonexistence; there are no other viable options presented to us."

Boys learn that it is okay for girls to have feelings. They also learn that it makes peers, parents, and other adults uneasy if boys express their feelings. *Feelings are not masculine.* The refrain of boyhood is reinforced repeatedly: "Don't be a baby. Don't cry when you are hurt. Don't whine. Be a big boy now and wipe those tears away; big boys don't cry." Aaron Kipnis sums up the demand to be masculine as "*Men should suffer alone and in silence!* It's like an ancient, evil spell that hangs over us."[108]

The result may be domineering, insensitive men who are covertly angry. This is the way men are trained to carry their anger.[109] A cool head is the model for men: keep your cool, cool down, chill out, keep it all together, stiff upper lip, don't blow it, back off, don't get uptight. This conditioning directs men not to express their strong emotional experiences except in the positive modes associated with winning and triumph, the hero experience. "If a man is angry, it is seen as a shameful exposure of his inability to be the victor . . . The dominant male ethic perceives both tears and anger as expressions of failure . . . Often our anger is just the cap on a deep well of grief."[110]

This conditioning for the hero role prepares men to attempt to extend themselves beyond the natural limits of their bodies, hearts, and minds in an attempt to achieve some ideal of manhood and productivity. As Kipnis says, they become "success objects." Surrendering to this heroic ideal may feel "powerful and invulnerable." However, "the price is alienation, isolation, stress induced mental or physical illness, injury, and an early death."[111]

Mediated by environmental conditioning, the role played by biological factors in aggression is species variant. Aggression in animals is largely dependent upon physical strength. In humans, the imaginative construction and use of weapons decreases dependence upon biological endowment for combat success. A puny person with a gun can eliminate a physically stronger opponent. As well, human social organization diminishes the importance of internal structural characteristics for aggression. At the social level, aggressive power derives from organized collective action.

For individual and collective survival, vicarious learning is crucial. If organisms relied solely on learning from the consequences of their actions, the number of fatal errors would reduce the odds for survival. The more costly the mistakes, the greater is the reliance on observational learning from competent models.[112] Especially for aggression, trial and error can have deadly outcomes. To alleviate the high risk of individual experimentation, "by observing the aggressive conduct of others, one forms a conception of how the behavior is performed, and on later occasions, the symbolic representation can serve as a guide for action."[113] In this way, the cultural symbolism of violence is able to influence behavior by providing symbolic representations for action.

Observational learning is divided into four interrelated subprocesses.[114] First, attentional processes direct the exploration and perception of modeled activities. These initial perceptions are followed by the second process of memory representation of the observed modeled behavior. The influence of modeled behavior would be negligible without a memory of it. By coding into images, words, or other symbolic modes, transitory modeling influences are altered for memory representation into enduring behavior guides. The capacity for observational learning increases with the increased capability for symbolizing experience. These symbolic representations must then eventually be transformed into appropriate behaviors. The third process, motor production, regulates the integration of constituent acts into new response patterns.

Social learning theory makes an important distinction between the *acquisition* of behaviors that are potentially destructive or injurious and *factors* that determine whether or not persons will enact what they have learned. *Not all learned behavior is enacted.* Individuals can acquire, retain, and possess the capability to act aggressively, but the behavior rarely may be expressed if it has no functional value for them or is negatively sanctioned. If appropriate circumstances and stimulation occur on a later occasion, persons then put into practice what they have learned. Thus, the fourth incentive and motivational processes regulate the enactment of observationally learned responses.

In contemporary culture, aggressive modes of behavior can be learned from three main sources. One primary source is the aggression modeled and reinforced by family members. Family violence reinforces violent types of conduct, as shown by similarities in child abuse practices across several generations.[115] For instance, a convicted rapist, when asked why he replied that the "great pain" women experienced when he raped them was "a good feeling to me," he returned, "I guess it goes back to my childhood, when I'd seen my father do the same thing to my mother."[116]

A second source of modeled aggression is the social network within which the family is situated. The subculture of daily interaction is an influential matrix for modeling. "The highest incidence of aggression is found in communities in which aggressive models abound and fighting prowess is regarded as a valued attribute."[117] For instance, in studies of rape in tribal societies, Peggy Reeves Sanday concludes that violence is not biologically programmed, but is a means by which men socially programmed for violence express their social selves. "Men who are conditioned to respect the female virtues of growth and the sacredness of life do not violate women."[118]

A third source of modeling for aggressive conduct is the mass media. As has been indicated already through the example of the contrary findings to the cathartic theory of media, additional research shows televised violence teaches aggressive modes of behavior, changes restraints over aggressive behavior, desensitizes and habituates people to violence, and conditions people's images of reality that influence behavior.[119] The stained glass windows of medieval churches simply have been replaced by spectacular media images that serve a parallel didactic function: to tell the story of what is valued in the culture.

Flight *and* Fight

From the perspective of anger and violent behavior, frustration or anger arousal is a "facilitative, rather than a necessary, condition for aggression." Frustration subsumes too wide a variety of conditions for aggression, ranging from physical abuse to insults. The relationship between the emotional experience of anger or frustration and the behavior exhibited includes an analysis of the origin of the angry feelings and the factors controlling the enacted behavior.

There are two classes of variables that intervene between the objective situation and the person's aggressive action. One variable is the emotion of anger. Anger is regarded as the motivational construct serving to heighten the likelihood of aggression. Anger is considered an inborn reaction to goal blockage.[120] The second variable is the interpretation of the situation. These include such socially learned expectations as the punitive incentives for aggression and the social cost of aggressive behavior.

Leonard Berkowitz argues that aversive events are the root of angry aggression.[121] Aversive events may arouse fear and an inclination to escape or avoid an unpleasant situation. They also arouse many of the expressive motor reactions and memory responses that are associated with the experience of anger. Whether or not the aversively stimulated person is consciously aware of these reactions and responses at the time, these internal reactions produce a tendency to attack the perceived source of unpleasantness. Said differently, aversive events elicit responses to flight *and* to fight, and the emotional experiences of fear and anger may accompany these arousals. Prior learning and the circumstances of the aversive event determine the strength of these experiences and their associated action tendencies. As well, prior learning may influence the instigation to attack such that the aversively stimulated person is inclined to injure a suitable target.[122] This phenomenon, variously described in psychoanalytic and philosophical theories as an aggressive compulsion to repeat, is in the discourse of trauma theory, the spontaneous reenactment of unresolved trauma memories associated with posttraumatic stress disorder.

Posttraumatic Stress Disorder

Posttraumatic stress disorder (PTSD) is an obverse instance of the "angry" aggression response in an aversive situation. A traumatic or uncontrollable aversive event that instigates flight and fight arousal may result in chronic dysregulation of nervous function.[123] A high percentage of combat veterans, rape victims, sexual abuse victims, and survivors of catastrophic events experience symptoms of PTSD.[124]

Traumatic events have primary effects on the psychological structures of the self and the systems of attachment and meaning that link individual and community.[125] They destroy the victim's fundamental trust assumptions about the safety of the world, the positive value of self, and the meaningful order of creation.[126] Victims of trauma experience damage to the self in the violation of autonomy and basic bodily integrity, and develop contempt for autonomy and dignity compounded by shame and doubt.[127]

The psychological reactions to trauma consist of hyperreactivity (startle reactions, explosive outbursts of anger) and recurrent intrusive recollections of the trauma (flashbacks, nightmares) alternating with a compensatory psychic numbing, constriction of affect and social functioning, and a loss of a sense of control over one's destiny. The traumatic stressor is defined as an aversive stimulus that mobilizes so much painful affect that psychological adaptive mechanisms are overwhelmed, initiating the alternating responses of hyperreactivity and hyporeactivity.[128]

The actual trauma event may be quite brief but result in long-lasting, at times lifelong disturbances. The recall of the actual trauma may be impaired and occur as memory traces of flashbacks, nightmares, or intrusive images. Aspects of the traumatic response, such as lack of trust or hyperarousal, may persist or reappear after an unrelated stressful event, or seemingly without provocation. PTSD indicates that long-lasting neurobehavioral responses and memories are formed as part of the traumatic response, in contrast to the easily forgotten thoughts and response patterns of daily life.[129]

The capacity of a stressor to elicit a state of helplessness is critical to its capacity to produce psychological traumatization.[130] The inescapable stressor (IS) response, or learned helplessness model appears to be an invaluable model for investigating the interaction of biology and behavior in traumatic disorders. A study of animals exposed to severe or repeated inescapable aversive stimuli showed that IS exposure produces an initial alarm response, followed by conditioned alarm states and exaggerated reactivity to previously tolerated stressors.

The negative symptoms of PTSD, like impaired concentration, loss of interest in people and activities, and psychomotor retardation, are similar to the negative behavioral changes found in IS exposure. Some PTSD symptoms may be produced simply through activation-induced disturbances in homeostatic neuronal systems and not as goal-directed learned responses. In contrast, stress-induced dysregulation may produce learned behavioral syndromes that adaptively dampen arousal through mechanisms such as phobic avoidance or cognitive mechanisms that decrease the level of arousal.

The autonomic, or spontaneous, conditioning hypothesis of PTSD may involve mechanisms akin to those in animal studies that investigate the startle reflex by conditioning. A visual stimulus, a light, is paired with an electric shock to condition the shock response to the light. When the light stimulus is subsequently paired with a loud noise, the resulting startle response is greater than the response produced by the noise alone. In veterans with PTSD, the exaggerated startle response and increased autonomic responses to stimuli such as loud noises may reflect a conditioned enhancement of these responses through previous pairing of the loud noise with life-threatening situations.[131]

In a combat situation, conditioned stimuli include the sounds of gunfire, mortars, helicopters, enemy sightings, wounded combatants, odors of gunpowder, napalm, and the damp jungle. Unconditioned stimuli include unexpected explosions, physical assaults, and horrific

visual scenes such as mutilated or decomposed bodies. The conditioned responses to these stimuli include physiological reactivity, defensive behavior (e.g., "taking cover" at the sound of a car backfiring),
explosive rage, startle, and vivid imagery or flashbacks.[132]

Patients who suffer from a trauma syndrome form a certain type
of transference in the therapy relationship. The experience of terror
has deformed their emotional responses to anyone in a position of
authority. Hence, traumatic transference reactions have an intense, life-
or-death quality to them. "A destructive force appears to intrude repeatedly into the relationship between therapist and patient. This force,
which was traditionally attributed to the patient's innate aggression,
can now be recognized as the violence of the perpetrator."[133] The transference does not reflect a dyadic relationship, but a triad. "The terror
is as though a patient and therapist convene in the presence of yet
another person. The third image is the victimizer, who . . . demanded
silence and whose command is now being broken."[134]

The transference reflects the experience of terror and abandonment, creating the need for an "omnipotent rescuer." Often the patient
may develop idealized expectations of the therapist to be this rescuer.
When the therapist fails to live up to these expectations, as he/she
inevitably will, the patient is often overcome with fury and the need
for revenge. Because the patient feels that his or her life depends upon
the rescuer, there is no room for tolerance or human error. This is the
displacement of rage from the perpetrator to the caregiver, for the loss
of safety the perpetrator took away in the threat to life.

Judith Lewis Herman states, "Trauma is contagious."[135] In the
role of witness to disaster or atrocity, the therapist can be overwhelmed,
experiencing to a lesser degree "the same terror, rage and despair as
the patient." This is known as "traumatic countertransference" or
"vicarious traumatization."[136] The therapist may begin to experience
symptoms of posttraumatic stress disorder.

Vicarious traumatization, also termed "secondary trauma," refers to the effects in people who care for, or are involved with, those
who have been traumatized directly.[137] These secondary trauma victims are spouses, family members exposed to the trauma victim, or
even nontraumatized children who play with traumatized children.
This also includes family members who were not born at the time of
the traumatic event, resulting in "intergenerational transmission" of
trauma.[138] In the empathic identification with the victim, caregivers
also may become victims of the originary trauma.

Traumatic countertransference includes the therapist's emotional
reactions to the victim and to the traumatic event itself. For therapists

working with survivors of the Nazi holocaust, there has been observed "an almost impersonal uniformity of emotional responses . . . The Holocaust itself, rather than the individual personalities of therapists and patients, is the primary source of these reactions."[139] For Herman, this shows the shadow presence of the perpetrator in the patient-therapist relationship and traces countertransference, like transference, to "its original source outside of a simple dyadic relationship."[140]

The patient cannot trust the therapist due to the experience of trauma. There is no confidence in the therapist's benign intentions. The therapist may eventually react to these hostile attributions in unaccustomed ways. "Drawn into the dynamics of dominance and submission, the therapist may inadvertently reenact aspects of the abusive relationship . . . Once again the perpetrator plays a shadow role in this type of interaction."[141] This dynamic has been attributed to the patient's defensive style of "projective identification." The patient's projective identification of the shadow perpetrator with the therapist now assumes the role of perpetrator for the victim.

In the role of witness, the therapist may be caught in conflict between victim and perpetrator as being able to identify with the feelings of the perpetrator.[142] This may be profoundly horrifying to the therapist, as it challenges his or her identity as a caring person. The therapist's own identification with the perpetrator, or aggressor, may have several forms. The therapist may doubt the patient's story, or minimalize or rationalize the abuse. The therapist may find the patient's behavior revolting or disgusting and become extremely judgmental in the victim's failure to live up to expectations of how a "good" victim would behave. The therapist may feel contempt for the patient's helplessness or paranoid fear of the patient's vindictive rage. There may be "moments of frank hate and wish to be rid of the patient."[143] The therapist may be required to examine their own capacity for violence. "What we cannot own up to, we may have to reject in others."[144]

A recurrent theme for treatment of PTSD patients and their caregivers is the search for meaning in terrible experience.[145] For Vietnam veterans the struggle to formulate meanings of their experiences may cause them to become psychologically isolated.[146] It is estimated that in the U. S., 30 million people, or 13 percent of the total population, have served in the armed forces, and 50 percent have a first-degree relative who is a veteran.[147] Over half a million American Vietnam veterans suffer posttraumatic stress disorder years after returning from war.[148] Rehabilitation therapies include support groups, buddy systems, family therapy, social networks, and integration into society.

Purposeful Distanciation

Many Vietnam veterans felt that they had changed and no longer
fit into the society when they went to war.[149] Their personal struggle
to sort out the meaning of the war experience brought about greater
sensitivity to issues of justice, fairness, equity, deceit, phoniness, lies,
the use of power, and principles of morality. The realities of war, life-
and-death situations, intense bonding with buddies, the exercise of
important decision making and the day-to-day struggle to survive
caused them to ask philosophical and psychological questions their
families and friends at home would find difficult to understand. The
struggle to formulate meaning and the fear of stigmatization if others
found out about the atrocities of guerilla warfare brought about psychological isolation for veterans. They feared that no one would understand what the war was about and that no one would understand
them. The need to connect with fellow humans conflicted with the
need to protect themselves from emotional vulnerability.

"Intimacy conflict" occurs when the symptoms of PTSD prevent
the establishment or maintenance of trusting interpersonal relations.[150]
Anger toward a loved one often is accompanied by anxiety about the
attachment, as these feelings are elicited in the same circumstances. The
risk of loss in intimacy attachment is heightened for the veteran and is
managed by "purposeful distanciation" as a coping pattern developed
as a response to the death or injury of a member of a military unit.[151]

Purposeful distanciation allows the individual to control the
degree of emotional attachment by partially numbing feelings and by
not permitting personal disclosure that would lead to the formation of
friendship or deeper levels of caring for others. "Emotional numbing,
when combined with hyperarousal states, ensured that during combat
the function of behavior was survival."[152] The "confrontation with death
and the realities of war" led to purposeful distanciation, while it also
created a need to know oneself more fully and genuinely be close to
others. Yet the survival of war demanded emotional numbing to
maintain a psychologically safe distance.

Survivor guilt about having been the one to survive, instead of
one's friends, also leads to self-blame and recrimination which make
it difficult to view one's life as worthwhile in view of the loss of life.
This phenomenon is acutely evident in survivors of mass trauma, such
as the Jewish Holocaust in Nazi Germany. Upon return from the war,
an individual was likely to have difficulty establishing intimate ties
and integrating into a community with a sense of belonging. Thus the
extreme form of purposeful distanciation has consequences of loneliness and alienation.

A paradox of PTSD for veterans lies in the ego-defensive quality of purposeful distanciation. In order to have truly intimate interpersonal relations, an individual has to learn to trust; disclose personal concerns; and render oneself potentially vulnerable to hurt, rejection, and failure. However, the presence of hyperarousal states creates defenses against vulnerability. Both openness and unpreparedness are threats to the self. The ingrained cycle of survivor adaptation, of co-experienced feelings of distance, distrust, and vulnerability makes it extremely difficult to integrate such trauma behavior into the self.

The survivor mode of functioning (i.e., hyperarousal leading to emotional constriction, depression, affective flooding, or sensation seeking) always works against feelings of vulnerability, perceived threats, and being in a position of unguardedness. Thus, the paradox of PTSD is that in order to recover from the stress disorder the individual must "let go" of survivor mode functioning in order to come to terms with the unassimilated elements of the trauma. *However, it is an extremely difficult process to accomplish because survivor mode functioning is what led to survival in the first instance.* Intrapsychically, then, to give up survivor mode functioning is often subjectively experienced as death anxiety because of the unconscious belief that without it the individual self will die or be injured.[153]

The repetition of survival mode can be traced back to the situations of traumatic events from which the behavior arose. Events in the present act as functional equivalents of the first instance and activate hyperarousal and cognitive programs that direct adaptive behavior. Thus, love relationships, the illness of a child, a partner's frustration about the relationship, loss of work, or other stressors may activate PTSD and "increase the likelihood of purposeful distanciation without fear of loss, rejection, repudiation or humiliation. The result, more often than not, is conflict over intimacy."[154]

As well, the emotional numbing and prevention of disclosure of the self in the trauma victim mitigate against the expression of anger within an intimate relationship. Conflicts that are not resolved thus create a repression of anger that weakens the relational bond. The self can enact a covert inner rebellion that is expressed as indirect anger in all aspects of the relationship.[155] Or, as in the case of trauma victims, the threat to the vulnerable self in an anger/anxiety intimate relation may activate the PTSD symptom of explosive rage. In this respect, aggression is tied, not to an unruly drive according to Freud, but to the "fracture of human connection," a "sign of failure of relationship."[156]

A key adaptive function of survivor guilt and aggression is to reaffirm the world as a just and compassionate place. It is a means to restore lost human values and one's own human image. In the case of Jewish Holocaust survivors, "both guilt and aggression serve to restore a feeling of justice and security in relation to the world" that contrasts directly with "the denial and rejection of any kind of guilt by the mass murderer . . . and the silently acquiescent world."[157] The acquiescence of the "world" to the acceptance of violence by the perpetrator is illustrative of an indirect consensual acceptance of violence. The ability of the victim to interpret the traumatic experience and accept the scope and meaning of survivor guilt through the therapeutic process is crucial to constructively transcending or overcoming it, in the same manner of transcending *identification with the aggressor*.

Identification with the Aggressor

The phenomenon of identification with the aggressor reflects a fundamental aggression against the self through acts of self-alteration and hostile self-judgement.[158] In the event of aggression, the other's hostile gaze is redirected by the self toward oneself as a defense against the devaluation undergone as an object of the hostile gaze. It gives the self an illusory sense of control because while the self is the object of the devaluing gaze, the self is simultaneously its own powerful spectator (internalized aggressor) observing and judging oneself. The self thus feels in control when, as the object of the *aggressor's* control, it gains the aggressor's approval and when the self, as internal aggressor and observer of self, feels satisfied that the commands are being followed.

Identification with the aggressor is characteristic of any "slave system" of domination/subordination of one person over another. Andrea Dworkin characterizes this dynamic where the "slaves" internalize the oppressor's view of them which results in pathological self-hatred.[159] Such self-hatred then wreaks vengeance on its own kind as the internalized aggressor's gaze is directed toward one's own. The oppressed become isolated from each other and their common condition becomes obscured, which makes united rebellion and resistance inconceivable. The oppressor is able to divide and rule. The power of the aggressor becomes incontrovertible, as it is protected by civil law, armed force, custom, and divine and biological sanction.[160] Within Western culture, the rule of the aggressor is reflected in the myth of the hero as social savior wielding sanctioned violence.

The dynamic of the slave system is a form of institutional trauma that is distinct from the act(s) of assault or violation usually associated with trauma experiences. From the previous discussion of symbolic modeling and vicarious learning, it can be seen how institutions, as loci of collectively acceptable behavior, may perpetuate trauma through support and promotion of oppressive and hence injurious beliefs and behavior, such as racism or sexism. Institutional trauma reflects the extent to which the symptoms of assault, for instance wife battering, function in a larger interplay of social influences. The devaluation and subordination of women may be reflected in the therapeutic situation. For instance, justifiable anger at professionals may be interpreted as "resistance," or actual patient powerlessness may be seen as "depression."[161]

The silence surrounding the devastation brought about by the Holocaust held second-generation Germans hostage in secondary trauma. They had been raised not to ask questions, not to feel and to think that such a horror could be dealt with unemotionally.[162] The conspiracy of silence was translated into a cultural protocol as improper behavior, where postwar children were considered improper if they asked their parents questions about the Third Reich.

Such an appeal to normalcy is in accordance with the "poisonous pedagogy" of parental enforcement of obedience and suppression of a child's feelings. Alice Miller's analysis of the father (the same applies to the mother as parent) who misuses his power by suppressing his children's critical faculties, shows his weaknesses by staying hidden behind his fixed attributes of uniqueness, bigness, importance, and power. In this respect, Miller attributes Hitler's legendary influence over the men who surrounded him to his symbolic likeness to their fathers. "They will submit to this man, will acclaim him, allow themselves to be manipulated by him, and put their trust in him, finally surrendering totally to him without even being aware of their enslavement."[163]

One of the things the history of the Third Reich teaches us is that the "monstrous is not infrequently contained in what is 'normal,' in what is felt by the great majority to be 'quite normal and natural.'"[164] This insight is acute in the discussion of trauma transference and Girard's monstrous double in chapter 5. Such benign acceptance, as an indirect acquiescent consensus, is also characteristic of the acceptance of the assumption that violence is innate and that it requires social controls. This demand for social control legitimates a complex system of beliefs and social practices as normal and natural that fundamentally undermines trust relationships of the individual, the validation of emotion and anger, and collective growth in violent social stasis.

FIGURE 3

U.S. Military Police on Patrol, Chu Lai, Vietnam, 1969

Photographer: Clinton C. Whitmer, U.S. Army Spec 4 Medic during September 1968 through October 1969 Tour of Duty, Chu Lai, Vietnam.

2

Violence and Legitimation

In the previous chapter, the assumption of normal or "natural" violence was contrasted with the social motives for interpersonal conduct in social learning theory. "Natural" violence assumes intrapsychic factors, such as instincts, brain centers, or so-called aggressive energy influence what is labeled "aggressive motivation" and "violent behavior."[1] In contrast, the social learning theory and posttraumatic stress disorder models discuss anger and the psychoneurological learned responses to aversive stimuli. Violent behavior is a cognitively and neurologically mediated response to perceived aversive stimuli, regulated by social and moral sanctions of appropriateness. The motivation for aggression is a conditioned response to aversive stimuli (other responses might include withdrawal, substance abuse, or constructive problem solving). The enactment of violent behavior in social practices is mediated by the cultural context of expectations and acceptability or tolerance for the expression of violent behavior.

The discussion now turns to the discourse of how social practices are labeled "violent" and how these practices become socially legitimate. The use of coercion by an individual or collective may be labeled "aggression" or "violent behavior" when it is not legitimated by social norms and values. An individual who is labeled "aggressive" is "tantamount to being blamed for antinormative action, and social costs might be incurred by the actor."[2] The estimated value of social costs may inhibit the actor from engaging in violent behavior or coercion. If these costs are low or the goal is very valuable, the actor still may use coercion. "Impression management techniques" may be used to relieve the actor of responsibility and serve to displace blame to the victim, as often occurs in wife assault. "The availability of justifications for using coercion and the economic and political organization of society appear to be directly related to the frequency of coercive acts in a culture."[3]

The effectiveness of coercion is increased, and the negative impressions associated with its use are removed by legitimation of the action. It is not the number of punishments or their magnitude that leads observers to view coercive behavior as aggression, but "the violation of norms or lack of justification."[4] For example, R. J. Light claims that in Colonial America, a father not only had the right to kill his children, but also to call upon colony officers to assist him.[5] Today, such extreme violence against children is unacceptable. However, though there is increasing intolerance for child abuse, the legitimation of violence against children continues in the "poisonous pedagogy" that enforces the child's obedience to parents and the suppression of the child's feelings. Psychological, verbal, and emotional abuse often have longer devastating effects on the victims. In a culture that includes a victim-victimizer dynamic in expected social practice, the availability of social justifications for aggression "tends to facilitate or inhibit the individual in issuing threats and punishing others."[6] In this manner, violence against children under the poisonous pedagogy retains social legitimation.

Violent acts can be delimited between justified and unjustified violence as well as between violent and other forms of behavior. For Freud, civilization attempts to prevent excesses of "brutal violence" by "assuming the right to use violence against criminals."[7] Freud distinguishes between *legitimate* violence as a right of socially acceptable authority to control the *illegitimate* violence of the individual that is not socially sanctioned, and hence is a threat to society.

The division of violence into legitimate and illegitimate behavior indicates a contrast between *social right*—validated by law, status, custom, or social acceptance—and *moral justification*—validated by appeal to religious precepts, ethical principles and reasoning, or consensual moral judgments.[8] A legitimate but immoral act may be performed by someone in a position of legal authority. Conversely, an illegitimate but moral act may be performed by a principled member of a perceived evil social group.

The evaluation of whether violence is legitimate or illegitimate is conditioned by belief. As we have seen, beliefs and evaluations about violence vary according to time, place, and setting. Beliefs as cognitive definitions and evaluations as appraisals of desirability go hand in hand.[9] A positive evaluation of a particular act may obscure any reference to the act as violent. An acceptance of a definition of violence that includes "infant malnutrition caused by poverty" may lead to an increased negative evaluation of income distribution within society. The process of discerning legitimacy or illegitimacy of an action is definitional or classificatory, such as labeling or naming.[10]

Violence and Behavior

The three components in judging an act to be aggressive are the following: an action is observed, an intent to harm is inferred, and the action is judged to be antinormative. The judgment or appraisal of the action is an evaluation of its desirability as social behavior once its identification has been made. Simply identifying the act and forming a belief about the behavior as violent is usually insufficient. An evolution of the behavior contextualizes the act as good or bad, desirable or undesirable, appropriate or inappropriate, necessary or unnecessary, and tolerable or intolerable.

The acceptance of the act varies with the "legitimations" and explanations that attempt to make comprehensible otherwise inexplicable behavior. These explanations translate plain *behavior* into *conduct*.[11] Justifications are explanations for behavior where the actor accepts responsibility for the outcomes or consequences and yet maintains the positive motives or values that led to the behavior. "Justifications attempt to reverse or neutralize initial negative impressions formed by observers, have the interpersonal function of avoiding blame and associated negative reactions of others, and align the actor with the norms or rules that govern conduct in the group."[12]

Violence that otherwise would be condemned, may be rendered "justified" by a diffusion of responsibility to other persons or circumstances involved. Individual responsibility may be transferred *systematically* to a collectivity that depersonalizes the actor as a representative of, and allows him/her to blend into, the norms of the group.[13] Legitimated use of coercion, as well as being effectively influential, is one tactic to prevent others from establishing negative opinions of the actor. In the United States, death row contains a disproportionate number of the poor, African Americans, and the mentally challenged and disturbed. The words of Supreme Court Justice William Douglas continue to be relevant: "One searches in vain for the execution of any member of the affluent strata of our society."[14] For these purposes, the availability of justifying norms and values facilitates and encourages the use of coercion.[15] As a result, violence as a legitimate use of coercion is *not* perceived as aggression. The Rodney King arrest in Los Angeles in 1991 was an example of the legitimate use of violence as law enforcement crossed over to police brutality.

A society is able to solve the threat of antagonists external to the group and internal to the group who may be deviant. "If accepted patterns are to be seen as normal, we need a theory of abnormality. The solution is to *include* both normal and abnormal inside the dominant beliefs."[16]

Blaming the Victim

When violence is legitimated by the beliefs and evaluations of the group as justified conduct, the blame for the violation of the norm of the group is refocused from the aggressor/victimizer to the victim. The role of definitions, labeling, and naming is crucial when responsibility for violence shifts to "blaming the victim." In order to maintain the values and beliefs of the group as legitimate when this legitimacy is called into question, a solution to the threat to legitimacy is *"denial* that a given set of acts is properly classified in a socially suspect or disapproved category."[17] A defense against charges of illegitimacy is to *"exclude the persons injured from the universe of morally protected entities."*[18]

Thus, the object or target of violent behavior or aggression is rendered "fair game" by being defined within the belief system as a nonmember of the moral community. As nonmembers, or "outsiders," they pose a threat to the status quo even though they may not be physically dangerous, but simply different than other members of the collective. A static belief system requires the category of "outsider" in order to pre-empt the possibility of change to the system by projecting all possible alternatives onto the nonmember. The outsider is integrated into the belief system of the society and legitimates existing institutions. The outsider is the *illegitimate* excluded model of challenges to the social order. Behavior may be evaluated according to these models and labeled acceptable or unacceptable accordingly. Persons may be labeled and "justifiably" harmed or killed when categorized as "mere animals," or inhuman monsters with abominable traits, or with heinous political views (Fascists, traitors, Communists), or as having a different biology and thus not "human" (i.e., persons of color or women). "By reducing their humanity we emphasize our own."[19]

The object of violence can be transformed in ways that make the violence done to the victim socially acceptable. For instance, a claim for the justification for rape may be that the victim was provocative and "caused" a spontaneous aggressive impulse reaction in the violator, instead of the aggressor being held responsible for his/her own actions. The target of violence might be considered outside the realm of social valuation and protection and not "really human," or uncontrollable by nonviolent means, or a deadly enemy to society. The assumption becomes, "If our society is just, the victims *must* have provoked the aggression, deserved their fate; it follows that the objects of violence inflicted by the Good Authorities (police, etc.) must be bad persons."[20] Collective violence legitimated as a last resort to "rectify injustice" by the "bad" outsider is "necessary" violence, where "violence is necessary now to avoid greater violence."[21] This is a justification of Freud's collective containment of the "aggressive" individual.

The effects of the legitimating logic of the cycle of violent trauma is sentiently portrayed in Michael Ondaatje's *The English Patient*.[22] This pastiche of posttraumatic victims in the aftermath of World War II confronts us with drastic juxtapositions of life and death: the immobile pilot burned beyond recognition watching the whirling desert dance of a youth. Within interlaces of racism, nationalism, imperialism, the Villa San Girolamo provides a momentary sanctuary from systemic cruelty for those suspended in the confusion of its justification as legitimate brutality.

A different means of coercive and punitive authority may be used to victimize disadvantaged segments of society by "arbitrary denial or discriminatory administration of beneficial resources to which they are entitled."[23] An example is inappropriate labeling of battered women as "hypochondriachal," "crocks," or hysterics. This "legitimates nonintervention, isolation, perfunctory treatment, and punitive care" and tells the woman that she, and not the assailant, is the source of the problem.[24] Institutional violence can be defined negatively, as *nonaction* or failure to respond to the needs of social participants due to a devaluation of their significance as participants. This abdication of responsibility is similar to nonaction in personal relationships in the violence of neglect or abandonment.

Labeling that is inappropriate devalues the violence done to the victim. It has a flip side of inaction that denies rectification of the violence that is done to the victim because the victim has effectively been removed from the moral realm and hence has no "legitimate" claim to justice. The absence of authority to support the claim of the victim translates into a tolerance for the violence done to the victim and an acceptance of the belief in the legitimacy of such violence. This is the violence of compliance, the indirect acquiescence to the legitimacy of violence that prevents the trauma of violence from effective resolution. It keeps the victim isolated and without means for restoring trust and membership in the collective. It allows the reenactment of trauma to continue as prescriptive social behavior.

The reversal of responsibility in "blaming the victim" can be elaborated in the example of battered women. Research literature supports the view that abuse is brought about over conflict over women's stereotypes rather than by family history, psychopathology, or personality deficits.[25] One such stereotype is the role of tension management by wives for their husbands.

On the job, the "masculine mystique" is the hero ideology of patriarchal capitalism that teaches men to repress many of their feelings,
particularly alienating and hurtful feelings related to being subordinate
in a chain of command.[26] It is not in the interests of patriarchal capitalism for these feelings to be expressed and dealt with at work or translated into political activity, such as union demands. Feelings of self-doubt,
fear, anxiety, shame, and longings for affection and emotional support
are not allowed validation, which is reinforced from an early age by the
media, schools, and family interaction. As a result many men do not
know how to express these feelings, let alone identify them.

At work, the hierarchy of superiors often results in subordinates
being blamed for discomfort or problems experienced by the superiors. As well, in domestic hierarchy, men often expect their wives to
meet all their emotional, physical, and sexual needs. As one member
of a program for abusive men says, "My wife was there to make me
feel good. 'Why didn't you fix my supper the way I wanted it?' That
sort of thing. In any number of ways that was her primary role I
think—feeding me, nourishing me emotionally. And after a period of
time, I became very inept at nourishing myself."[27]

Abusive men who lack emotional skills tend to fuse any repressed
feelings into one emotion they are not comfortable in accepting or
expressing: rage.[28] Their unrealistic expectations that their wives manage the tension created by their own repression of their feelings becomes stated as "She should know what I want when I want it, and
I shouldn't have to tell her." As a result, the wife cannot meet the
unrealistic demands of the husband, he explodes into violent behavior, his discomfort disappears, and he has re-asserted control over the
supposed cause of his problems: his wife.[29]

A battered woman describes her experience of marital rape: "It
was a very brutal marriage. He was so patriarchal. He felt he owned
me and the children—that I was his property. In the first three weeks
of our marriage, he told me to regard him as God and his word as
gospel. If I didn't want sex and he did, my wishes didn't matter. One
time . . . I didn't want it so we really fought. He was furiously angry
that I would deny him . . . he said I was his wife and had no right to
refuse him . . . he just held me down and raped me."[30]

The husband's rage often is replaced by remorse and contrite
behavior, until the tension builds up again and the cycle is repeated,
with an escalation of violence. Most abusive men are extremely jeal-
ous and possessive of their wives, and in the need to control them
(and hence the husband's problems) the men are willing to do anything to keep them, including maiming or killing them. Surveillance

systems are set up to monitor their wives' every activity. This analysis is supported by evidence of abusive husbands themselves in treatment programs and of abused wives.[31] In Canada, according to a 1993 Violence against Women Survey, 29 percent of women, or 2.7 million, who have ever been married or lived common law had been physically or sexually assaulted by their partner.[32] Many of these women suffered emotional abuse, while others were emotionally abused without physical violence.

In conformity with the erosive controlling patterns of abusive men, one woman was relentlessly stalked, harassed, and assaulted following attestations of infatuation over a period of months until she "wearied of the endless assaults and reluctantly became involved" with him.[33] His abuse increased in extreme control over her time, energy, and emotions, forcing her to sever ties with personal friends. Her repeated attempts at escape were followed by stalking, beatings, and threats to kill her and members of her family. The abusive man was careful to refrain from abuse in public, and beat her where bruises would not show. She submitted to marrying him. One month later she was involved in a near fatal car accident. A concussion, multiple contusions, a broken wrist and knee, massive internal injuries, and a tracheotomy had her in intensive care for weeks. Days after being moved from intensive care, the abuser raped her in her hospital bed. The psychological, emotional, sexual, and physical abuse continued for nine years, even after she secured a divorce and relocated to another state. The abuser remarried and recently was shot and killed by his wife.

The rationalizations used by men reflect the denial of men's responsibility and blaming the victim: "I never beat my wife. I responded physically to her."[34] Abusive men deny their behavior is criminal and justify it instead: "It wasn't unprovoked, you know what I mean? It was almost like she was being an asshole at that particular time. I think for once in her life she realized that, you know, it was her fault."[35] Battering men minimize the injuries they inflict. They respond to direct questions of whether they hurt their wives by saying, "[She was] not injured. She bruises easily."[36] Another batterer rationalizes, "Not really. Pinching does leave bruises. And, I guess, slapping. I guess women bruise easily too. They bump into a door and they'll bruise."[37] In one study, 94 percent of men receiving counseling for wife beating excuse their physical violence by claiming something "made" them "lose control."[38] Blaming the victim, they use rationalizations of their wives "failing" them in some way—not cooking properly, being unavailable for sex, not being submissive or silent—to explain why it was acceptable to verbally abuse, beat, punch, kick, assault the women in their lives.[39] Some men think themselves entitled to judge and regulate women's behavior. Therefore, violence against women is characterized by extreme male dominance and control.[40] This dynamic of exploitive dominance and submission is central to the myth of the hero (discussed in chapter 5).

In a comparison of assault and other problems that battered women have, it was found that abused women experienced a higher risk of alcoholism, attempted suicide, mental illness, and child abuse only *after a history of assault is presented*. Thus, "battering is the context for the psychopathology, not the reverse."[41] The battered or assaulted woman who is inappropriately labeled "mentally ill" would belong in the "abnormal" category of socially acceptable behavior and values. Here mental illness is conceived according to dominant cultural beliefs.[42] She would then be placed outside the realm of moral protection by the group and represent a challenge to the norms of the society. In the instance of rape, the testimony of a raped woman is minimized when deemed barely credible by police and goes against the "cherished male assumption that female persons tend to lie."[43] Hence, female persons again are typecast as outsiders who undermine the "truth" and its cohort, goodness, and hence the morality of the system.

Blaming the woman in instances of violence against women neutralizes a threat to the legitimation of gender stereotypes within the society, such as the male hero. The focus is shifted away from the offender and internalized into self-blame by the victim. Even the way we name the experience "wife assault" places the focus on the victim, not the perpetrator. Call it what it is: husband violence. The device of blaming the victim allows society to reduce, buffer, or mystify the direct impact of what violence does to victims. The device of displacement to the victim transforms the violent act into violence legitimated by the social value of the subordination of women. Thus, women's testimonies which go against the social value are deemed "illegitimate," discounted, categorized as "abnormal," and integrated within the social belief system. In other words, psychopathology does not determine society. Rather, "society limits and directs pathology for its own purpose."[44]

Psychoanalysts refer to blaming the victim as a displacement from self to other in "projection," where impulses found intolerable and unacceptable in ourselves are projected onto a "scapegoat."[45] The outsider is the mysterious one, the irrational and uncontrollably violent one. However, "projection is a mechanism, not an explanation" for why the projection is made.[46]

The labels, definitions, and categories that are applied to the scapegoat are not simply the negation of the self externalized. The scapegoat as an internal or external nonmember of the group serves a role for the *members* of the group. The behavior attributed to the scapegoat demonstrates to the average individual what behavior he/she ought to avoid and avoid being mistaken for doing. The scapegoat defines for the member the limits of normality by producing a boundary only within which can the members be secure. Abusive names for other groups—honkies, queers, bitches, niggers—are used "particularly inside our own group to reassure our companions and ourselves where our loyalty lies."[47] In this respect, abuse is a means to gain acceptance and affirm identity for self and with others.

The mentally ill within our own group are perceived as "in a state of chaos and non-meaning" where even though their rejection of the dominant social values is *not* intentional, they serve as a "model for such rejection" and serve as a threat to security.[48] Similarly, prejudice as stereotype is a mechanism of rejection, not an explanation for why a certain prejudice exists.[49] As mechanisms for rejection, projective scapegoating and prejudice serve inversely to define and reinforce the boundaries of acceptance.

Rape

When the status of women is lower relative to that of men in the same society, the rape rate is higher, which suggests that gender inequality contributes to a social climate conducive to violence against women.[50] Further, this relationship is believed to exist because, "in a male-dominated society, rape both reflects the low valuation of women and contributes to their subordinate position in the gender stratification system."[51]

The testimony of Elly Danica is an illustration of several of the phenomena we have discussed. These include the brutal impact of the devaluation of women as subordinate by four sadistic men, the identification with the aggressor in the mother's collusion, the victim's purposeful distanciation of mind from body in action, and the twist of an appeal by the aggressors to the authority of male justice in a realm of moral legitimacy from which the victim is excluded:

> This is the one I want most to forget. This is the time it all came apart. This was the night of my death. Eleven. Beautiful girl child . . . She wakes me. Come, she says, He wants you now. Barefoot. Cold. Walking behind my mother . . . Be quiet. Do what he says. Don't talk unless he tells you to. Do exactly what he says . . . Three men. Strangers. And my father . . . Take your panties off . . . I peel myself out of my skin. I am no longer myself. I am someone else. Someone I don't want to be . . . A body sits there naked. The body tries to cover itself . . . The body is no

longer capable of response. The man is between the body's legs. He tries to put something between the body's legs. He tries to put something into it. It feels his fingernails and it screams. He's hurting me, he's hurting me . . . No! No! No! Shut up a voice snarls. No. No. No! He slaps its face, hard . . . It tries to get away. It can't move. The hand at the throat. It chokes. They don't stop . . . Suddenly it stops . . . At last, it is over . . . The man in the blue suit will now have his turn . . . He spreads its legs apart. Again. It's going to happen again . . . What is this? Why do they want to hurt me? . . . Harder and harder he pushes into it. It feels like something is ripping. The body thinks it will die. It hurts so much. The hand over its mouth barely muffles its screams. It chokes. It bites. It bites as hard as it can. He takes his hand away. The body throws up. He hits it again . . . It's not over. The other man and my father will have a turn. So it's fair I hear them say. Fair.[52]

Indeed, labeling women who protest against male violence as "abnormal" or mentally ill may be seen as a way to delegitimate a perceived challenge to dominant cultural beliefs.[53] In the context of male violence as rape, one challenged assumption is that "a woman's body is a man's *right*, and if violence occurs while the rapist is exercising that right [the act itself not being defined as violence, remember], it is because the woman attempts to deny him his due. In the case of rape, right justifies might."[54] A woman's body is perceived as a valued commodity by men, and "taking it" is considered "human nature."[55] The woman's "disobedience" and resistance to rape would thus be perceived as a denial of the man's "right" to rape.

The idea of rape as a right is akin to the medieval chilvalric idea of vengeance. A knight who suffered what was perceived to be a wrong had to inflict an equal wrong to prove the dignity of his position in the hierarchy of society. Once done, the wrong was canceled and evil was not integrated in the personality of a knight. An updated version of chivalric vengeance would view the act of rape not as violence, but as heroic justice and the affirmation of the subordination of women in male hierarchy.

Such a "right to rape" is motivated by power over women. One rapist who confirmed power over women was his goal went further to say "It was to humiliate them. That's what the goals of rapists are— to humiliate. To me it was more like a revenge kind of thing."[56] And later in the interview, "Since I have this anger through my home life, why I gotta take it out on women. That I don't even know."[57] Another rapist affirmed that what led him to rape was wanting to get back at all the "domineering" women in his life.[58] And yet another rapist says, "It's mostly anger that you feel. What you're doing is taking out that anger on her."[59]

And finally, one rapist says, "I killed them even before I fucked them. I would stab them first, kill them, fuck them, and then beat the body with my fists . . . I would hit them, strip them, rip their clothes off, and stick them in front of a mirror. I'd hold their mouth and stick a knife in their chest while they were awake." To the interviewer's question, "You put them in front of a mirror so they could watch themselves being murdered?" the rapist replied, "Yeah, that made me very hot—watching their reactions being stabbed." His response to "Why?" was, "Because every time I went to see a decent girl, she always refused me. So I took it upon myself to punish them."[60]

When the idea that men will rape is taken for a "legitimized given, part of nature,"[61] and that a woman's body is a man's right (to take or to punish) is teamed with the idea that sexual violence is an appropriate means to express anger against women, the result is a devaluation of women as autonomous sexual beings. Further, the legitimation of rape becomes an unfortunate social right for which, if the woman denies that right, the *woman*, not the rapist, is to blame, as scapegoat. As well, men learn that they are able to deal with anger toward women only through violence. Thus, to use Mary Douglas's concept that "cultural themes are expressed by rites of bodily manipulation,"[62] the cultural themes of the devaluation and subordination of women and violence as a means to express anger are enacted in the rite/right of rape.

The discussion of violence and legitimacy showed how a violent act could be "transformed" through the lens of social right and moral justification into socially acceptable behavior that reversed responsibility of the act to the victim. "Nothing seems easier than to develop the conviction that those who oppose our purposes and who block the satisfaction of our desires are immoral."[63]

The system is able to protect itself by maintaining the authority of the belief that violence is innate, a natural given, and that a collective restraint of innate violence, itself violent, is necessary. This is a tautology of violence between individual and collective. Applying the dimensions of the discourse infrastructure shows this tautology to be a symbolic duplication of the paradigm of the mind/body split, where the mind orders society and constrains the violence of the disruptive body. Its cultural representations are replicated in gender relationships and the subordination of women and others who represent the "illegitimate irrationals" who differ from the legitimate rationality of the system. For example, an excerpt taken from the fifteenth-century Catholic church publication entitled "Rules of Marriage," reads: "Scold your wife sharply, bully and terrify her. If this does not work, take up a stick and beat her soundly, for it is better to punish the body and correct the soul than to damage the soul and spare the body... Then readily beat her, not in rage but out of charity and concern for her soul, so that the beating will redound to your merit and her good."[64]

Foucault analyzes the political anatomy of the body in his work on the birth of prisons in the sixteenth century. He articulates the discipline, not only of women's bodies, but of bodies in general through what he calls a "mechanics of power." This mechanics of power "defined how one may have a hold over others' bodies, not only so that they may do what one wishes, but so that they may operate as one wishes, with the techniques, the speed and the efficiency that one determines. Thus discipline produces subjected and practised bodies, 'docile' bodies."[65] Foucault writes that it is from an attention to the details of observation of the body "for the control and use of men" that emerges from the classical age that from such "trifles" "the man of modern humanism was born."[66]

Where violence is considered innate to the body, within a system structured to discipline and to contain this body of violence, then the cause for an instance of an outbreak of violence would be relegated to those devalued and illegitimate bodies outside the bounds of legitimacy, yet within the system. The system would be able to constrain the protests of the victims as abnormal, and they would not be valued as challenges to the belief system. They would be contained within the parameters of discipline, custom, and protocol. In this way, the system is able to rationalize both the violence and the victimization without having to alter itself. Those devalued by the mind/body dualism in the hero myth, "insane" women and unheroic perpetrator "criminal" men, are institutionalized accordingly.[67] The tautology of violence could remain in place. However, if the tautology is usurped by questioning its assumptions, the system becomes vulnerable to change. The core authoritative beliefs and their legitimacy come under scrutiny. The ideology that explains them and legitimates them can be contested by alternatives. Some of these alternatives may be labeled "deviant" or "illegitimate" claims, such as with Galileo, where his "deviant" geocentric views questioned ideologically legitimate heliocentric belief. These alternatives make a categorical shift from illegitimacy to legitimacy in the cultural imagination, in the play of social discourse and belief. This shift occurs in a dynamic of ideology and alternative belief, or utopia.

The Dynamic of Ideology and Utopia

The intersection between the discourses of ideology and the discourses of alternatives, or utopia, is depicted as a dynamic in the cultural imagination described by Paul Ricoeur. Ideology and utopia are "deviant attitudes toward social reality."[68] Deviancy in either extreme of ideology or utopia is a "criterion of noncongruence." This disparity assumes individuals and collective groups may relate to social reality without distance, as congruent, and also with distance, or noncongruence, and may take various forms. The two-sided assumption is the work of social or cultural imagination that operates either in constructive or in destructive tones, elements both of ideology and of utopia. It is possible that there is a complementarity to ideology and utopia, where the constructive side of one may enhance the distortive, or deconstructive, side of the other, and vice-versa. The distortions of ideology may complement the aura of possibility in utopia, and the coherent, socially adhesive aspect of ideology may complement utopia as a subversive force in society.

Ideology is generally understood as a pejorative concept, concealing and distortive, as illustrated by Karl Marx in *The German Ideology*. Ricoeur uses Marx as an example because Marx focused upon persons in real material conditions in contrast to Hegel's idealist species-being as the basis of social reality. Ideology is "a sphere of representations, ideas, conceptions" in opposition to the "sphere of actual production."[69] It is the discrepancy between the imaginary and the real; appearance and actuality. Assuredly, this demonstrates a gap between the "unactual representation in general (religious, political, juridical, ethical, aesthetical, etc.) and the actuality of the life-process."[70] In Marxist theory, the gap curtails human action and subjects it to a vicious circle of class conflict dependent upon technology for abatement.

Ricoeur quotes Marx as declaring that "each new class which puts itself in the place of one ruling before it is compelled merely in order to carry through its aim, to represent its interests as the common interest of every member of society."[71] Ricoeur identifies the relation of interest to its ideal expression as one of motivation, not causation. Legitimation is introduced as the prime concern for social activity. A process of justification needs to exist in order "to represent a particular interest as general, as the only rational, universally valid one."[72] Dominant beliefs are expressed as the interest, or belief of all, to motivate acceptance and legitimation of these beliefs.

Ricoeur incorporates Max Weber's work on the problem of domination. In reference to the political power upheld by the state, Weber says that "it is an induction from experience that no system of authority voluntarily limits itself to the appeal to material or effectual or ideal motives as a basis for guaranteeing its continuance. In addition, every system attempts to establish and to cultivate the belief in its 'legitimacy.'"[73] Legitimacy may be perceived in a context of human action motivated by enculturated beliefs. Indeed, the belief in a legitimate order of existence relies upon the validity of motives for meaningful action.

There is a breach between a claim to legitimacy and a belief in legitimacy, or the claim held by authority and the beleif in that claim by individuals.[74] This gap is filled by authority's excess of claim over belief or ideology. Ideology is intended to reinforce belief so that it alleviates the demand for legitimacy. This "credibility gap" is the source of distortion and deviation between claim and belief. This distortion is required by the claim of authority to legitimacy that fills the credibility gap.

As equal participants in social activity, the meaning of any one person's beliefs is as valid as any other's. Each has equal authority in their prejudices or life experiences. When it comes to having a *shared* belief there become discrepancies in meaning and authority simply because of the discrepancies in individual experiences. The shared beliefs of a society ensure the stability and cohesion of institutions which provide for social needs and the continuity of the society. In order to accept one belief instead of another, and so share a belief, the authority of a shared belief must be validated in its now unequal status to retain its place as representative of the interests of all.

The development of discourse is not a static process. It is a continual development of communicative understanding and action. Any claim to meaning is vulnerable to change in the freedom of individuals' activity. The life of a society requires continuity in the form of institutions. The claim of meaning that was one of many possible meanings becomes instituted in society as authority and representative of all. A change takes place in meaning that is an authoritative claim in contrast to meaning that is still possibility. Authoritative meaning is static in its position as preserving social and cultural values in the continuity of institutions. Possible or alternative meaning has the dynamic potential to displace authoritative meaning and change institutions and social activity. The conceptual bridge that sustains authority through history is ideology.

From Authority to Violence

Authority depends upon the social participant's consent to belief in the authority's legitimacy. This assumes a consent to the legitimacy of power underlying authority. These relationships differ from strength, force, and violence. Power refers to an ability to act in concert. It belongs to the domain of the group, not to the individual. When someone is said to be "in power," what is meant is that he/she is empowered, or given permission, to act in the name of the group.[75] If the group disappears, so does the power of the person "in power." Thus power rests upon acceptance and support in the group context.

Strength, in contrast, refers to the singular, the individual. Strength is the property inherent in a person or object and belongs to its character. It may prove itself in relation to other things, but it is independent of them. The *strength* of the individual may be *overpowered* by the many.

Force, often considered a synonym for violence as a means of coercion, is indicated by the energy released by physical or social movements, as in the "forces of nature," or the "force of circumstance."

Authority is defined as the phenomenon of "unquestioning recognition by those who are asked to obey." Authority may be vested in persons, as in the relation between parent and child or teacher and pupil, or institutional office, such as the office of a senator or a priest. Respect by those expected to obey is required for the person or office to remain in authority.

What distinguishes violence from power, strength, force, and authority is its instrumental character. As a phenomenon, violence is closest to strength. The means of violence, like other tools, are designed to multiply natural strength until they eventually can be substituted for it.[76] This does not distinguish between violence as destructive behavior and the technology used to carry it out, and does injustice to both concepts. Violence associated with technology as an instrument of destruction displaces responsibility for violent behavior on technology, not the agent of action. As well, technology becomes associated with violence as an instrument of destruction, instead of an augmentation of an agent in action with predelictions to use technology in certain ways. From a cultural perspective, human agents and technology both belong to a history of social values and practices which influences current and future behavior and use.

Violence relies both upon power and upon authority. When authority breaks down, where commands are no longer obeyed, the question of obedience to authority is not decided by the command-obedience relation, but by opinion and the number of those who share it: "Everything depends upon the power behind the violence."[77] The breakdown of legitimate power in the form of a revolution shows how civil obedience to laws, rulers, and institutions is simply the outward manifestation of support and consent. Authority rests upon power that in turn rests upon the consent and the beliefs of the people that *respect* the power. This consent is granted in direct and indirect assumptions of consensus discussed previously. These assumptions incorporate explicit agreements and agreements supported by tradition and convention within the context of cultural symbolic discourse.

Ideology works from the base of symbolic discourse. Beneath the level of ideological "distortion" we discover systems of legitimation that meet the claim to legitimacy demanded by a system of authority. This fills in the gap between belief and authority. And beneath this level we find yet another system of symbolization which constitutes action itself. This torte of ideology is a means to pattern, integrate, and consolidate an order of action. It provides stability in society, whether a ruling class, system of authority, or stable community. Ideology is the cohesion for human order that is susceptible to splintering by the disparate interests at work in nature and history. "All the pathology of ideology proceeds from this 'conservative' role of ideology."[78]

Utopia as Otherness and Alternative

The possibility of disruption to a given order is an alternative to the given order. This is the function of utopia, to present the voice of subversion to ideology. Utopia is to existing society what invention is to scientific knowledge. Utopia excels in imagination, in creativity. Utopia is the language of "another"—another society, another reality, another world. Inventive imagination shuns integrative functions for a world of "otherness." The search for otherness is not thematic, but rather includes a diversity of claims. Another family, another sexuality may mean monasticism or sexual community. A different way of consuming may be asceticism or sumptuous consumption.[79]

The imaginative possibilities of utopia may be likened to a nowhere. Coined by Thomas More as a literary term for a place with no place, *utopia* has retained its meaning as a ghost place in the imagination. This holds a significant function for society. As an open possibility, utopia provides a porthole for looking in on reality. Through the glass of utopia, we can be separated from our accustomed ways of living. These are not as familiar anymore, for nothing is taken for granted with this possibility beyond actuality. In a range of alternative ways to live, utopia contests what is. Utopia as social subversion counters the integrative function of ideology.

Utopia interrogates given systems of authority. Ideology reinforces authority by providing legitimation structures for it. The credibility gap is pried open by utopias that indicate other ways of using power in social, political, religious, or economic life. Utopias call established systems of power into question.[80]

The opposition between the stabilizing role of ideology and the subversive power of utopia involves corresponding pathologies in legitimating or contesting a system of power. In contrast, the positive aspects of both reflect in ideology as conservation and utopia as a schema of perfection. This latter view of utopia may appear as eccentric or erratic, as a decentering device. However, what decenters us also brings us back to ourselves. This is the paradox of the utopian imagination.

In the dynamic of ideology and utopia, one is needed for the other to realize itself. The need for ideology to mediate social ties, to reinforce belief, identifies a gap for potential utopia. This dynamic process highlights the "healthy" function of ideology to cure the "madness" of utopia and the critique of ideologies from the point of view of "nowhere." The social system becomes a flexible human negotiation of these beliefs, attitudes, and practices as elements of continuity and change.

There is no getting rid of the ambiguity of interpretation, as ambiguity is necessary for the cohesion as well as the transformation of society. The implications of the interpretation of symbolic discourse and action are significant as a shift away from the mind/body dualism of Western culture through which we have perceived the environment and ourselves. Authority is configured in the beliefs—such as the hero myth, innate violence, and the subordination of women—by which experience is prioritized and orients action to socially acceptable behavioral expectations and responses. To question the assumption of innate violence from the dynamic of trauma reenactment and the utopia of interdependence, respect and trust would reshape responsibility and accountability, the keystones of trusting relationships that bind a society together. In a sense, this text portrays the dynamic of the "ideological" violence mythos and the "utopian" interdependent mythos in the cultural imagination.

To contextualize this dynamic, the story of the violence mythos is placed in a history of cultural precedent based upon authoritative beliefs about violence. We now turn to an inquiry into the transmission of values and beliefs about violence through the myths and symbolic discourse of tradition.

FIGURE 4

Light Observation Command Helicopter (LOCH), Chu Lai, Vietnam, 1969

Photographer: Clinton C. Whitmer, U.S. Army Spec 4 Medic during September 1968 through October 1969 Tour of Duty, Chu Lai, Vietnam.

3

Myth and War

Myths are cultural stories that embody symbolic discourse and authoritative beliefs in a culture. Myths about violence include an overview of authority and tradition. How authority functions in tradition and culture is shown in the transmission of authoritative beliefs from one generation to the next and from one culture to another. These concepts inform how myth has historically been used as a model for collective learning and social intercourse. Myth provides cultural unity and continuity, in getting members of the collective believing similar concepts with similar attitudes and behaving in similar ways with similar expectations. In this way, myth transmits values in tradition through symbolic discourse and models for action.

Authority and Belief

Symbolic discourse and accepted behavior, or institutions that constitute a society, reflect the authority of culture in the direct or explicit agreement of social assumptions by consensus. Authority in culture is the history of selective judgments interpersonally acknowledged and substantiated by grounds offered by reason. Authority reflects the priorities of a culture for its survival. Giving reasons and discussing consequences establishes these priorities and their appropriate authority. The values of a culture are reflected in priorities, and hence, in authority. The root of authority is in the consent of the person asked to respect authority. Authority lives not from dogmatic power, but from acceptance.[1] The concession to a superior knowledge and insight provided by authority shows that one believes that authority is right. Authority may reflect a vicarious knowledge that may help others to survive without taking the risks of testing that knowledge themselves. The status of authority may be reflected in reputation, or the trustworthiness of authority acknowleged and substantiated by others.

The indirect consensus of social assumptions signified simply by their enactment includes tradition, a form of authority that is "nameless."

Our finite historical lives are characterized by the fact that the authority of what has been transmitted, beyond what is clearly grounded in reason, has power over our attitudes and behavior.[2] Hans-Georg Gadamer cites morals as a case in point. Morals are "freely taken over, but by no means created by free insight or justified by themselves. This is precisely what we call tradition: the ground of their validity."[3]

The two modes of authority as acquired knowledge (direct, explicit authority) and tradition (indirect, implicit authority) apply both to *social right* as validated by law, status, custom, or social acceptance and to *moral justification* as validated by appeal to religious precepts, ethical principles and reasoning, or consensual moral judgements.[4] These two forms of authority inform the influence that myths and symbols have within a culture.

Because individual and cultural development is an ongoing process of adaptation to uncertain circumstances, any claim of valuation is vulnerable to change in the course of the activity of individuals. Like interpersonal relations, the system of society, because it is a symbolic construct of interpersonal interaction, demands a continuity to sustain itself. Interpersonal relations have a history of interaction or habits of relating over time. So do institutions. Interpersonal relationships cease when a participating party exits the relationship, through choice or death. Institutions have a symbolic life, an abstraction of a history of habits of relating among many people, such as a university. The leaders and members of these institutions may change over time. The institutions themselves, which symbolize the collection of actions, beliefs, ideas, purposes, buildings, called a "university," continue. Any one of these elements on its own does not constitute a university. Nowhere can one point to one object and say "That is the university." As long as the belief in their value is transmitted from generation to generation and the commitment of resources is made to uphold the matrix of elements, the institutions will then also survive generation to generation. An institution survives on the basis of authoritative belief in its value. Similarly, the claim of myth or symbol to valuation becomes instituted in culture amidst other symbolic representations. Their cultural survival depends upon acceptance by those who enact the models provided by the myths and symbols through institutions. For instance, the myth of the hero persists through the willingness of men and women to engage in modeling and supporting hero characteristics in social practice in family, educational, economic, and political institutions, even to the extent of censoring and denying the extensive private brutality to the self and others of this paradigm as inconsequential, and hence not a priority of authoritative discourse.

Myth and History

The status of an authoritative belief within a tradition of myth and symbolism raises the question of the distinction between myth and ideology. To elaborate upon myth, myths are primarily stories or narratives. The words *story* and *history* once had the same meaning but are now distinct.[5] 'Story' connotes a dimension of fantasy that makes their representation of actual events improbable. On the other hand, 'history' designates a verbal structure that has a satisfactory correspondence with events that actually occurred. Myth as narrative suggests the two inconsistent dimensions of "this is what is said to have happened" and "this almost certainly is not what happened, at least in precisely the way described."[6]

As previously discussed, in most societies at the center is a nexus of "serious" stories that are claimed to have happened as important stories particularly urgent for the community to know.[7] Their structure is not different from other stories, but they serve a different social function. The more serious stories "become the cultural possession of a specific society: they form the verbal nucleus of a shared tradition."[8] The heroic stories of Homer had this serious status for Greek culture, as did stories of the Bible for Christian Europe, at least until the eighteenth century. Since the scientific revolution of the sixteenth and seventeenth centuries, the stories of science, from Copernican heliocentrism to genetics and biotechnology, have become the serious stories for Western culture to know in their ability to explain and alter life. The revolutions in America and France have become archetypes for democracratic political interaction. For social interaction, the hero myth predominates in Western culture.

Myths that tell the tradition of a culture tell the stories of "ultimate meaning and destiny of human existence."[9] What is being spoken about is not what has already happened, but rather that which is to happen, because "it must happen." This differs from history, which is limited to an understanding of the past as a process of causally related, meaning-laden unrepeatable events "out there."[10] Myth tells about what has happened and what will happen in the future, beyond the present.

Myths are stories that tell about an all-inclusive whole. More specifically, myths are stories that are told about symbols.[11] In Christianity, the symbols "resurrection" and "cross" came to have stories told about them, as in Paul's sermon in Acts. Myths are already an expression of "differentiated thought." Of the many meanings of symbols, select meanings are chosen and elaborated as a means to "legiti-

mize the world." Here myths attempt to give meaning and shape to
the world and communicate what is "really real, self-founded, true,
and good."[12] In the United States, the myth of the cowboy hero is a
transition from the classical war hero to mobile pioneer in the "war"
against nature. The lone cowboy conquers both new territory and the
war against mistrustful, exploitive civilization, in exercising an ethos
of individualism and freedom that denies/silences human loneliness
and responsible social connection.

Myths are stories that speak from and in turn legitimate the moral
authority of tradition. As preservative of tradition, myth serves an
ideological function as a way to understand mysteries. Myth provides
a form of *reasons* to guarantee certain associative interpretations of
symbols as continuing to be authoritative for moral justification in
society. Myths also operate as forms of warranty for specific modes
and patterns of behavior that are normative for the subject.[13] Myths
are used as a set of reasons or appeals to invoke consciously and
explicitly a sacred authority in support of given practices.[14]

Consciously invoking authority to support given practices takes
myth into the institutional realm of social rights. Rights are permission to do something and obligations on others not to interfere.[15] As
regards myth, there is a permeability in the distinction between social
right as validated by law, status, custom, or social acceptance and
moral justification as validated by appeal to religious precepts, ethical
principles and reasoning, or consensual moral judgments.

In the West, this was illustrated in the shift from the "divine
right of kings" to the "rights of man" formulated in natural law theory.
The warrant of sacred authority remained in natural law as the modified belief in the divine design of the universe accessible by universal,
not monarchical, reason more suitable to democracy. Included in the
divine design were natural rights that were self-evident for any rational man (sic), of which the king was but one. Thomas Jefferson used
Montesquieu's equation of law with geography to justify America's
"natural right" to security and territorial (continental) expansion. This
was translated into the well-known phrase *manifest destiny* in 1844 as
a legitimation for the right of white men to the land, believed to have
been accorded to them by God for civilization.[16] By default, this legitimation also included the legitimation for sexism, racism, and imperialism by according social sanction for a select group to enforce its will
over those unlike them, or those who contested their "rights." In its
day, the myth of manifest destiny wielded tremendous power to enforce and sustain a social, economic, and political system protective of
the ideals of a few and the perpetuation of the nightmares of many.

Myth and Archetype

The distinction between ideology and myth may be made clearer. Ideology, as a preservative function of authority, provides legitimation for authority (implicitly consensual power) by an appeal to the past, and is thus historical. Myth, as warrant for behavior and narrative of tradition, incorporates the past with its structures of legitimacy *and* extends into the future, as a paradigmatic story about what is crucial for the continuance of the culture. The discourse of the use of violence may be justified by appeal to myth rather than ideology as a justification for future violent behavior. Hence, myth as model may serve as a form of legitimation and justification for violence as ritual and social practice.

Ritual as practice has a divine model, an archetype.[17] Rituals are practices that repeat the act believed to have been performed at the beginning of time by a god, a hero, or an ancestor. In this way, an act becomes real, or "meaningful" through repetition. The mechanism of the transformation of human into archetype through repetition can be approached through the examination of the extent to which collective memory preserves the recollection of a historic event.[18] In the example of epic poetry, the historical character of the persons celebrated undergoes a change. To be preserved in the collective memory, the historical event approaches a mythic model. In this respect, "myth is the last—not the first—stage in the development of a hero."[19]

The recollection of a historical event or a real person only survives in popular memory for two or three centuries at the most.[20] Collective memory finds it difficult to retain individual events and real figures because the structures by which it operates are different. Collective memory uses categories instead of events and archetypes instead of historical persons. "The historical personage is assimilated to his mythical model (hero, etc.), while the event is identified with the category of mythical actions (fight with a monster, enemy brothers, etc.)."[21] The "historical truth" which epic poems supposedly preserve has less to do with the persons or events than it does institutions, customs, and landscapes. In this respect, the historical truth represents traditional forms of social and political life in archetypal structures that form more slowly than does the individual.

The memory of historical events and its associations are altered such that they can enter the archaic mentality, "which cannot accept what is individual and preserves only what is exemplary."[22] There is a shift in memory representation from individual intention to eternal essence. Myth is able to present characters in action without offering a causal explanation for their behavior. Myth "empties human conduct of historical meaning, thereby transforming history into nature."[23]

Christianity and Paganism

A regressive archeology of the myth of the war hero to Greek antiquity reveals the layers of reinforcement in the historical valuation of violence. The transformation of history into the givenness of nature is reflected in the history of the development of the myth of the war hero. This development occurs parallel to the events to which it applies, namely war and conflict. The interpretation of these events in their time may yield insights into the valuation of the war hero for culture. For instance, G. W. F. Hegel's philosophy on the dialectic of spirit operant in history from the nineteenth century provides a fascinating window on how the war hero ethic becomes prescriptive not only for individual development, but for the culture as a whole in the pursuit of the spiritual life.

In Hegel's dialectic of Spirit, history is a movement of Spirit actualizing itself in history through reason. Reason, as the capacity for reconciling antithetical or contradictory manifestations of Spirit, is the conservator and expansion of Spirit. Reason conserves the truth, which is annulled in the reflection of Thought and reconciles the truth of the known with the truth of the alien, generating a new manifestation of Spirit unfettered by restraint of contingent will or external authority.

The dialectic of Spirit includes a process of negation which severs all sensual ties in the movement of Thought toward truth and divinity. This process exemplifies a split between the mind and body, where Spirit negates bodily existence and the emotional power of bonding with another, and forsakes sensual relationship for individual spiritual growth. Individual consciousness "has to show that it is liberated entirely and generally from its sensual nature."[24]

Mark C. Taylor elaborates on the dialectic of self-formation where all-powerful God and self, master and slave, engage in a life-and-death struggle inspired by an "absolute fear" from the encounter of the other as *other*.[25] The encounter with the other seems to disrupt self-identity through the mirroring of the self reflected in the other. Such a duplication is self-alienation. This "confrontation with the other as other leads to the encounter with the *self* as other."[26] In face of the all-powerful master the self realizes it has lost itself, for it finds itself as other. The self as slave to the other remains outside the self as the other has not "given him back" to the self by recognizing the self. This reveals that the other has recognized the self and shown the self that the other depends upon the self and is not "absolutely other than he."[27] The encounter with the other thus discloses the self's estrangement.

According to Taylor, to regain self-possession, the self rebels against the other, in a negation where identity secures itself by *excluding* difference.[28] The slave's offensive assertion is defensive. "Aggressive action is actually a reaction that grows out of impotence."[29] For Hegel, "the relation of the two self-conscious individuals is such that they prove themselves and each other through a life-and-death struggle. They must engage in this struggle, for they must raise their certainty of being *for themselves* to truth."[30] For Hegel, the staking of one's life is the process by which freedom is won. "Just as each stakes his own life, so each must seek the other's death."[31] Through this "trial by death" the two opposed shapes of consciousness exist, one as an independent consciousness to be for itself, and the other a dependent consciousness to live for another, forming the master and slave, respectively. The self that works to find its identity attempts to "surmount the threat that the other poses to its autonomy by dissolving alterity and assimilating difference. The act of aggression is simultaneously hostile and erotic."[32] For Taylor, this means that rather than an exercise through which the self finds itself and greater autonomy, the dialectic of self and other reveals that "no longer can a unique and individual identity stand autonomously upon itself."[33] Hence the dialectic reveals the dependency in the relation between self and other, not its severance, yet in a philosophical rendition of the dynamic of identification with the aggressor.

From the perspective of the violence mythos, the point is not the status of the relation between self and other in the dialectic, as independent or dependent in the process of realization of Spirit. The point is that for Hegel the negation in the progression of Spirit must be made through a life-and-death struggle through trauma. In seeking the death of the other in the early stages of negation, Hegel is not necessarily advocating violence, but requires violence for the negation, and hence violence becomes sanctioned as a necessary part of the process of the dialectical realization of Spirit.

For Hegel, the power of the negative is the means whereby the male individual negates himself as connected with every existential form, including that of the larger community and, more intimately, woman. Through this negation the freedom of the ethical self as the worth of the youth is openly acknowledged in war. In war, it is "physical strength and what appears as a matter of luck, that decides on the existence of ethical life and spiritual necessity."[34] In a sense, trauma determines truth.

Karl Löwith interprets Hegel's work as a description of the ultimate liberation of Spirit that is a result of the irruption of Christianity
into the pagan world.[35] The coming of the Christian principle shows
that the earth belongs to the spirit. "Only the Christian God is truly
man and 'spirit' at once. The spiritual substance becomes the subject
in an individual historical person."[36] The history of Christianity is the
unfolding of the power of free decision and equality. It is accepted by
the Germanic peoples through the hegemony of the Roman Catholic
church and Protestant Reformation which signals a reconciliation of
church and state, conscience and law.

This history of the Christian world that is a progressive transcendence of antiquity is a fulfillment of antiquity as well. The world of
ancient Greece and Rome is both elevated and abolished in the Germanic and Christian world.[37] Löwith describes Hegel's ontology both
as Greek and as Christian logos, or understanding.

Hegelian discourse, which emphasizes the necessity of the moment of war for the actualization of Spirit, is a cultural product of
theoretical discourse, derived from the cultural values and symbolism
of the eighteenth and nineteenth centuries, a time of Prussian promi-
nence. The valuation of physical strength in war mentioned by Hegel
can be traced to a time previous to Hegel, during the formation of
feudalism in medieval Europe between the eighth and the twelfth
centuries. These values were themselves based upon the heroic myths
of Greek antiquity.

According to Norman Cantor, there were three central values
that served feudalism and the feudal lords.[38] First, military prowess
was valued because only the strong man (sic) could provide peace and
protection. Second, it was believed that the bonds of personal loyalty
were the ties of the social order and only the relationship of one man
(sic) to another could give sanction to political and legal obligations.
Third, these bonds of loyalty were arranged in ascending and de-
scending order, permeating society and onward to the heavenly spheres
in the medieval world view.

These values reflected and reinforced the social order. The hierarchy of social bonds allowed feudal relationships to gain the acceptance of the ecclesiastics accustomed to the doctrines of hierarchy. The
clerics endorsed this value and made it more rigid than it already was.
Personal loyalty was the glue of the social order that proved of use to
kings and lords who sought to impose sovereign power over landed
society in the eleventh and twelfth centuries. The value of military
prowess became transformed into the ideal of aristocratic leadership
in society and the belief that "the man on horseback was the natural

leader." "Feudal recognition of the intrinsic goodness of physical strength was perpetuated in the moral sanction of the stronger over the weaker that became essential to the operation of the European states system from the twelfth century to the twentieth."[39] In nineteenth-century America this warrior ethos was translated into the myth of manifest destiny and imperialism that justified the exploitation of nonwhite peoples who were considered inferior. Representative of this Anglo-Saxon attitude was the racist rationalization that "God has not been preparing the English-speaking and Teutonic peoples for a thousand years for nothing . . . He has made us the master organizers of the world . . . to finally lead in the regeneration of the world."[40]

The value of personal loyalty as bonding for social order came from the dissolution of kinship ties of the Germanic tribes in northern Europe. During the period of the Germanic invasions, (400–600 C.E.), kinship bonds were weakened as a result of strife between relatives. The social bonding of the kinship groups was steadily transferred to the relationship of "lord" and "man," of which no blood tie was necessary, only loyalty. This change in social organization paralleled and enhanced political changes, with a form of kingship resting not upon the "folk" but upon military prestige. The war leader who could provide the spoils of war had the allegiance of his followers, even if they were not of the same kindred as their "king."[41]

The most illustrative and historically accurate record of the nascent values of feudalism in changing northern Europe is the Anglo-Saxon epic poem *Beowulf*. *Beowulf* was composed between the age of invasions/migrations and the late eighth century C.E., when it was written down by a cleric.[42] Although there is a prevalent Christian overlay, the poem details the ideals and mores of upper Germanic society. *Beowulf* indicates the meeting of the Christian and the pagan cultures in formative medieval Europe.

The main story of *Beowulf* is that of a hero of extraordinary physical strength who braves two life-or-death ordeals against monsters who had killed all previous opponents, and dies in a final encounter with a dragon, whom he slays. According to the translator, the main subject of *Beowulf* is the human challenge of death. The focus is not upon the hero's three successful battles with monsters, but upon "a hero defending mankind against its enemies."[43]

Although transcribed by a Christian cleric, as foremost an oral epic of nature and heroism, *Beowulf* was not conditioned by the traditions and needs of the Christian church.[44] Nature represented the unified structure of society and cosmos that was a result of the organic relationship that formed the basis of human experience since earliest times.[45]

Central to the organic theory was the identification of nature, especially earth, with a nurturing mother. There were two identifications
of nature as female. First was that of a kindly, beneficent female who
provided for the needs of humankind in an ordered, planned universe. Second was that of wild, uncontrollable nature that could render violence, storm, droughts, and general chaos. "The metaphor of
earth as a nurturing mother was gradually to vanish as a dominant
image as the Scientific Revolution proceeded to mechanize and to
rationalize the world view."[46]

   In parallel with the three values of strength, loyalty, and hierarchy
of feudal society, the transition from organicism to mechanism includes
three variations of the organic theory of society. First, the medieval
society was perceived as a hierarchy. The body politic was a metaphor
of the organic unity of the human body and presented a conservative
view of the social order that resonated with the experiences of feudal
lords and the church. Second, the tendency to the leveling of hierarchies
through political loyalties had traces of the organic village community
of blood ties. Third, in protest to a mechanistic ethos, a revolutionary
form of organic theory advocated the overthrow of all social hierarchies
for a return to harmony with nature.

   The Christian transcription of the oral *Beowulf* epic signals a larger
cultural transition from the values of organicism to the values of the
mechanistic world in the conflict between paganism and Christianity.
Indeed, for Lynn White, "the victory of Christianity over paganism
was the greatest psychic revolution in the history of our culture."[47]
According to White, "Christianity, in absolute contrast to ancient paganism and Asia'a religions (except, perhaps, Zoroastrianism), not only
established a dualism of man and nature but also insisted that it is
God's will that man exploit nature for his proper ends."[48] In destroying pagan animism, Christianity made it feasible to utilize nature with
an indifference to the feelings of natural objects. This effectively entrenched "man's monopoly on spirit in this world."[49]

   In medieval Christianity, the task became one of attempting to
understand God's mind by understanding how his creation operated.
"From the 13th century onward, up to and including Leibnitz and
Newton, every major scientist, in effect explained his motivations in
religious terms . . . It was not until the late 18th century that the hypothesis of God became unnecessary to many scientists."[50] For White,
"modern Western science was cast in a matrix of Christian theology."
White also claims the Christian dogma of transcendence over nature,
in the mind/body split, was realized through technologies developed
to master nature.

In the encounter between Christianity and paganism, Beowulf's battles with the monsters Grendel and his mother mirrors the Christian tradition of the martyrs who drove the evil forces of Satan away from the cities and the monks who chased them into the wilderness to battle them single-handedly.[51] From 789 through 1157 C.E., the Slavs sent out military expeditions to Germany in lieu of the absence of the kings and their nobles and soldiers who were on their own military ventures. In order to keep the pagan Slavs in check, a holy war, or crusade against these pagans was advocated by Bernard of Clairvaux, who saw the battle as one between the forces of God and the forces of Satan.[52]

The concept of 'holy war' included the concept that warfare could be meritorious and benefit those who undertook it. The doctrine that those who kill were obliged to observe penance was changed into the doctrine that "those who killed in the name of Christ were absolved from the need for it."[53] It was believed that God had instituted a holy war so that "the knights and unstable multitude who used to engage in mutual slaughter in the manner of ancient paganism may find a new way of gaining salvation."[54]

Hence, Beowulf's battle with the monsters (perceived as the forces of Satan) as an organic myth may be viewed as a transition narrative from trust to trauma in the Christian struggle with paganism. Symbolically, the protective mother, Grendel's dam, was the trustworthy caregiver of her son, the natural man rebelling against the replacement of natural bonds of trust with the duties of mercenary lordship loyalties in the shift to a hero mythology. A mythology of heroic mistrust and the dynamic of domination/submission invades her organic domain and drives her to a death far under the surface of somatic interchange.

In the shift from paganism to Christianity, the symbiotic relation of nature and humans is replaced with the reinforced subordination of nature and woman in the social hierarchical order. Nature and woman, no longer symbolic of embodied connectivity, themselves become a dual split of mind and body into the values they previously represented holistically, that of nurturance and wildness, into the symbols of sublimation/irrationality and the madonna/witch. These are both subordinate and inferior to the male hero/aggressor principle of physical strength as a military and moral good sanctioned by God for use against them and the enemies of God. The reverence of Mary was a striking element of popular piety in the twelfth century. During the same time, witchcraft was a craze resulting from social pressure. "The hatred of certain elements in society for certain other groups was formulated in a mythology of evil, which was at least in part accepted by those against whom it was created. The witches, accused again and again of demonolatry, gradually came to fulfill the expectations of their accusers."[55] In the erosion and marginalization of organicism, it is not surprising that of the several goddesses of early Teutondom, from which evolved the Anglo-Saxon myths, "*not one* is to be found among the Anglo-Saxons."[56]

The pagan maternal principle and the Christian paternal principle were contradictory deifications. The maternal principle of universality which knows no barriers gives over to the paternal principle of restriction, to limitation to specific groups. The idea of motherhood that produces universal fraternity among humans dies with the development of paternity and its individuation.[57] Both contained a collective memory of individual personages and events that were converted into archetypes, which then converted this history into nature, as unalterable and given. The transition from paganism to Christendom may be seen as contradictory and identical relationships of deification, which it is the task of myth to resolve. Myth attempts to resolve a "catastrophe" and expresses deep-seated human concerns, fears, and aspirations. This transition utilized another dimension of myth narrative, where it "moves forward in time even as it points toward a timeless dimension."[58] The personages of the resolution enact events that occur in a moment that is nonrevertible. The pattern is everlasting.[59]

The success of Christendom in "taming" the northern peoples included the appropriation of the hero/warrior myth of the intrinsic goodness of physical strength and the devaluation of nature and women represented by paganism. The Roman Catholic church, as "molder of our [Western] civilization," through many centuries sought to "convert, tame, and unite the Northern peoples. Her success was Christendom."[60] The moralization of medieval society into general categories of right and wrong and general modes of understanding right and wrong gave rise to a code of law that replaced the particular bonds and fractures of an older paganism.[61]

Violence and Salvation

The Christian/mechanistic/industrial framework came to replace the organicism of pagan animism. The symbolic representations of a cultural sanction of violence through traumatic torture and martyrdom may be explored further in the deeper layers of history, in the discourses of salvation and heroism.

The demand for self-sacrifice in the encounter with the other was illustrated in Hegelian self-transformation, the *Beowulf* epic, and the Christian conflict with Satan. Self-sacrifice enables one to transcend and actualize oneself. It is resonant with martyrdom in the New Testament tradition. In this tradition, the martyr bears witness to his/her faith by undergoing torture. The unmerited punishment is a duplication of the crucifixion of Jesus Christ. On the human level of exploitive somatic interchange, "men try to force other men to agree with them and the force is literal not metaphorical."[62] Sanctity was obtained by accepting evil as an opponent, and conquered by submitting to it.

In the fourteenth century, violence was official as well as individual.[63] Torture was authorized by the church and regularly implemented to uncover heresy by Inquisition. In daily life, pedestrians passed decapitated heads and quartered bodies impaled on the stakes of city walls. In church, people saw didactic pictures of saints undergoing varieties of atrocious martyrdom inflicted from swords, spears, arrows, and fire. The crucifixion with its nails, spears, thorns, and dripping blood was prevalent. "Blood and cruelty were ubiquitous in Christian art, indeed essential to it, for Christ became Redeemer, and the saints sanctified, only through suffering violence at the hands of their fellow men."[64]

In chivalry, the idea of suffering for sanctity leads to the dominant idea of vengeance. A knight who suffered a wrong had to inflict an equal wrong to retain his social position. Evil was believed to be a "force existentially independent of human beings."[65] It was perceived as detached from those who committed it. By "equalling" the wrong, it was cancelled and the evil annihilated.

Violence seemed "transferred from the cosmic to the human plane as having an independent existence of its own." According to George Boas, through the eras of martyr and knight into the eighteenth- and nineteenth-century philosophy of Kant, Fichte, and Hegel, evil was accepted as an opportunity to assert oneself and to "realize" oneself. In regard to consciousness, particularly in the thought of Fichte, after the ego posits itself, it posits the nonego, or nature, for two reasons: (1) a term obtains meaning by contrast and opposition with its contradiction, and (2) in order to have an antagonist to overcome. A saint without worthy opponents does not merit canonization. Thus, "aggression turns into a good in that it furnishes the occasion to rise above one's normal humanity."[66] This heroic campaign is reflected in the dialectic of self-actualization described by Hegel.

The notion of striving for the goal, not the goal itself, in the struggle with the opponent, gives rise to the "heroic life." Fighting is a virtue, and violence is not to be slighted. Physical strength is valued as an intrinsic good. If what one says is right, that which threatens one is evil and a source of frustration, and a challenge to one's authority that requires elimination. This intolerance of difference corresponds to the idea that those who thwart one's goals and desires are morally wrong, and hence the victim of one's violence is to blame.

The counterpart of the active hero is the passive hero who suffers, the martyr, the one to whom violence is done. To suffer demands that something be done to one, the act of an aggressor. Thus war, aggression, and violence also provide the opportunity to suffer and become great through "conquering" the opponent in righteous submission, a passive aggression.

War on Hegel's philosophical battlefield incorporated both aggression and suffering.[67] The process of the realization of Spirit could become an apologetics for violence and aggression, as it is only through a life-and-death struggle with an opponent that one actualizes oneself. "The negative is necessary for the affirmative," which posits an enemy over and against one, with life a prolonged battle of defeating this enemy.

The Classic Hero

The archetype of *Beowulf* is the mythic epic poem of the classic hero ethic issuing from Greek antiquity.[68] The archetype is the warrior of extraordinary physical strength who fights on behalf of the preservation of the social order. Hektor in *The Iliad of Homer* is one such historical hero. During a brief reunion with his wife, Andromache, and child, Hektor prays to the immortals: "Grant that this boy, who is my son, may be as I am, preeminent among the Trojans, great in strength, as I am, and rule strongly over Ilion . . . and let him kill his enemy and bring home blooded spoils, and delight the heart of his mother."[69]

For Joseph Campbell, the redeeming hero is one whose shining blade, existence, touch, will "liberate the land." He is positioned against the tyrant-monster of "uncontrollable impulses to acquisition within himself."[70] In myth, the hero is proclaimed a "man of self-achieved submission," to which Campbell queries, "submission to what?" Submission to the heroic deed. Campbell cites Arnold Toynbee as observing that the schism in the soul, or social body, can only be resolved with the birth of something new. In the soul and body social there must be recurring births to nullify the recurrences of death. Akin to Hegel, through the crisis of "detachment" and "transfiguration," a higher spiritual dimension is attained. The first step of detachment or "withdrawal" shifts the emphasis from the external to the internal world. It is a retreat from the "waste land to the peace of the everlasting realm that is within."[71] For Campbell, this is the retreat to the "infantile unconscious" that we carry within ourselves forever, all the "life-potentialities" that did not manage to be realized while we were adults. If a portion of the lost totality could be realized, or a forgotten memory of our whole civilization brought to light, then we would be "the cultural hero of the day." The first work of the hero is to retreat from the world scene of secondary effects to "the causal zones of the psyche where the difficulties really reside." Next, the hero must clarify the difficulties, eradicate them for himself, and break through to undistorted direct experience and assimilation of the Jungian archetypal images. However, in contrast to Campbell, this "withdrawal" appears to be an instance of purposeful distanciation by a war(rior) veteran. And the "transfiguration" to an "everlasting realm within" seems to be an attempt to resolve traumatic dissociative emotional numbing and isolationist detachment from the vulnerability of the interpersonal bonds of intimacy.

The proximity of experiences of purposeful distanciation in battle and divinity as inward turn is shared by Hegel. Hegel saw philosophy as beginning with the "annihilation of a real world ... Reconciliation is a reconciliation *not in reality, but in the real world*. In Greece, philosophers withdrew from the affairs of state; they were idlers, as the people called them, and fled into the realm of ideas."[72] Yet the associations of war followed them, as is evident in Aristotle's description of the limited and unlimited nature of bodies in the *Physics*: "If fire were limited, the air unlimited in quantity, and if there were *any* ration of equivalence whatever between the assimilative power of a given volume of air and that of an equal volume of fire, then obviously the unlimited volume of air must vanquish and destroy the limited volume of fire."[73]

A strong motive for withdrawal from the polity, or state, was found in the "disparagement of the body."[74] The Neoplatonist, Plotinus, had been a soldier before he became a sage. He criticized civic virtue and thought the savior of the state a rascal. However, "as life is in the body, it cannot be rejected outright. And as life must be affirmed, the most complete philosophies ... must find some ultimate way of affirming what has been rejected."[75]

Classical Greece found ways to affirm the rejection of the body and affirmation of the mind or spirit in the war experience. This happened in a larger symbolic sense of a flight from the bodily maternal bonds of peaceful security and earthly abundance to the paternal right of individualism and heavenly light. Traumatic grief and sorrow became governed by reason. Woman and her symbolic associations with the body were omitted from the realm of speech and left to the realm of animal inarticulate violence. Affirmation was found in reason/divinity/strength/speech/man through war and the reenactment of violence. Affirmation came through an increasing militarism and war experience that destroyed human relationships and created a distanciation from intimate attachment and bodily experience that initiated the mind/body split refined in the shift from the interconnectivity of the maternal goddess to the individuated paternal god.

As a distant reflection of modern individualism distinct from the holism of organicism, the inward turn of the hero to find peace within himself instead of the consolation of his community indicates a modern maladaptive, not classic, definition of peace. In antiquity, *eiréné* (the etymology of the word *irenic*) derived from the root meaning "linkage." Peace was a state of order, coherence, and security, and its imagery was commonly agricultural.[76] As more than an absence of war, peace represented prosperity associated with kindred, wealth, health, and pleasure.[77]

In antiquity for the Hebrews, peace was a gift of Yahweh. For the Greeks and Romans, peace was personified. Some deities, such as Athena, protectress of Athens, were once warlike and grew peaceful. The owl of Athena's battles transformed into a symbol of wisdom, and Niké, the goddess of victory, sponsored the warrior and the musician. Justice was considered the rectification of injury to life and good. Despite their many wars, the Greeks considered warfare a tragic interruption of ordinary life.[78]

From Maternal to Paternal

J. J. Bachofen writes of a turning point in the shift to Hellenism in the time of Alexander the Great: "The Pelasgian culture derives its stamp from its emphasis on maternity, Hellenism is inseparable from the patriarchal view."[79] The establishment of paternal right was an act of the uranian solar hero, whereas the mother right was the first duty of the chthonian mother goddesses. Gerda Lerner evaluates the changes in the development of plow agriculture as coinciding with increasing militarism that brings changes in kinship and gender relations.[80] The development of strong kinships and of archaic states brought changes in religious beliefs and symbols. The pattern is first a demotion of the Mother-Goddess figure and the ascendance and later dominance of her male consort/son, then his alteration into a Creator-God. Wherever such changes occur, the power of creation and fertility is shifted from Goddess to God.[81] The Hellenic man wishes to achieve goals by his own efforts, and in struggles becomes aware of his paternal nature. In the echoes of Hegel, "In battles he raises himself above maternity to which he had wholly belonged, in battle he strives upward to his own divinity."[82]

Aaron Kipnis investigates the role of the Earth Father, prior to the Sky God of agricultural cultures dominated by invaders.[83] He explores the mythology of the Earth Father god imagery that is a complement to the Earth Mother, and is intimate, sexual, deep, life-affirming, fierce, spiritual, and feeling. This Earth Father suffers the pain of attachment and loss, and natural embodiment. He refers to Plutarch, the first-century Greek moralist, and Plutarch's description of the sculptures of the god Hermes as featureless below the head, except for the erect penis in bas relief. The reason for this was that "the body was not important. In order for a man to be potent only the brains had to be alive and fertile. Men became disconnected from their feelings; intellectual split-ting from the body was encouraged."[84] For Kipnis, the contemporary resistance to expressing pain and grief is a fear of rejection by women and others if men present themselves unheroically. A reclamation of Earth Father imagery for masculine identity could give men a spiritual source of response-ability and permission to grieve as natural men.[85]

Lerner critiques Bachofen as evolutionist and Darwinian, and as regarding the ascendency of patriarchy as superior religious and po-litical thought.[86] However, she regards his contribution as the claim that women in primitive society developed culture and that there was a stage of "matriarchy" that led society out of barbarism.

The movement of distanciation-idealization is the beginning of what Carolyn Merchant describes as the nature/culture distinction that identifies woman and animality with lower forms of human life. The contemporary rebuttal of the concept that women's place was with nature and man's with God has been focal in eliminating the sexual oppression of women. As regards war, "a female victim of rape in war is chosen not because she is representative of the enemy, but precisely because she is a woman, and *therefore* an enemy."[87] Merchant describes the place of women in the order of nature as identifying women and animality with a lower form of human life.[88] The histori-cal role for women as subjects is problematic because maleness is the norm, and femaleness constitutes a deviation from that norm. Man is the subject, or absolute, and woman is the other.[89] "As the unifying bonds of the older hierarchical cosmos were severed, European cul-ture increasingly set itself above and apart from all that was symbol-ized by nature."[90] The absence of reunifying the human hero in the bonds of the collective occludes the trust relationships upon which interdependent life depends and perpetuates a fragmentation of rela-tionship in a paradigm of exploitation.

From this Western seedbed springs a kind of science that is fragmentary and empirical. Its focus is upon observing objects and leads to "a split between idea and feeling that was carried to its conclusion in Auschwitz or in the slave trade."[91] As an established culture of hero warfare, modern European society would be "particularly liable" to mental splitting and projection. In this way, the mind/body dualism was a symbol that reflected not the experiences or wishes of individual childhoods, as suggested by Campbell, but the experiences of "adult social life experienced communally."[92]

The flight from reality promotes the rejection of the physical, psychic, and emotional feelings of the body in the experience of pain and rage in the war experience and the relationships which caused them, leading to a devaluation of intimacy, personal relationship, women, vulnerability, pain, trust, and interdependency. The inescapable violence of war then could be idealized and legitimated into a violence necessary for the actualization of the inner self, the inner sanctum from a hostile world. Peace that had formerly represented interpersonal order and security was now internalized and represented intrapsychic security. The experiential distanciation was changed into a symbolic representation of the transformation of the self. The consequences of this transformation were neglect of interpersonal relations and responsibility toward the private/intimate realm of the family. The violence done to women and children as a result of modeling war behavior or instances of rage resulting from posttraumatic stress disorder would be viewed as necessary, natural results of the process of self-actualization. Those who interfered with this process, namely women and children, would thus "deserve" the violence done to them. It would be the price they would pay for expecting the man to be heroic. They would be viewed as interfering with the man's rightful path toward internal divinity. Such devaluation of the body is expressed in the Augustinian theme that the earthly life does not greatly matter.[93] "Woman may be raped in body but cannot be polluted in spirit. Men may be killed, but those who destroy the body have nothing more they can do to the soul."[94] In the twentieth century, we now know that rape and war can destroy body and soul in lasting debilitating states of victimization and suicide.

The passive resistance toward the destructive goals of the warfare system is an updated version of martyrdom. Pacifism that starves the body and submits to torture for the sake of ideals and concepts is the other side of the same coin of the heroic mind/body split that sacrifices the body for the purposes of the mind.

In passive resistance, violence to self and body may be justified by the internalized mind/body split in the denial of the body. In active resistance, violence to the self and the body is justified by the destruction of the body in war, the externalized mind/body split. Either way, the split between idea and feeling is maintained and the person is susceptible to the reenactment of the myth of heroic sacrifice by martyr or warrior. When this is implemented as a global strategy, it may be a means to "destroy the village in order to save it."[95] Jean-François Lyotard's observation is acute:

The system can count severity among its advantages. Within the framework of the power criterion, a request . . . gains nothing in legitimacy by virtue of being based upon the hardship of an unmet need. Rights do not flow from hardship, but from the fact that the alleviation of hardship improves the system's performance . . . It is not in the nature of force to be ruled by weakness. But it is in its nature to induce new requests meant to lead to a redefinition of the norms of "life." In this sense, the system seems to be a vanguard machine dragging humanity after it, dehumanizing it in order to rehumanize it at a different level of normative capacity.[96]

The integration of feeling and idea, body and mind is the reconnection of the bonds broken in trauma and war in the history of Western culture. Integration requires a dissolution of the association of anger with violence, where anger is recognized as an emotion that signifies a need for change in aversive circumstances and violence is recognized as one possible behavior. Anger can do its work of signifying a need for change or an obstacle in relationship that needs to be confronted in order to preserve or change relationship. Anger then can be restored to its function as an emotion that primarily seeks to *preserve* relationship, not destroy it. Violence becomes a behavior that is a particular expressive act of destruction. As a behavior, violence becomes *one* possible chosen means to express beliefs and values.

The flip side of the dissolution between anger and violence is the revaluation and feeling of loss, pain, and vulnerability for men and the revaluation of anger and active initiative for women. This other side may be difficult to conceive in Western culture, because the male goal-oriented cognitive schema of separation is directed to achievement, acquisition, and individuality. To integrate sorrow, grief, or helplessness into acceptable feeling modes means to admit loss, failure, and the loss of property and attachment in relation. These are feelings that need to be felt and processed in order to regenerate and open oneself to new possibilities. Women need to allow anger and rage to be acceptable feeling modes that signal the need for assertion of self in relationships through autonomous external expression, instead of internalizing anger against the self, which often results in a preoccupation with how the self is perceived by others (Naomi Wolf's beauty myth[97]) and encourages eating disorders and substance abuse. Assertiveness goes against the traditional values of submission, compliance, and self-sacrifice, the rejection of which may mean the loss of relationship.

The mythological and symbolic tradition of the violence mythos includes beliefs in necessary violence in famine and war; necessary violence as innate in violent instincts; salvific violence; the hero, attitudes of subordination and devaluation of women, nonwhite peoples, animals and nature; the institutionalization of war as the primary mode of social change, and the philosophical discourses of distanciation. The alternatives to this tradition will be discussed in the discourse of the interdependent mythos.

The panoptic gaze on the body as object of war described by Foucault reflects the surveillant power relations of war that deprive its receptor of response. However, the gaze issues from its own body, however distanced in discourse. The body that is scrutinized has eyes to see, power to speak, and a body to act. This is the power women and men must claim if they are to resist the identification with, and enactment of, the aggressor, and the pervasive symbolism that suggests and reinforces valuing violence in culture, increasingly as entertainment, whether in electronic games or in media.

The valuation of violence in Western culture is the outcome of historical events where the authoritative legitimation of beliefs in necessary and natural violence has had survival value. From the analysis of social learning theory and posttraumatic stress disorder, it has been shown that anger and violent behavior are foremost responses to aversive events deemed appropriate for survival. The maladaptive quality of trauma reenactment by humans in their environment for the purposes of survival may make a shift from relationships between self and world as a violent dialectic of opposition to a restoration of trust in responsive socially mediated interchange. Now that we have looked at the symbolic discourse of violence in the tradition of the hero, we turn to cultural symbolization and theories about the tradition of violence in contemporary discourses.

PART II

VIOLENCE AND THEORETICAL DISCOURSE

FIGURE 5

Rite of Passage

Photographer: Clinton C. Whitmer

FIGURE 6

Vietnamese Boy, Viet Cong Village of Antaan, Vietnam, 1969

Photographer: Clinton C. Whitmer, U.S. Army Spec 4 Medic during
September 1968 through October 1969 Tour of Duty, Chu Lai, Vietnam.

4

Freud and the Aggressive Impulse

Feelings do not have behaviors. Feelings are felt experiences. If and how a person expresses feelings is mediated by the social circumstances, expectations, acceptance of behavior, and choice that re-present the emotional value of an experience for the self to others. If one is attempting to gain acceptance and belonging among those who value or approve of aggressive behavior, such as street gangs or war compatriots, then such behavior achieves the status of legitimacy in that social setting. The initiative of aggressive behavior is based upon socially mediated choice, not upon an innate impulse.

A collapse in the distinction between anger and violent behavior results in an illusory connection between anger and violent behavior. A false connection between anger and violent behavior results in an identification of anger or rage as aggression, with the premise that violence is an expression of innate aggression, or an aggressive impulse, rather than a response to an aversive situation.

Early Freudian Instinct Theory

A theory of aggressive impulse is found in the work of Sigmund Freud. Freud's most explicit statements about an aggressive impulse, or "death instinct" as it became commonly known, came toward the end of his career, in his work "Instincts and Their Vicissitudes," "Beyond the Pleasure Principle," and most notably *Civilization and Its Discontents*. Freud was a pioneer in the area of mental health whose work traversed both discourses of physiological or organic and environmental or functional causes of mental activity.

A qualifying statement about the translation of certain terms Freud used is in order. Bruno Bettelheim distinguishes between Freud's use of the words *triebe*, which is usually translated as instinct, and *instinkt*, which Freud used to refer to the inborn instincts of animals and shunned when speaking of humans.[1] A closer rendering of the meaning of *triebe* for Bettelheim is the word *drive* which refers to basic biological impulses or urges on the order of self-preservation, hunger, sex, and so on. *Impulse* as an impelling force would even be a better rendering than instinct.[2] Bettelheim suggests a different title for the standard translation of "Instincts and Their Vicissitudes" to be "Drives and Their Mutability." Drives may be changed in various ways. They may be altered into their opposites, directed against the self by oneself, suppressed, or sublimated. *Instincts* is the wrong word to describe this phenomenon, as instincts are inborn, unconscious, and basically unalterable.[3] According to Bettelheim, Freud never believed that the most important aspects of human behavior were unalterable, otherwise, there would be no point of psychotherapy.

The most unfortunate casualty of this mistranslation for Bettelheim is the "death instinct," something of which he claims Freud never spoke. Rather, Freud referred to "a mostly unconscious drive or impulse that provokes us to aggressive, destructive, and self-destructive actions."[4] Bettelheim qualifies this watering down of the "death instinct" by claiming, "Some of us are certainly driven toward death—our own death or death inflicted on others."[5] As a case in point, he questions how else one could explain suicides such as those of affluent American adolescents that are not due to incurable sickness or other like causes.

However, Bettelheim's translation and interpretation of Freud must be considered carefully. Some of his assumptions do have counterexplanation in the work of Alice Miller. For instance, she offers an alternative explanation for troubled adolescents in her exegesis of the "poor rich child."[6] These gifted patients have been praised for their gifts, talents, and achievements. As the pride of their parents, they should have a strong sense of self-assurance, but the truth is to the contrary. Behind this lurks depression, a feeling of emptiness and self-alienation, and a sense that their life has no meaning. As soon as they are not "on top," the drug of grandiosity fails, and they experience the feeling that they have failed to live up to some ideal image and measure to which they think they must adhere. They are plagued by anxiety or deep feelings of guilt and shame. Miller describes how these patients have a complete absence of real emotional understanding or serious appreciation of their true needs—beyond the need for achievement.[7] A basic assumption in treating these patients is that a child has a need to be regarded and respected as the person he or she is at any given time, as the center and central actor of one's own activity by one's caretakers. "In contradistinction to drive wishes, we are speaking here of a need that is narcissistic, but nevertheless legitimate, and whose fulfillment is essential for the development of a healthy self-esteem."[8] This is an example of the reworking of Freudian theory in attachment theory and will be discussed more fully in chapter 8.

The discussion of Freudian theory and its internal dynamics of a struggle between life and death drives comes very close to being instinctual by animal standards. Acknowledging Bettelheim, the following references to "instincts" will be meant as "mostly unconscious drives."

Freud theorized that humans have basic instincts and drives that if repressed erupt, cathect their energy and return to constancy. An aggressive instinct, or impulse to aggress, offered an explanation for perceived and disguised aggressive behavior. Drives differ from instincts in that drives vary per individual while being common to all members of a species. For instance, nutrient ingestion is performed in a variety of ways, yet by all living things. Drives indicate generality of a certain form of behavior.[9] For Freud, "Civilization has to use its utmost efforts in order to set limits to man's aggressive instincts and to hold the manifestations of them in check by psychical reaction-formations."[10]

A theory of aggressive impulse has social consequences such that an innately violent individual must be controlled externally through cultural prohibition and through restraint and must learn to internalize these restraints in order to protect the self and the continuous unity of the community. In other words, the phylogenetic (species) trait of human aggression would exemplify itself in the ontogenetic aggressive behavior of the individual. The "natural" impulse to self-destruction of the individual would be directed externally into the social realm and there must be channeled into nondestructive behaviors for the culture as a whole.

In the early years of Freud's work on the theory of psychoanalysis, the central concept was the 'unconscious.'[11] Later, around 1920, the unconscious was redefined from being the largest and most important area of the mind to being a kind of mental phenomenon. What had earlier been relegated to the unconscious became the id, and the structural distinction between the unconscious and consciousness was replaced by a three-part organization of the personality as three systems: the id, the ego, and the superego. Freud's goal was to infer or to guess how the mental apparatus is constructed and what forces interplay and counteract in it.

Between his earlier and later theories Freud shifted models, where the original opposition between the ego instincts and the sexual instincts proved to be inadequate.[12] It appeared that there was not a clear-cut distinction between the two, and that a portion of the ego instincts was sexual, or libidinal, and that sexual instincts, probably with others, operated in the ego. The "old formula" which held the

sexual instincts and ego instincts in conflict, needed to be reformulated so that the distinction, "which was originally regarded as in
some sort of way *qualitative*, must now be characterized differently—
namely as *topographical*." This original opposition also included an
equation of the ego-instincts with death instincts, and sexual instincts
with life instincts.[13] "Our views have from the very first been *dualistic*,
and today they are even more definitely dualistic than before—now
that we describe the opposition as being, not between ego instincts
and sexual instincts but between life instincts and death instincts."[14]

The unconscious was an important concept in that it attempted
to explain the unknown causes of behavior. What was unconscious
was what was unknown. As a locus of the unknown, the unconscious
as part of mental activity was at odds with the prevalent understanding of mental activity as consciousness. Freud changed the description
of mental activity. Unconsciousness as a description of consciousness,
or a state of consciousness, shifted to the unconscious as a dynamic
mental activity distinct from consciousness.[15]

Freud distinguished between two types of stimuli to the nervous system: external or environmental, and internal or instinctual.
The nervous system is an apparatus which serves to get rid of stimuli
that reach it or reduce the stimuli to the lowest possible level, or
maintain itself as an unstimulated condition. This was Freud's principle of constancy.[16]

The principle of constancy was coupled with the pleasure principle, which regulated mental events in the direction of an avoidance
of unpleasure or a production of pleasure.[17] Further, satisfaction of
an instinctual impulse is always pleasurable. When an instinct meets
with resistances which render it inoperative, it enters a state of repression.[18] Repression is a preliminary stage of condemnation, something between flight and condemnation, to turn something away and
keep it at a distance from the conscious.[19] Such is Freud's "economic"
view of the instincts.

The nervous system undertakes complex connections in order
for it to keep off stimuli, as "they maintain an incessant and unavoidable afflux of stimulation."[20] Freud concluded that instincts are the
"true motive forces" behind the development of the nervous system.
Instincts are in part "precipitates of the effects of external stimulation,
which in the course of phylogenesis have brought about modifications
in the living substance."[21] Hence, instincts have a historical component, as they are influenced by the historical environment in which the
organism finds itself.

Life Instincts and Death Instincts

By 1930, Freud saw culture as rising out of love and common work. Love is to be understood as stemming from a primary hostile narcissism that regards every other person as a "potential enemy, rival or inhibitor of one's freedom; the aggression aroused in defense of this narcissism is only by reaction-formation turned into the ambivalent love that characterizes society."[22] He revised his theory of instincts into a dual-instinct theory, where aggression is an instinct drive on equal footing with the sexual instinct.[23] According to Robert Paul, aim-inhibited object love and the narcissistic identification that forms group bonds rest upon the surface of a "repressed current of hatred and destructiveness." Western civilization's interest in beauty, cleanliness, order, and compassion betrays the more fundamental work culture must do to inhibit and defend against "the violent and anal sadistic urges that arise when narcissism is infringed."[24] In his description of the opposition between "the ego or death instincts" and "the sexual or life instincts,"[25] Freud gives an example of a similar polarity between love (or affection) and hate (or aggressiveness). The influence of the sadistic component of the sexual instinct is such that it can, when perverted, dominate an individual's entire sexual activity. In refuting a Darwinian view of sexual reproduction, he refers to the extraordinary violent instincts whose aim it is to bring about sexual union.[26] The opposition between libidinal and ego instincts is thus transformed into an opposition between life instincts (eros) and death instincts (thanatos).

Freud analyzes the two classes of instincts, the sexual instincts or eros and the death instinct of which sadism is representative. The sadistic instinct is an *"instinct of destruction* directed against the external world and other organisms."[27]

The individual deals with the "dangerous death instincts" internally in various ways.[28] They may be fused with sexual or erotic elements and rendered harmless. They may be diverted toward the external world in the form of aggression. Or they may continue their internal work uninhibited.

The work of the death instincts takes a curious turn when it comes to morality. Morality, defined as instinctual control, is problematic for the ego. Freud describes the id as totally nonmoral, while the ego strives to be moral, and the superego could become "super-moral and then become as cruel as only the id can be."[29] The relationship between the id and the superego is like that of a balloon which when squeezed at one end becomes larger at the other end. The more a person attempts to control or subdue individual aggressiveness toward the exterior world, the more severe or aggressive the person becomes in his ego ideal.

Freud believed the more a person sought to control her aggressiveness, the more intense became her ideal's inclination to aggression against her ego. The ego is flanked by danger from three unrelenting masters: the external world, the libido of the id, and the severity of the superego. By sublimating the dangerous instincts into an acceptable form for consciousness, the ego's work results in a defusion of the instincts and a liberation of the aggressive instincts in the superego, in which its struggle against the "libido exposes it to the danger of maltreatment and death."[30]

However, the attacks of the superego upon the ego destroy the ego by that which it helped to form. From the point of view of culture, Freud explains that the "turning back of sadism against the self regularly occurs where a *cultural suppression of instincts* holds back a large part of the subjects' destructive instinctual components from being exercised in life."[31] Further, he states that "the situation is usually presented as though ethical requirements were the primary thing and the renunciation of instinct followed from them."[32] For Freud, it seems to be the other way around. The first instinctual renunciation is enforced by external powers such as parents (or surrogates) and cultural factors, and it is only this which creates the ethical sense, which expresses itself in conscience and demands further renunciation of instinct.

The Civilizing of Instinct

The eros (life ego) and thanatos (death) instincts were derived to accommodate the conflict Freud found in human psychology. With the recategorizing of instincts in "Beyond the Pleasure Principle" in 1920, by the time of *Civilization and Its Discontents* in 1930, aggression was considered an instinctual drive on par with the sexual instinct. Freud still saw culture and society as arising out of love and common work, but this love was to be understood as a derivative of a primary narcissism that regarded every other person as a potential enemy rival or inhibitor of one's freedom.[33]

The aggression instinct was considered virtually primitive and independent of other instincts.[34] The aggression aroused in defense of narcissism is only by reaction formation turned into the ambivalent love that characterizes society. To preserve itself from the destructive aggressive impulse, civilization had to foster and sustain affection between human beings. If humans were left to realize their aims, they would create an environment too hostile for civilization to go forward.[35] Morality and conscience are the ways in which civilization disarms the individual's propensity to aggress. Hence, relationships become a secondary defense against a primarily aggressive individual.

However, for Freud cooperation meant binding a civilized society's members together libidinally. These ties among social members were necessary as a check to their own hostile impulses.[36] Cultural continuity was maintained through the encoding of the prohibition against aggression in the cultural symbolism of loving one's neighbor as oneself.

The objectives of civilization, in the sum of its achievements of human efforts, are to protect humans against nature and to adjust their mutual relations.[37] The first part, that of making the earth serviceable to humans via technology, Freud deems easy, and has made humans as a kind of "prosthetic God." Yet Freud reminds us that the human in this Godlike condition is still not happy. He proceeds to the second part, an analysis of the regulation of the relationships of humans. Freud points out that without regulation, these relationships would be subject to the arbitrary will of the individual, specifically "the stronger man" who would act on the satisfaction of his own interests and instinctual impulses.

Freud claims that community life is possible only when a majority that is stronger than any one individual comes together. This majority can then protect itself from any of the individuals. As mentioned previously, the "right" of the community is set up against the "brute force" of the individual. This is a substitution of power of the community for the individual that constitutes "the decisive step of civilization." This step leads to the rule of law, where all sacrifice their instincts, in the form of sublimation, suppression, repression, or other means, and leaves no one at the mercy of brute force.

The regulation of libidinal ties in the community is depicted in the commandment to love thy neighbor as thyself. Freud concludes that the stranger in reality has more claim to one's hostility and hatred than love, as love would be valued among one's own people as a sign of one's preferring them, and it would be an injustice to them to put a stranger on par with them. He then speculates that the neighbor, when bidden to love one as himself, would answer as Freud has and repel him for the same reasons. The "truth behind all this, . . . is that men are not gentle creatures who want to be loved . . . They are, on the contrary, creatures among whose instinctual endowments is to be reckoned a powerful share of aggressiveness."[38] Thus, the neighbor is an enticement for the satisfaction of aggression. "As a rule this cruel aggressiveness waits for some provocation or puts itself at the service of some other purpose, whose goal might also have been reached by milder measures."[39]

This aggression also can rise spontaneously and reveals man as a "savage beast" to whom consideration toward his own kind is something alien. Because of this "primary mutual hostility of human beings" civilization is perpetually threatened with disintegration. Not even work in common would hold it together. "Instinctual passions are stronger than reasonable interests." Civilization must set limits to human aggressive instincts and hold their manifestations in check by psychical reaction formations.[40] Hence, civilization uses methods to lure people into aim-inhibited relationships of love, restrictions on sexual life, and the commandment to love thy neighbor as thyself. By these measures civilization hopes to "prevent the crudest excesses of brutal violence by itself assuming the right to use violence against criminals, but the law is not able to lay hold of the more cautious and refined manifestations of human aggressiveness."[41] The twist of the matter is depicted when Freud claims it unfair to reproach civilization with trying to do away with strife and competition, which he claims are indispensable: "Opposition is not enmity; it is merely misused and made an *occasion* for enmity."[42]

For Freud, the death instinct exists alongside eros and represents "the ubiquity of non-erotic aggressivity and destructiveness" deserving of "its due place in our interpretation of life."[43] He concedes people would not want to hear that there is an "inborn human inclination to 'badness,' to aggressiveness and destructiveness, and so to cruelty as well."[44] In compensation, he suggests a "low bow to the deeply moral nature of mankind" which will "help us to be generally popular and much will be forgiven of us for it."[45] With this, Freud states that the instinct to aggression is an "original self-subsisting instinctual disposition" in humans, and presents "the greatest impediment to civilization."[46]

In the end, civilization seems to be a necessary culprit that at once inhibits instinctual satisfaction, and yet in its numbers and ideals protects the human species from the threat of annihilation by the aggressive individual. The collective bodily repression of the physical force of an aggressive individual also, through cultural symbolization, could be internalized as a form of individual psychic repression as the superego. Hence, Freud acknowledges that help for civilization might come from a change in the relations of human beings to possessions more than in ethical commands.

Psychoanalysis and Hermeneutics

Thus far, Freudian psychoanalysis has been assessed as describing mental functions of neurological disorder. We will now engage further in theoretical discourse to show the depth of the influence of the violence mythos through the work of Paul Ricoeur on Freudian theory.

Ricoeur distinguishes between a hermeneutics of symbolic meaning and a Freudian energetics of psychoanalysis as organic where energic cathexis of pleasure and unpleasure determine behavioral responses. Freud elaborates his theory in the discourse of physics transposed to a dynamics of ideas. This dynamics of ideas is described by Ricoeur as a topographic-economic explanation of psychical processes. He characterizes it as an energetics, not a hermeneutics (interpretation). Energetics adopts the explanatory terminology of instincts that are psychical, not biological. Instincts are not represented by but rather represent organic energies that originate in the body and reach the mind. Instincts are psychical representations interpretable by the mind.

Freud sought to develop a scientific account of mental activity in a biological organism. The objective was to explain what appeared in mental illness as a distortion of mental activity without apparent alteration of the biological functioning of the organism. "Organism" here refers specifically to a human being. The conventional intellectual climate perceived human beings as having degrees of consciousness, as agents of self-present conscious activity, and as unconscious in sleep or an un-conscious state of being (e.g., a result of a blow to the head). It reflected degrees of "wakefulness." Un-consciousness was used to describe or predicate a degree of consciousness, not to describe a substantive unconscious distinct from consciousness. The latter was eventually Freud's conclusion.

For Ricoeur, Freud takes the descriptive concept of the unconscious as an observable state of being conscious (e.g., sleep) and shifts it to an internal system of motivation "behind" consciousness. Ricoeur compares the descriptive move to a substantive unconscious to Edmund Husserl's phenomenology of intentionality. For Husserl, every conscious process is a consciousness *of* something. However, Freud understands consciousness itself as the aim of psychic instincts. As the *aim* of instincts, Freud reduces consciousness to an outcome of psychic instincts issuing from the unconscious. Thus, consciousness is decentered from its previously privileged position of cognitive reflection. Methodologically, consciousness moves from the solipsistic reflectivity of the Cartesian cogito to the Husserlian intentional consciousness to the Freudian decentered topographical consciousness, a consciousness that is part of a process of transgression beginning in the unconscious.

The division between the unconscious and consciousness becomes evident from the clinical observation of posthypnotic suggestion, hysteria, the psycho-pathology of everyday life, and other mental activity attributed to unconscious ideas. The method of psychoanalysis formulates the idea that "thoughts" are kept from consciousness by forces that prevent their reception. There are unconscious psychical acts which may or may not become conscious. The difference between what does or does not result in becoming conscious is the division between the unconscious and consciousness hardened through the repetition of repression into a barrier of resistance. Becoming conscious as a process of transgression is the crossing of a barrier, a penetration into consciousness. The shift from an adjectival unconscious (as a degree of consciousness) to a substantive unconscious (distinct from consciousness) establishes the unconscious as a system with its own laws and regulatory apparatus.

Freud's topographical view of the unconscious consists of three occurrences. The unconscious (Ucs) is part of the activity of becoming conscious (Cs) which may or may not occur. When becoming conscious occurs without resistance or difficulty, this is termed preconscious (Pcs) activity. When this activity is "cut off" or forbidden, it is an unconscious activity. The three agencies of the id, the super-ego, and the ego have three topographical places (Ucs, Pcs, Cs) because there is a barrier which excludes from or provides access to consciousness.[47]

Ideational Representation

Ricoeur's interpretation of Freud focuses upon the problem of ideational representation. It is the interpretation of meaning through meaning or what is signified and what is intended to be signified. The breakdown of meaning through meaning and its systemic explanation is conducted in two movements. First is a movement *back to* instincts as a dispossession. Reflection completely separates itself from the illusion of consciousness. The second movement *starts from* the ideational representation (that which passes into ideas) of instincts. This is a reappropriation, the recapture of meaning through interpretation.

In other words, reflection is decentered from its conscious locus of meaning to the disguised meaning of the signs of desire. These signs lend themselves to interpretation. Desire is accessible to reflection only through an interpretation of the signs of desire. These two movements of interpretation are the hermeneutic of suspicion and subsequently retrieval. In contrast, Freud's primary and secondary processes are biological in nature. The primary process is directed toward the free discharge of quantities of excitation (energic quantification of desire). The secondary process is directed at inhibiting this discharge and transforming this cathexis (bound energy) into a quiescent one.[48]

The problematic of ideational representation concerns how desire is represented or signified, and how it is nonsignified. Instinctual representatives in the nucleus of the unconscious seek to discharge their cathexis energy. These affective representatives are distinct from ideational representatives. Psychoanalysis is the borderline knowledge of the ideas which, in representation, do not pass into consciousness.[49] The nonsignified desire transcends, passes, and may evade disclosure and only be explained indirectly. The quantitative energic cathexis is mute, the unnameable root of speech, the substrate that cannot be symbolized in desire as desire. The unnameable root of speech is the limit the unconscious transposes upon the linguistic transcription that would claim to be without remainder. This limit of the unconscious developed by Freud is countered by Ricoeur. He argues that meanings are overdetermined in the distortion that occurs in the meeting of force and meaning, or energy and significance. It remains characteristic of Western culture to describe life energy as belligerent and overpowering. In a fundamental way, the ignorance of the trauma process has left us devoid of a sensitivity to the simple willingness to live, to aspire to life and enjoy it.

The lack of a perceptive system of selection for the internal protection of psychical processes from "dangerous excitations" is filled by the primary and secondary processes. The divergence of these two principles stems from the absence of the flight/fight apparatus regarding dangers from within. For Ricoeur, "The notion that perception is a selective system regarding excitations from the external world, whereas desires leave us unprotected, is a profound one."[50] It becomes Ricoeur's task to develop an internal selective system which protects us from internal dangers, primarily desire. This selective system becomes the rational interpretation of the signs of desire in symbolic discourse.

In the violence mythos and its symbolic discourse of the mind/body split, the interpretation of the meeting of force and meaning is a crucial intersection of symbolized cultural value and felt experience. How force is interpreted depends upon the values that have been placed upon the mysterious, the unknown, the uncontrollable. The subtlety of interpretation imbues force in Western parlance as that to be feared, arising as it does from the experience of the body, as it holds a chaotic threat to the order of logos, even as mutant logos. This intersection, in the West, usually has meant the instantiation of some form of control or repression—the assignment of a sign of negative social value—which presents interpreted force in a socially acceptable form. Yet force may shirk this insecurity of logos and reveal itself in playful spontaneity, welcoming the evasion of restriction, not as outlaw, but as inspiration to happy growth and expansion, beyond the drama of tragic logos (trauma). Force may be considered a life force that seeks and relies upon affirmative interaction, bonding, and attachment for its survival; an interdependent force between beings. This interpretation of force draws upon the integration of mind and body in the organic tradition that is subsumed in the dualistic instrumentality of the violence mythos.

In Freudian theory, the mechanism of protection, or selection, hinges upon the equilibrium of unpleasure accompanied by the rise of tension on the one hand, and pleasure and the lowering of tension on the other hand. Repression as a primary defense is the removal of cathexis from a hostile memory image. As we shall see in the next chapter, the hostile memory image as the shadow perpetrator, not a "death instinct," is the motivation to the compulsion to repeat destructive acts to self and others in trauma transference.

The pleasure-unpleasure apparatus begins to break its internal boundaries when external factors such as food and sexual partners are brought into play. The experience of satisfaction comes to the fore, which is achieved by external assistance. As a kind of "test experience," that experience of satisfaction relates to reality testing and marks the transition from the primary to the secondary process.

In contrast to theoretical reflection, dreamwork includes two ideas, one of a "violent change of place" and one of distortion, change of place, disfiguring, and deformation which makes something unrecognizable. Distortion or transposition splits dreams off from the rest of psychic life where the discovery of dream thoughts relates dreams to waking life.

Dream thoughts have a particular character. It is regression that leads us from concepts of meaning to concepts of force by the "relation to the abolished, the forbidden, the repressed."[51] Regression to repressed wishes is the close connection between the archaic and the oneiric, for the realm of dream fantasy is the realm of desire. In the timelessness of the unconscious with its reserves of desire, the archaic is vented in the oneiric. Because of the narrative structure of the discourse of dreams, the relation of dreams to desires and wishes is one of energy, conatus, appetition, will to power, libido. Dreams, as expressions of wishes, "lie at the intersection of meaning and force."[52]

Interpretation in the Discourses of Meaning and Force

The intersection of meaning and force is where interpretation enters the scene of action. Interpretation as meaning is a movement from the manifest to the latent, a displacement of the origin of meaning to another region. In this movement interpretation "uncovers another distortion, that of desires into images."[53]

Ricoeur explicates the regression from meaning to desires, from meaning as narrative discourse to wishes repressed by force. The displacement of conscious meaningful discourse to the discourse of distortion of unconscious impulses is not a displacement into a realm of unintelligibility. Ricoeur undercuts the deterministic structure of desire by the displacement to images of desire. The distortion of desires into images is an act of interpretation. It is the nexus of the reversal of regression to the retrieval of interpretation of symbols.

The concept of 'distortion' is correlative to the concept of 'censorship.' Distortion is the effect of censorship. On the one hand, censorship deletes subversive items in discourse and displaces them to "harmless out-of-the-way spots," leaving blanks, word substitutions, a lacuna in discourse. On the other hand, censorship is the bold expression of power as political power which refutes an opposing element by curtailing its expressive capacity. Censorship works in the discourse of meaning and force by altering meaning when it expresses a force and represses a force by disturbing its expression.

If we focus upon the notion that the three modes of distorted expression (condensation, displacement, representation) reveal the dream as a work, we come to see interpretation as a work. The distortive character of censorship at the intersection of force and meaning is like metaphor that, in an attempt to name something new, distorts the original meaning and retains it as hidden in the new meaning. The distortion of expression by repression in dreamwork is an activity that is different for the condensation and displacement of dream content.

To strip elements of their psychical intensity by displacement and condensation results in an overdetermination of representations. This multiple determination is a meaning of meaning, the result of distorted desire, the result of which is symbol, a double-meaning expression which is the pivotal point of interpretation. "If symbol is the meaning of meaning, then the entire Freudian hermeneutics should be a hermeneutics of symbols inasmuch as they are the language of de-sire."[54] Consciousness is never transparent to itself, for there is the excess of the unreflected of the unconscious that is co-intended in reflection and persists as the remainder of the nonexperienced.

The rupture in consciousness as self-knowing forms a fissured consciousness co-intended with the unconscious. The human becomes primarily a "'concern for things,' 'appetition,' desire and the quest for satisfaction."[55] Instinct is the frontier between the mental and the so-matic, as psychical representatives of the stimuli that originate from within the organism and reach the mind.

Entwined with this possibility of the human as primarily desire is the notion of the mode of being of the body as model for any conceivable consciousness. The body is not a representation in me nor a thing outside of me, but is a mode of existence. A "meaning that exists is a meaning caught up within a body, a meaningful behavior."[56]

The ambiguity of embodied existence is a correlation to "every mode of being conscious (that) is for subjectivity a mode of being unconscious."[57] Ricoeur extends this ambiguity into the dialectic of presence and absence, in which the gap of co-intention of the uncon-scious with the conscious is indicated by cosignification in language. Presence and absence are signified in language primarily by meta-phor, and more generally by words intended to signify an absent presence. The implicit absence in signification parallels the absent presence of the unconscious in consciousness, the lacuna in language.

Freud's systematization of the psychical processes is solipsistic and deficient for Ricoeur because the thematization of the "vicissi-tudes of instincts" occurs within an isolated psychism. Rather, "the situation and relations analysis speaks of and which speak in analysis are intersubjective."[58] Ricoeur moves from the Freudian abstraction of a solipsistic topographical understanding of psychical processes to the concrete situatedness of dialogue, the exchange between participants. Ricoeur shifts the exegesis of meaning out of the framework of iso-lated desire to dialogic interaction. Isolated desire remains constant and determines thought and action through unconscious motivation. The change to the realm of the intersubjective characterizes psychical activity as intersubjective in the symbolic constitution of the psyche through the concrete dialogic situation.

Authority and Symbolic Discourse

The shift from the solipsistic to the interpersonal requires further elaboration in terms of the concept of 'authority.' The movement of the repression of desire is the positing of the other of desire itself, that is, authority.[59] This is accomplished by focusing on that which re-presses. The repressing agency reveals itself to be the psychological representation of the social facts of cultural phenomena.[60] These in-clude such historical figures as the family, the mores of a group, tra-dition, education, political or religious power, penal or social sanctions. Authority as repression is an agency internal to desire itself. Repres-sion as a primary defense acts as a selective system within desire. Perception shields us from the dangers of the external world. How-ever, perception is lacking in the internal world of desire. Authority thus attempts to fill this lack of the limitation of desire by positing a limit to desire. Because authority is not given, as perception is, author-ity must disguise itself and present itself over and against desire.

The impact the historical figures of authority have on an indi-vidual does not depend upon their objective influence, but on the rela-tionship the individual has with the representatives of authority and the symbolic significance of the discourses that compose these figures in the attempt to reflect the individual's experience. The symbolic discourse that composes both the individual's understanding of oneself and the claims to authority of the historical figures serves as a mediating ground between the two, in which the self-understanding of both may be al-tered, through the acceptance of authority by the individual and through the alteration of authority by the creativity of the individual. It is through the mediation of the symbolic discourse, and not an independent agency of repression as authority, an other author, as desire meeting desire, that the limit to desire is posited. Thus, there is no authority in history that works its way into the internality of desire and poses its limit through the overdetermination of symbols common to history and desire. Ricoeur adopts Clifford Geertz's notion that "culture is public because meaning is" because it "clearly indicates that symbolism is not in the mind, not in a psychological operation destined to guide action, but a meaning incorporated into action and decipherable from it by other actors in the social interplay."[61]

For Ricoeur, authority posits a limit to desire in the unconscious. Desire in the unconscious is timeless where nothing ends or is forgot-ten. This realm of the "indestructible" has no history. The unconscious is the timeless wellspring of desire. Yet, the repressive agency of au-thority does have a history, it *is* history.[62] It is the individual's history from childhood to adulthood, and humanity's history from prehistory to history. Freud's project is to coordinate an ontogenesis and a phylogenesis: the genesis of the characteristics of individuals and those of humanity. As historical, the agency of repression produces an ontogeny and a phylogeny that subordinates all other histories, those of institutions, beliefs, and mores.

The thematic shift from what is repressed (desire) to the agents of repression (authority) entails a thematic displacement. The shift is made from the first topography (Cs, Pcs, Ucs) of desire to a second topography of repressive agents of desire. No longer by itself, desire has its "other" in authority. Desire always has had its other in the repressive agent internal to desire itself. What is repressed has no history. However, the repressing agency is history, a person's history from infancy to adulthood and human history. The agencies of the id, the ego, and the superego are not "places," as in the first topography, but rather "roles in a personology."[63] These roles are learned and internalized from external representations in history.

The second topography does not correspond to the first topography. The ego is not the same as consciousness, nor the id the same as the unconscious. Rather, the second topography is a threefold variation on a grammatical subject in relation to the anonymous and the suprapersonal in the individual's coming to be. The "person" is a historical designation of id, or what has not been named, as not yet "known"; the ego is what is believed; and the superego is more than the personal. The "person" is a temporal composite of changing relationships constituted through symbolic discourse.

The theory of agencies is an attempt to bring authority into the history of desire, making authority appear as "a 'differentiation' of desire."[64] Authority discriminates between desires and the appropriateness of their expression. Consider authority as external to desire. If desire is posited as an absolute with authority external to it, behavior is reduced to a desire/motive causality. Such a causality indicates a continual repetition of certain desires with certain behaviors, for that same structure is repeated in every instance of individual genesis where that desire demands expression. The limits to desire are thus forms of external authority (taboos, prohibitions) that must keep it in check. It is not mediated through interaction and discourse with other individuals. For Freud there is no medium for recognition of desire in others, only in oneself as desire made conscious.

For Freud, desire that constitutes oneself is always a repressed, distorted desire of the unrecognizable expressions of the unconscious. Desire is thwarted by the external roles of repression historically represented in configurations of the person's id, ego, and superego. For that reason, the Freudian schematic is not only pathological but pessimistic. Without a mechanism of recognition between persons, the historical agencies of repression within the individual are in relentless conflict with the internally uncontrollable unconscious.

The Signs of Desire

Ricoeur criticizes Freud's determinism of desire. For Ricoeur, authority is part of the internal semantic interpretation of desire. He interjects a semantics of desire, a mixed discourse distinct from the "motive-cause" alternative.[65] Behavior is not a single motive-dependent variable observed from outside the body. It is an expression of changes in the meaning of a subject's history disclosed in psychoanalysis. There is not a single causal link between motive and behavior. Behavioral expressions are signifiers for the history of desire, a history constituted through the overdetermination of symbolic signification. As expressions to be interpreted, there are no "facts" for psychoanalysis, for the analyst does not observe, the analyst interprets.[66] What is interpreted is the subject's history of desire that has been symbolically and intersubjectively constituted over the course of the person's life.

Because "wishes are a demand on another person, a speaking to another" they can enter the psychosocial realm of taboos, refusals, prohibitions, that is, frustrated demands.[67] Expressions of desire occur in relation with another person, within a social context. The other person is the aim of the demand, and the subject is also the *recipient* of the *response* from the other person. The interpretation of the subject's demand may be varied. The demand may or may not be recognized, fulfilled, refused, accepted, or returned with a demand from the other person. In order to discern whether the demand has been fulfilled, the subject must be able to interpret the response from the other person. As was discussed by Erikson, the degree of success or failure of this interpretive interaction relies upon the degree of trust in the relationship between participants. The subject must also be able to recognize the response of the other person as a response to one's demand. The demand of desire and the response to desire require language as a medium to decipher the signs of desire of both parties. Therefore, the interpretive mode of the analytic situation is intersubjective. The drama to be untangled can be transposed through the process of transference in the dual relationship between analyst and analysand. "The possibility of transference resides in the intersubjective texture of desire and of the desires deciphered within that situation."[68] The reference to the other person is present in desires, in wishes, and in the psychical as instinctual representatives. The intersubjective reference is the transition from the solipsistic to the symbolic, where desires are demands— albeit they are unrecognized as such, they are implicitly intersubjective and potentially recognizable as a desire in the context of other persons with the capacity to respond to and thereby satisfy one's desires, and with their own desires.

The demands of desire are signified in the overdetermination of meaning (the primacy of the unreflected over the reflected) that delimits the finitude of reflection. The human becomes primarily appetition, desire, and the quest for satisfaction. The abundance of unreflected experience is of the order of fantasy or imagination operative prior to language. The imaginative is the realm of distortion, where symbolism borders the unconscious. It is the interpretation of symbolism which suggests a correlation of hermeneutics and energetics on the level of praxis (activity). There is a "correlation between the art of interpretation and the work against the resistances: 'to translate' the unconscious into the conscious and 'to do away with the constraint' . . . are one and the same thing. To interpret and to work coincide."[69] Working through resistances as transference is an indication of the intersubjectivity of desire as an unanswered demand.

Authority enters into the history of desire as an acquired differentiation of desire, which gives rise to a special type of semantics. The semantics of ideals is where unsatisfied desire aims toward satisfaction in another desire. The semantics of ideals is explicated not in terms of a desire-pleasure/unpleasure relation that would retain desire in a strict economics of cathected impulses achieving constancy at the sacrifice of satisfaction. Rather, this semantics is expanded in terms of a desire-desire relation were "self-consciousness attains its satisfaction only in another self-consciousness."[70] A semantics of ideas resituates the context of goal-directed instinct from the aim and conversely an objective of pleasure external to the self, to a dialectic of desire itself, where the desire to have and the desire to be like come together in a recognition of difference and sameness.

The discourse of the unconscious becomes meaningful, as Ricoeur sees it, in the dialogic situation of analysis. The "talking cure" is that by virtue of which "the constitution of the subject in speech and the constitution of desire in intersubjectivity are one and the same phenomenon."[71] Thus, desire becomes meaningful in human history where history is constituted by speech addressed to the other.

The self's desire removes itself from the desire of things by seeking itself in the other. Desire is desire only if life manifests itself as another desire, a certainty found through the process of reflection, the reduplication of self-consciousness. The reduplication makes it possible for self-consciousness to become manifest in the midst of life.

Infinitude becomes part of the process of mutual recognition as "infinitude realizing itself in and through consciousness."[72] The opposition of desire seeking another desire is an infinite movement in the "restlessness" of life raised to reflection through opposition and struggle, for "it is only in this struggle for recognition that the self reveals itself as never being simply what it is—and therefore as being infinite."[73] Desire thus becomes an infinite dialectial movement through recognition and identification in otherness. Mastery of the negative becomes a possibility when put into play in symbol.[74]

Satisfaction of desire is "attained only through another history, that of recognition."[75] In this appropriation of Hegelian teleology, the dialectic of desire consists of a dialectic of archeology or the regression to origins, and teleology, the overcoming of origins in the progression of co-intentions carried in thought by the same symbols operative in praxis. Language is the milieu of recognition of the signs of desire, of the transference of the meaning of desire to self-consciousness. In transference, desire is both unsurpassable and overcome. It is a struggle of otherness that resides in life where life becomes the other, "in and through which the self ceaselessly achieves itself."[76]

Symbol is the conduit from abstract reflection to concrete reflection. The arrival at the concrete is a labored task involving the revival of archaic means and the anticipation of new meaning wrought from the overdetermination of authentic symbols. This task is not limited to dreamwork. Rather, the symbolic relation is the work of culture and formed within language.[77]

The innate constitution of aggressive impulse as instinct becomes a symbolically mediated interpretation of desire, and hence the shift is made from solipsism to social participation. However, Ricoeur's analysis is not a radically discursive analysis of self-understanding, as he assumes the recognition of a common desire between participants, be they between individuals or between the individual and historical figures of authority derived from the idealist concept of 'subjectivity.' The experience of desire cannot be experienced by the other; the self can only *signify* the expression of the experience of desire to the other. Ricoeur does not make the linguistic turn to symbolic discourse and to the recognition of the signs and symbols of particular desire in the discourse of unique participants. The meaning of meaning has significance only insofar as it is signified. His theory of a hermeneutic of desire remains within a methodological reductionism to an internal universal origin of desire paralleled in Freud's theory of an aggressive impulse for self-formation and language. In this framework, although the models of authority and cultural ideals are internalized through learning, it is ultimately faulty desire that determines human aggression. The theories both of Freud and of Ricoeur reflect the exploitive logos of innate violence in the violence mythos. Self-formation is motivated by and attained through conflict and struggle, with an unconscious impulse to aggress in the struggle for self-realization with another.

Let us reconsider for a moment instinct on the frontier between the mental and the somatic, as psychical representatives of the stimuli that originate from within the organism and reach the mind. Ricoeur accurately emphasizes the role of the body and meaning where meaning that exists is meaningful behavior both as conscious and as unconscious. Ricoeur uses the body as an intersubjective bridge to symbolic discourse as shared discourse between dialogic participants capable of recognizing the same desire expressed in this symbolic discourse. He also posits authority as a limit to desire as history mediated in symbolic discourse. The repressing agency as authority is the psychological representation of the social facts of cultural phenomena. The roles in a personology of the id, ego, and superego are learned and internalized from external representations in history. With Freud, desire is posited with authority external to it, indicating a repetition of certain desires with certain behaviors kept in check by authority as desire becomes conscious.

Ricoeur makes an important move when he shifts to images of desire in the intersection of meaning and force. When he shifts the exegesis of meaning from isolated desire to dialogic interaction, he introduces the possibility of symbolically mediated desire in psychical activity. He brings the mental together with the somatic through the linguistic. The repetition in the reduplication of consciousness indicates the movement of the struggle for recognition and identification as mastery of the negative/otherness put into play in symbol. Desire reduplicates itself through linguistic symbol. Both Freud and Ricoeur attempt to control compulsive desire: Freud through external force as authority, Ricoeur through symbolic force as authority. They both posit a "legitimate" mode of force as collectively recognized authority to control the "illegitimate" force of unknown and hence unrecognized desire. There is a particular kind of dynamic at work in these theories: the attempt to control the assumed destructive force of desire.

The frontier of the somatic is particularly significant in the early stage of human development: infancy. According to Erikson, it is in infancy that a child establishes the fundamental orientation to the world through the "unmistakable somatic interchange" with the caregiver. The child's memory is visual and enactive, relying upon sensory and image perceptions of the caregiver's face and body to develop pscychoneurologically, and appropriate responses to and expectations of itself, others, and the world. The child internalizes models of caregiving as trustful or mistrustful in developing an estimation of itself, others and the world. This somatic memory is prelinguistic and the basis of core identity formation in the dependency stage of getting the child's survival needs met. The success or failure of this early stage of negotiated somatic development is reflected in basic trust or basic mistrust.

It is this frontier of somatic memory to which the body reverts in times of overwhelming trauma terror. In the shattering effect of trauma to the person's inner cognitive schemata, the linguistic encoding of memory is inactivated and the central nervous system reverts to sensory and iconic forms of memory from early life. "The earliest steps are preserved in the deepest layers."[78] Early mistrust is accompanied by an experience of "total" rage, with "fantasies of total domination or destruction of the sources of pleasure and provision . . . [that] live on in the individual and are revived in extreme states and situations." If the basic orientation to the world is mistrust, "the human being may regress temporarily to partial mistrust whenever the world of his expectations has been shaken to the core." This contrasts to basic trust, with its accompanying sense of faith, hope, and an interrelated goodness between inner and outer worlds.

Trauma shatters the mind's ability to process new information and update the inner schemata of self and world. "Unassimilated traumatic experiences are stored in active memory which has an intrinsic tendency to repeat the representation of contents."[79] Trauma is resolved only when the survivor develops a new mental "schema" to understand what has happened. Reliving the trauma experience carries with it the emotional intensity of the original event, whether in intrusive memories, dreams, or actions. "Adults as well as children often feel compelled to re-create the moment of terror, either in literal or disguised form . . . with a fantasy of changing the outcome of the dangerous encounter . . . (and) may even put themselves at risk of futher harm."[80] For Freud, the propulsion to re-create seemed to defy conscious intent and resist change. Freud could not find a life-affirming explanation for it and evolved the "death instinct."[81] Theorists now reject this and appropriate Freud's earlier concept of an attempt to master the traumatic event. The compulsion to repeat represents spontaneous unsuccessful healing attempts to restore efficacy and power.[82]

The shattering of the inner schema that is organized through linguistic significations is the shattering of the cognitive layer of organized memory. Linguistic signification requires a level of abstraction that allows the literal/somatic to be signified symbolically and applied to new experience as pattern of expectation and response. This allows the self to learn vicariously and cope by increasing the chances of survival through not having to experience life-threatening events itself, but to learn from the "successful" survival experiences of others.

When the self does experience a life-threatening event, the threat to survival reverts mental functioning to primary memories of survival: somatic images of basic trust or mistrust relationships. The compulsive reenactment of trauma is an attempt to restore effective trust relationships, and hence an effective understanding of the self, a reorganized inner schemata that will allow the self to cope with such experiences in the world and survive. The inner schema is linguistically organized. Until there is a means to signify the trauma event, to name it, to understand it, there will be a perpetual repetition of unassimilated trauma experiences as somatic memories without linguistic representation/signification in the mental/cognitive memory of the inner schema in relation to the outer world.

The "action of telling a story" in "the safety of a protected relationship can actually produce a change in the abnormal processing of the traumatic memory."[83] As well, "with this transformation of memory comes relief of many of the major symptoms of posttraumatic stress disorder. The physioneurosis induced by terror can apparently be reversed through the use of words."[84] In resignifying , resymbolizing, reabstracting the somatic memory traces, the self is able to reconstruct an inner schema that reconnects the inner and outer worlds of understanding. Done in the safety of a trust relationship, the self is able to reaffirm its basic trust orientation to the world developed from its earliest somatic memories, and rebuild its cognitive understanding as a new trust of self, others, and world. In this sense, knowledge is empowerment, where the traumatized person is relieved simply to know, to learn the name of the condition. The survivor begins again the process of effectivity with a language for the traumatic experience that has been experienced by others. The survivor is not alone, and is not crazy; trauma syndromes are normal human responses to extreme circumstances. And most important, the survivor is not doomed to suffer this condition indefinitely. The survivor can expect to recover, as others have recovered.[85]

However, survivors recognize social assumptions that rendered them vulnerable to exploitation in the past and may also identify sources of continued social pressure that keeps them confined in a victim role in the present.[86] While they must overcome their own fears and conflicts, they must overcome these external social pressures, "otherwise, they will be continually subjected to symbolic repetitions of the trauma in everyday life."[87]

Freud's "death instinct" is here redefined as a "healing instinct" to restore efficacy for survival. Without the combined elements of trust relationship and linguistic signification, the healing instinct cannot effectively engage a reschematization of inner cognitive understanding and the survival connections of trust relationships in the world. Without effective engagement, the self compulsively reenacts the trauma event as ineffective engagement that may put itself and others at risk for survival in trauma transference and countertransference. This ineffective engagement characterizes Ricoeur's dialectic of desire in a symbolic dialogue "struggle" for mastery of the negative in recognition and identification in otherness. Inscribed in a social context of control and mastery, of authority over desire, the dynamics of exploitation, Freud describes the somatic memory process of trauma, and Ricoeur describes its symbolic reenactment in interaction.

In a culture that does not have an assimilated understanding of trauma, and hence few symbolic associations or paradigms for the process of healing and effectively restoring trust, the individual reenactment of trauma through vicarious transmission eventually would become normalized as expected behavior, especially if there were masses of traumatized individuals from a trauma event, such as war. The culture would develop symbolizations of successful exploitive dynamics that resulted in survival, and pattern its expectations for social behavior on this paradigm. It would develop rationalizations for the exploitive dynamic and legitimations for authoritative control that permitted survival. In the dynamic of exploitive control, a cultural symbolic transference of blame to the victim recasts the healing instinct for survival as authoritative control of "destructive desire." This is a self-contradictory system, for its primary somatic/linguistic symbolization for survival is based on a primary somatic/linguistic interpretation of experience as destruction of survival. The abstract layer of "cultural schema" adapted for survival contradicts the prior layer of maladaption for destruction. The system cannot sustain itself on this basis; it cannot survive as an integrated whole, because it is based on the disintegrated trauma effects of victimization and internalized as self-destruction.

The somatic images of the unconscious are the imprinted survival images from infancy. They are mediated internalizations of impressions of caregivers and the world that develop into orientations of trust or mistrust. In basic trust, images that enhance survival are integrated into an effective schema of development. In basic mistrust, images that threaten survival are unassimilated with their extreme emotional associations as the self attempts to repetitively restore efficacy and hence ensure self-survival, not self-destruction, though these ineffective attempts may place the self at risk and result in self-destruction.

Replays of the trauma experience revert to and engage images of mistrust and images of trust, as these are the primary identification/attachment relationships of the self in the world. These relationships establish the self as interdependent for survival upon others and the world. In reliving the trauma experience in another relationship, such as a therapeutic relationship, the trauma transference activates these images as the self attempts to reschematize its shattered orientation to the world developed since infancy. The unassimilated images of the perpetrator become psychic images of a shadow perpetrator symbolizing mistrustful relationships. The assimilated, or internalized images of trusted caregivers are symbolized as psychic images of the rescuer, of reliant help for survival to whom the victim can appeal and depend. The external roles of these images are played out linguistically and somatically in relationship dynamics until the victim is able to assimilate the trauma experience into a new inner schema and effective relationships. The victim requires the safety and connection of a trusting relationship to do so. If the trauma experience is not assimilated, the roles are indefinitely repeated in the self's ineffective attempts to survive and may result in risks that lead to death. Unhealthy relationships deteriorate growth and enact isolated exploitation based on mistrust expectations. Healthy relationships promote growth and mutual responsibility based on trust expectations.

By focusing on a myopic maladapted dynamic of desire, both Freud and Ricoeur neglect the somatic survival impulse of effectivity and healing, and its negotiation, not *necessarily struggle*, in the trust process in the prelinguistic language of somatic interchange and its continual development throughout adult life. The dualistic dynamic of figures of authority is the symbolic condensation of the interdependent triad of self, other, and world into an exploitive dialectic of self and other. Both theories reveal the normalization of purposeful distanciation in the trauma dynamic externalized symbolically in authoritative control/mind over desire/body, reapplied to internal psychic processes, and hence repeat the cycle of exploitation they seek to explain. The intersection of meaning and force is a cultural misnomer for the linguistic/somatic expression of life attempting to affirm itself, others, and the world. Repression, in a cultural symbolic system of maladapted trauma traces that expect and demand control and exploitation oriented toward death, is reconceptualized as a protective boundary to assimilate understanding in respect and negotiation oriented toward life.

Violence in Language

The concept of 'private' violence and language is expanded in Ricoeur's work on metaphor and in the work of Edith Wyschogrod. Appropriating the Hegelian view of self-formation as struggle, Wyschogrod extends this dialectic of self-actualization to include a version of the self as "not only violent but also equiprimordially linguistic and thus able to restrain violence. This irenic function of language expresses itself as naming by designating the other in terms of kinship and in the use of proper names."[88] She views Hegel as the first to "comprehend completely" the intrinsic nature of death in human existence and for "fully self-conscious existence."

For Wyschogrod, the realization of death as its own possibility sets the human apart from the animal. The satisfaction of need in the animal is transformed into human desire. Natural animal existence has no concept of desire and cannot project something from memory into a future anticipation. Knowing in advance of the possibility of death, the human must be willing to risk its life in combat with the other. Such is "Hegel's figure to describe the origin of self-consciousness and social differentiation through violent encounter with the other . . . by means of violent confrontation with another."[89]

Enter language to restrain the violence. Without self-restraint, social existence would be nonexistent. Language does not supplant an anterior, or given, violence, however, nor is it a supplement to the residue of violence in society. "Language *is* the expression of this self-restraint." Even when provocative, language can be answered with language, an exchange that is not actual violence. Language is more than referential or informative; it is the "silent renunciation of violence." If *homo homini lupus* were the sole expression of social life, there would be nothing but reciprocal annihilation.[90]

As *irenic*, Wyschogrod, as does Ricoeur, applies this function of peaceful restraint to language. However, as the Frankfurt School's critique of instrumental reason has shown, language can be formulated into discourses of oppression. In this respect, Jürgen Habermas's claim that reason is *interested* reason disallows a privileged place to language as the expression of restraint. One person's restraint could be another person's censorship. Language seeks to value, discriminate, and associate signs in context. It is the history of these associations that speaks to humans particularly in the form of myth that has the power to do violence. The restraint of violence when injurious depends upon one's cognitive schema of acceptable violence. In the case of learned helplessness, the restrained discourse of the aggressor may simply reinforce self-hatred in the victim and perpetuate a cycle of internalized violence, because to oppose this discourse would be illegitimate and "wrong" according to the aggressor's rules. Nonparticipation in the aggressor's discourse may also be a form of passive resistance, a distancing dissociation through the deferral of discourse.

Both for Ricoeur and for Wyschogrod, the basis of self-formation is recognition between self and other in a Hegelian dialectic that has hostile undertones. For Wyschogrod language is the restraint of violence, the silent renunciation of violence. Let us now turn to a discussion of the role of violence in Ricoeur's symbolic discourse.

The reference to the necessity of violence in Hegel's concept of self-realization of Spirit shows the subliminal sanction of violence in cultural discourse. It must be kept in mind that it is not Hegel, Freud, or Ricoeur as a personality or author who advocates the valuation of violence in his discourse, but rather that through the symbolic associations in his discourse the cultural sanction of violence can be detected, as the logos of the violence mythos influences his theoretical assumptions.

Ricoeur's own *Symbolism of Evil* applies the hermeneutic of suspicion and retrieval to symbolic discourse with regard to violence as evil. According to Don Ihde, for Ricoeur it is symbol which reveals the originary experience of the body. Symbol reveals experience through expression, and myth interprets this expression. Through reflection on the history of a symbol, an analysis which began by reading evil upon the world in a primitive "realism" progressively interiorizes this understanding until at its other extreme evil is read in the subject as an ethical "idealism."[91] In this respect, a pure symbol is suggestive of a concept, whereby the symbol gives rise to thought.

The series of primary symbols of evil tends toward the concept of the *servile will*.[92] The servile will incorporates the quasi-nature of evil through the pseudo-concept of Augustinian original sin.[93] This quasi-nature is in the will, where evil is a type of involuntariness (such as desire), not over against the will, but in it, and this defines the servile will.[94]

This concept of the 'servile will' may be linked to a broader context of political discourse. For Ricoeur, political violence is where "individuals have begun and partly succeeded in overcoming their private violence by subordinating it to a rule of law."[95]

> Thus the rule of law which gives form to the social body is also power, an enormous violence which elbows its way through our private violences and speaks the language of value and honor.

And from here come the grand words which move crowds and sometimes lead them to death. It is through the subtle art of denomination that the common will conquers our wills; by harmonizing our private languages in a common fable of glory, it seduces our wills as well and expresses their violence, just as the juice of a fruit is expressed by squeezing.[96]

In articulating this lexicon of the heroic, Ricoeur questions whether this "misfortune" happens only in political language, and he answers that poetic language is less so: "And yet . . . it is at this furthest point of non-violence that violent particularity is accumulated," through the word, in the poetic capture of being by words, "things become and are."[97] Metaphor is the link in this capture of being. "The whole art of metaphor is to achieve the rapprochement that motivates the search for semes capable of identifying what was 'alien.' "[98] Metaphor is "enigmatic" insofar as it "says" two things, "the thing that lends its name and the thing that receives it" in the attempt to name.[99] Thus, there is "An openness that is a capture, such is the poetic word . . . The poet is the violent man who forces things to speak. It is poetic *abduction*."[100]

In this attempt to "capture" being, the human "possibility for evil" is revealed. According to David Klemm, this possibility rests on the condition that the human is "noncoincident" with itself. "Human freedom is so constituted that it must mediate between finite and infinite aspects of itself, and this makes it fallible."[101] Thus, Ricoeur's hermeneutics has its own assumptions about the nature of violence as internal to the human, based upon certain theological criteria and articulated in a theory of metaphorical discourse.

Ricoeur describes the encounter between violence and language as "human violence, the individual as violence."[102] He explains this violence in contrast to other forms of violence, such as a hurricane and murder. As with the hurricane, an "involuntary" form of violence, human violence is natural insofar as it is the violence of desire, fear, and hate. He does not distinguish between these emotional states and the possible behaviors that are chosen, as socially learned behavior, to express them. For Ricoeur, murder is a voluntary act, the will to dominate another, the attempt to deprive the other of freedom or expression. It is racism and imperialism. This violence becomes problematic for the speaking being, who in the speech act is pursuing meaning upon entering rational discourse. Violence gains its meaning from language, its opposite, or other. Violence that speaks is already a violence trying to be right, and begins to negate itself as violence. Hence, Ricoeur touches on the inversion of trauma memory traces through the act of telling a story, of signifying unassimilated experience into an integrated understanding.

Ricoeur's template for violence is one of a mind/body dualism, where violence has an innate dimension in that it arises from certain human emotions. In Ricoeur's formulation, speech is given a superiority, where violence is overridden by the superior faculty of rationality, as rationality imbued with the cultural value of enabling rightness, signifying conformity with the logic of cultural norms implicit in language use.

According to Ricoeur, even though persons who argue for violence contradict themselves, there is the world of falsified words that makes language the "voice of violence." It is not enough to examine the anatomy of language, for language is innocent and does not speak. It is in discourse, the spoken word, the use of language, that the dialectic of violence and meaning is born. Only in discourse will violence confront meaning. However, without the relational context of safety and trust, this confrontation may simply perpetuate itself as somatic conflict abstracted to symbolic conflict.

Metaphor

Language in use, as semantic, becomes a mediator that functions between human and human and human and world, and integrates the human into society and assures a relation between language and the world. For Ricoeur, "language is not a world of its own. It is not even a world." Yet because "we are in the world, because we are affected by situations," and we orient ourselves in those situations, "we have something to say, we have experience to bring to language."[103]

Metaphor functions as the mediator of this relation between experience and expression in language. Metaphor is "enigmatic" insofar as it says two things, the thing that lends its name and the thing that receives it in the attempt to name. The enigma of metaphor provides the possibility of new meaning in the activity of naming, the relation between language and the world.

For Ricoeur, the problem of language in confrontation with violence is not a problem of structure, but of rational meaning. The problem of meaning indicates the effort to integrate in understanding the relationship of human to human, human to nature, of existence and meaning. What Ricoeur calls the "loving struggle"[104] of the "hidden link between discourse and the violent particularity of the philosophical individual"[105] is where poetic metaphor attempts to capture meaning while itself remaining open to being captured. An openness to essential being and meaning, as well as capturing it through "poetic abduction," characterizes the confrontation with violence. The attempt to name, and therefore capture the being that is to be named while remaining open to the meaning of that being to be named, is an act of subtle violence for Ricoeur, as it is an act of will to dominate the other, to obtain its essence. Metaphorical statements are composites of the subject and the verb in a sentence that names. For Ricoeur, metaphors that express the intention of the subject admit of their own violence in the attempt to capture essential being, of the ontological condition of being in the world.

Recognition and Violent Desire

Ricoeur describes desire as intersubjectively constituted in the person through symbolic discourse through opposition and struggle with another. In the confrontation between self and other each recognizes the other as a self. Satisfaction of desire is "attained only through another history, that of recognition."[106] In mutual recognition, the negotiation of the self knows its limit and by knowing its limit knows how to sacrifice itself in order to continue its existence.

Hegel's dialectic of opposition and struggle is premised upon the capacity of two social existents to *recognize* each other. Recognition is the perception of something previously known. If we follow Ricoeur's analysis of self as interpretation, as constituted through symbolic discourse, then what two social existents recognize cannot be an ontological sameness, but a recognition of meaning mediated through intersubjective symbolic discourse within a cultural tradition. The other can be seen only through the meeting between the meaning of the signs of desire of the self and meaning of the signs of desire itself. The other is its own signifier of the meaning of the signs of desire. Social participants with similar expectations of engagement will recognize those facets in each other. In this way, the facets of trauma effects may be recognizable and draw victims to each other and subsequently reenact the exploitive dynamic of aggression/submission in an attempt to regain the efficacy that was lost in a previous traumatic experience. Hence, violent desire is a catachrestic lexeme for healing efficacy.

The nontransparency of consciousness and desire undercuts the Hegelian dialectic of opposition and struggle that *requires* the immediate identification of the consciousness of the other as *same*, as transparent. Given Ricoeur's argument for the discursively constituted self, such a demand cannot logically be made of the other, let alone the self. The attempt by metaphor to "capture" the meaning of the other through distortion and disguise is incomplete in making an identification of sameness.

Ricoeur can maintain the historicity of the self through symbolic discourse and the teleology of figures only if what is interpreted through the signs of desire as metaphor is the *same violent desire* for both participants, who can then through reduplication, or recognition, battle out the respective subordination/mastery dialectic of figures.

Ricoeur's assumptions that desire, fear, and hate are violent, or aggressive, and that there is a will to dominate another are in tandem with Freud's aggression theory. Freud claimed that humans have basic unconscious urges and drives that if repressed, erupt, cathect their energy and return to constancy. A universal impulse to aggress, or to act in a hostile or injurious manner, offered an explanation for perceived and disguised aggressive behavior. "Civilization has to use its utmost efforts in order to set limits to man's aggressive instincts and to hold the manifestations of them in check by psychical reaction-formations."[107] Here is Wyschogrod's *Homo homini lupus*.[108] Again, civilization becomes the necessary regulator of otherwise uncontrollable aggression.

It appears that Hegel and Freud describe an ontology of violence, of innate aggression and hostility in humans, particularly in men. Even those traits deemed life affirming are reduced to a more fundamental violence. Such are Ricoeur's signs of desire, the disguise work of metaphor that distorts a *universal* human impulse to aggression. However, the acceptance of the distortion of the impulse does not question the validity of the assumption about the universality or innateness of the impulse itself.

By positing an intrinsic linguistic historicity in contrast to a violent drive or desire in the unconscious, violence becomes part of the effective history of the social milieu of symbolic discourse that influences self-understanding and the context in which participants find themselves, as part of a preserved tradition in history, here that of the violence mythos.

Freud and Force

For Ricoeur, authority acts as a selective shield against the violence of desire by way of regulating the expression of desire in symbol and language where violence is transcended and transformed into meaning through the rationality of language, of discourse, as a violence attempting to be right.

A critique of discourse by Foucault shows that language loses its irenic function accorded it by Wyschogrod and Ricoeur and can be held suspect as in collusion with repressive histories of thought. Foucault analyzes the discourses of anonymous power in repressive histories of thought. He refuses analyses couched in the symbolic field or the domain of signifying structures and replaces them with analyses in geneologies of relations of force, strategic developments, and tactics. His own work incorporates the lexicon of the violence mythos. One's point of reference is shifted from language to that of "war and battle." "The history which bears and determines us has the form of a war rather than that of language: relations of power, not relations of meaning."[109] Here Foucault recognizes the import of somatic interchange obscured by preoccupations with linguistic meaning.

As body-in-relation, it appears the body is a convenience for something else at work in/on it. The body is the battlefield. It is the somatic war zone where Freud's project was to coordinate an ontogenesis and a phylogenesis: the genesis of the characteristics of individuals and those of humanity. As historical, the agency of repression produces an ontogeny and a phylogeny that subordinates all other histories, those of institutions, beliefs, and mores. For Ricoeur the agency of repression is the authority of rational truth and meaning (rendering the Freudian systematics a hermeneutics). The ontogenesis-phylogenesis reduplication is for Ricoeur a duplication of Hegelian self-actualization constituted through symbolic discourse intrapsychically in the individual. This is an attempt to recapitulate an ontogenesis in a phylogenesis that subordinates all other histories, including a liberating interpretation of efficacious life force and the reciprocal developmental influence of mind and body in linguistic/somatic interchange. Let us now turn to another version of the genesis of individual and species characteristics from the perspective of mimetic desire developed by René Girard.

FIGURE 7

U.S. Army Sergeant and Soldiers, Chu Lai, Vietnam, 1969

Photographer: Clinton C. Whitmer, U.S. Army Spec 4 Medic during
September 1968 through October 1969 Tour of Duty, Chu Lai, Vietnam.

5

Girard and the Trauma Victim

For René Girard, it is "not through words, . . . but by the example" or the somatic language of the mimetic process of what he describes as the shift from acquisitive to conflictual mimesis, that we see the process of trauma transference at work. We are able to appreciate Girard for his unknowingly accurate description of this process and its prevalence in Western culture. At the same time, we are able to update his misascription of this process to "innate aggression," and rename it "reenacted trauma transference" and the exploitation of interpersonal trust relationships.

At the symbolic level of discourse, this analysis corresponds to how the transference traumatology of the body and relationships has been interpreted in Western culture in the myth of the hero. The body is sacrificial, and relationships are dominated by the control of "innate aggression" through the legitimation of scapegoating as the displacement of blame from perpetrators of violence to victims. The creation of the hero role as the idealized model of human godlike self-sufficiency and restraint is imitated to control and prevent "illegitimate" violence through "legitimate" violence.

Mimetic Triangulation

Girard, a literary critic by profession, developed an analysis of novels that he later applied to anthropology. His analysis gave rise to the theory that a character's desire was not a singular pursuit of the desiring subject for the desired object. Rather, desire was triangular, mimetic, imitative. For Girard, as human desire copies or imitates the desires of others, a triangle is created where the object of our desire—knowledge, mate, position—is desirable by others who desire it as well. A mimetic triangle is created between the self, other, and object.[1]

The mimetic triangle differs from the interdependent trust triad in its assumptions. Humans learn how to interpret their experiences, and appropriate social behavior through imitation. Humans develop a basic orientation to the world through their early somatic interchanges that result in basic trust or mistrust. The mimetic triangle depicts the maladaption of mistrust and its expectations of exploitation, such that the mutual reciprocity of give-and-take in trustful needs negotiation is disrupted and needs are unfulfilled. This lack from unfulfilled needs is in effect a threat to the self's survival and is a form of trauma. Until the self is able successfully to negotiate its needs with others, the trauma dynamic will repeat itself in relationships with others. In the mistrustful mimetic triangle, obtaining the object is substituted for learning the process of trust negotiation.

In a description of a lover's heightened despair and the loved one's coquetry, Girard describes the unison of the process as the two sentiments are copied from each other. "It is the same desire, growing ever more intense, which circulates between the two partners."[2] The more they grow alike, the more different they imagine themselves. "The *sameness* by which they are obsessed appears to them an absolute *otherness*. Double mediation secures an opposition as radical as it is meaningless."[3] The dissonance brought about by the collision of illusory autonomous desires brings conflict and mystification. Conflict arises from the development of imitation in the form of the disciple's emulation of the model. A closing of the distance between the two results in rivalry, and when the other gets in the way of the desired objects, enmity occurs. However, the participants need not be aware that they are duplicating each other and converging toward the same objects. The fuller sense of imitation as a disposition or inclination to reproduce the actions and gestures of others is what Girard means by mimesis.[4] For Girard, what is commonly called "desire" originates in mimesis as an inclination that solidifies as a more distinct intention, or desire. Through literature, Girard presents the mimetic dimension of human behavior and its ability to produce cultural forms, or "the ability of mimesis to shape not only our actions but also our perception of our actions."[5]

Girard developed his insights on mimesis through his work on sacrifice in *Violence and the Sacred*. This book led to a theory of the origin of social order and a general theory of culture, considered in principle by most anthropologists as impossible, on grounds of the nonsubstitutability of categories for cross-cultural comparative studies.[6]

However, Girard claimed that mimesis is a universal characteristic of the human mind, where we copy each other's actions in being drawn toward the same objects and come into conflict. When enmity enters the stage of reciprocal imitation, the subjects progressively lose sight of the object of their desire and focus on each other. They do not see the imitative aspect of the process, but they do perceive "the aggressive and harmful attitude of their antagonist." Without intervention, this process "must necessarily lead to physical violence and from physical violence to death."[7]

Supposedly, there are only two ways to stop this process: through cultural institutions or through dominance patterns. Since mimesis is a universal human trait, it came about during our evolution "from animalhood to humanity." Hence the dominance patterns of the animal world do not apply to humans, and mimesis must have risen before cultural institutions existed.

For Girard, there is no halt to the mimetic process of violent escalation. Violence is "contagious," and once it has erupted, it has the ability "to spread." It has the ability to destroy all social institutions and the social order itself. The solution to this probable apocalypse is "the expansion and evolution of the very process of mimetic violence that creates the problem."[8] The expansion refers to the possibility of reuniting rivals through a common enemy, a surrogate victim upon which all can simultaneously vent their rage and have no fear of revenge from the dead victim.

As a result, the participants will see the victim in a distorted way, as the source of all violence (rage displaced from the community) and at the same time the origin of peace and order (calm restored to the community). Thus, this victimage mechanism becomes represented as "the sacred" by those who unwittingly perform it (as an indirectly accepted intersubjective assumption). To protect themselves from the return of the sacred (revenge), community members proscribe actions and gestures, now prohibited by the higher being, which originated the crisis and its development. Social institutions proceed from the victimage mechanism and ensure the continuity of sacred rules of relating, and myths preserve the memory of their origins. "The social order emerges from the self-regulating mechanisms of violence. It emerges as a means of protection against violence."[9]

Jean-Marie Domenach objects to the all-encompassing nature of Girard's theory. In keeping with the topic of sacrifice, there are examples of heroes who founded or revived states by assembling, not excluding. He calls to mind Henry IV and Augustus. "A golden legend runs through history in parallel to a macabre legend."[10] Sensitivity to the fragility of social institutions elicits oblations as well as ritual sacrifices. Domenach enlists Socrates who anticipated the law intended to sacrifice him and sacrificed himself for it. "Is there then to be no sacrifice but of victims presumed guilty—and not also . . . a sacrifice of self, stripped of cunning and illusion, just as there are desires whose object has not been designated for them by a third party?"[11]

Andrew McKenna summarizes Girard's explanation for the origin of the human species as the selection of a victim whose elimination ends the conflict of appropriative violence.[12] Appropriative violence occurs when the subject of our desire copies the model's aims and goals, then seeks to make this object of desire one's own *proper* and unique possession.[13] The violence of all against all, in which no community can form itself or survive, becomes the violence of the many against the one by arbitrarily singling some member out for destruction.[14] As evidence, McKenna refers to Girard's use of ethological studies of animal behavior that show instinctual brakes to violent behavior, but which, as shown by history, are lacking in humans. In place of an instinctual brake to violence, the victim is substituted, serving as a double or duplicate for the unanimous violence which produced it.

For McKenna, what occurs first is the victim as a product of violence followed by the sacred. The victim is representative of "deferred appropriation" on the part of indecisive community members about taking the victim for themselves.[15] The victim is desired by all and is thus taboo to all. This "irreducible paradox, this double bind or double bid issuing from doubles, accounts for the non-instinctual attention in which Girard postulates hominization. Humanity emerges from attention to the victim in the form of abstention from the victim, if only to bide its time, bid up the stakes, pounce anew."[16] The monstrous double that is projected onto the victim as scapegoat is a self that refuses to see a reflection in and as the self; the other's desire, the other's violence.[17] The self-inflicted denial of violence prevents the self from acknowledging a "violence born of (self) ignorance of which we stand as much a chance as any of being the arbitrary victim."[18]

Yet this analysis again assumes the sameness of desire, the sameness of violence, when in reality there are differences in desire and in the possibility of enacting violent behavior. It is simply not true that all are capable of the same behaviors. Much violence is not arbitrary, but occurs in relationships of familiarity. Each person develops a character and behaviors that are unique to themselves. How they cope with aversive circumstances may have social influences and certain patterns, yet their choices are unique to their history and themselves. There is a similarity of natural human psychoneurological response to trauma. How unresolved trauma is reenacted varies, for some it may mean attack behavior; for some it may mean suicide; for others it may mean a shadow life. What is similar about trauma experience is the violation of life and trust connections. A system that does not acknowledge the use of violence as relationship control and intimidation, and trauma coping differences, through assuming universal violence, risks allowing the exploitive dynamic of violence to perpetuate itself at great cost to itself.

Girard stages the victimage scenario with reference to the early hominization of humans, when our ancestors became carnivores and hunters: "Strong discharges of adrenaline are necessary at the critical moment of the hunt and these can occur in different conditions . . . under the effect of any sort of disturbance."[19] The resulting extreme rage becomes "centripetal" once it has been given "free rein," as it is never "centrifugal." This rage tends toward "those who are closest and most cherished," those normally most protected by the rule against violence.[20]

For Girard, Freud's emphasis on the control of sexual relations does not address the more fundamental problem of violence. He cites the use of weapons as a case in point. Animals can engage in rival combat without a fight to the death because instinctual inhibitions control the natural weapons of claws and teeth. Such control could not be applied to stones or other weapons when hominids began to use them. "The violence that goes unchecked by instinctual inhibitions because it represents no threat to disarmed adversaries will become fatal the moment these same adversaries become armed with rocks."[21] Hence, if chimpanzees learned to throw stones at each other their social life would be radically shaken. Either the species would disappear or they would have to impose prohibitions on their group. The victimage mechanism is such a prohibition for humans.

Mimesis and Reciprocity

The victimage mechanism is the means to prevent the escalation of violence brought about by mimetic rivalry. The basis for Girard's assumption is the following:

Once his basic needs are satisfied, (indeed, sometimes even before), man is subject to intense desires, though he may not know precisely for what. The reason is that he desires *being*, something he himself lacks and which some other person seems to possess. The subject thus looks to that other person to inform him of what he should desire in order to acquire that being. If the model, who is apparently already endowed with superior being, desires some object, that object must surely be capable of conferring an even greater plenitude of being. It is not through words, therefore, but by the example of his own desire that the model conveys to the subject the supreme desirability of the object.[22]

Desire is essentially mimetic in that it is a duplication of perceived desire directed toward an object through the actions of a model. This mimetic quality of childhood desire is "universally recognized." Adult desire is nearly identical except that an adult is usually "ashamed to imitiate others for fear of revealing his lack of being."[23]

Girard's statement is peculiar with the introduction of shame into adult desire, specifically male desire. Within a hero culture, where men are indoctrinated from birth that their feelings and bodies are not important, but should be sacrificed (ignore pain) in the relentless attainment of a heroic ideal in order to be loved and accepted by others,[24] are we surprised that as an adult a man would *feel* a lack of being, as bodyless, and be "ashamed to imitate others for fear of revealing his lack of being"? Girard's observation seems to say more about a hero culture than it does the epigenisis of identity.

Illustrating the mimetic character of learning, Eric Erikson describes the human infant's earliest encounters with the principal modalities of culture in the somatic interchange between infant and mother. "The simplest and earliest modality is *to get*, not in the sense of 'go and get' but in that of receiving and accepting what is given."[25] When it works, this is easy, yet disturbances show how complex this process really is. The groping and unstable infant organism learns this modality by learning to regulate the readiness to "get" with the methods of a mother who in turn, will permit the infant to co-ordinate the means of getting as she develops and co-ordinates her means of giving.[26] "But in thus getting what is given, and in learning to get somebody to do for him what he wishes to have done, the baby also develops the necessary groundwork 'to get to be' the giver—that is, to identify with her and eventually to become a giving person."[27] This establishes a sense of basic trust, a first and basic wholeness that the inside and the outside can be experienced in a basic goodness.[28] For Erikson, this mutuality is maintained through the mother's sense of wholeness as a member of a family and society, which she then is able to communicate, "in the unmistakable language of somatic interchange," that the infant may trust her, the world, and itself.[29]

In contrast to Erikson's co-operative give and take internalized by an infant that results in basic trust and a unity of the inner and the outer worlds, Girard's convergence of two desires results in conflict. "Mimesis coupled with desire automatically leads to conflict."[30] The problem is that the model perceived is too far above the disciple and the disciple too far below the model. To close the discrepancy and complete the reciprocal imitation, the disciple can serve as a model to the model. Within this relationship, the "universal human injunction,

'Imitate me!'" contains the counterorder of "Do not appropriate my object!" These contradictory signals between models characterize the double bind that brings the disciple into "violent conflict with a rival."[31] "He convinces himself that the violence itself is the most distinctive attribute of this supreme goal! Ever afterword, violence and desire will be linked in his mind, and the presence of violence will invariably awaken desire . . . Violent opposition, then, is the signifier of ultimate desire, of divine self-sufficiency, of that 'beautiful totality' whose beauty depends on its being inaccessible and impenetrable."[32]

To invoke Erickson once more, what Girard has described is the adult symptom of basic mistrust. The sum of all those diffuse experiences not successfully balanced by the experience of integration between child and caregiver is accompanied by an experience of "total" rage, with fantasies of domination or destruction of sources of pleasure and provision that live on in the individual and are revived in extreme states and situations.[33]

Rather than a signifier of ultimate desire, violent opposition is the signifier of unsuccessful integration that prevents a "basic wholeness" that implies that "the inside and the outside can be experienced as an interrelated goodness."[34] The idealization of inaccessibility and impenetrability may be seen as the defense mechanisms of isolation and withdrawal in trauma. In adults, a prevalence of basic mistrust is characterized by a form of "severe estrangement" which characterizes individuals who "withdraw into themselves when at odds with themselves and others."[35]

The invulnerable attributes of divine inaccessibility and impenetrability are paralleled in the concept of the 'idealized rescuer' in the relationship between trauma victim and therapist. The relationship of trauma transference often exhibits a displacement of rage by the victim from the perpetrator to the caregiver, and the need for an omnipotent, perfect rescuer to counteract the threat of the perpetrator. In the instance of a Vietnam veteran wounded in combat, the soldier felt that the medic, not the enemy, almost killed him.[36] Added to his helpless rage, characteristic of victims in terror of death, were humiliation and shame. Though in desperate need of the rescuer's help, he was "mortified to be seen in his defiled physical condition." In revenge fantasies against the rescuer, trauma patients often displace their rage to the therapist as caregiver. They fantasize that they can reduce the therapist to the same unbearable condition they have suffered, a condition unacceptable to one in the role of war hero.

Indeed, there is a desperate need for a idealized, omnipotent, perfect rescuer in the trauma experience. In Western culture, these attributes have been ascribed to Christian divinity. In a culture that has ignored the damage to person and community that results from the effects of the split between mind and body (purposeful distanciation, dissociation) from trauma, and has failed to develop traditions to legitimate and institutionalize recovery and restoration of the trauma victim to interpersonal trust relationships, and has rather adapted to glorify violence in the triumph of mind (divinity) over body (natural pain) and disseminate it culturally in symbolic discourse, there is one image that has been created to fulfill the mediating role between human and god as trauma savior: the hero.

The Hero and the Monstrous Double

Girard acknowledges the role of the hero as representing the victim of momentous and unexpected (traumatic) tragedy.[37] For Girard, the tragic flaw attributed to the hero is shared by the community, but "he alone must bear its burden in order for the community to be saved. The hero thus assumes the role of surrogate victim." Again and again in Western culture, the wounded human as hero (half-god) attempts to camouflage fear and pain by idealizing isolation and self-sufficiency as divine, as the ideal rescuer. Women as well as men may express a reluctance to ask for help in the belief that they would be exposed to rejection and humiliation, or reinforce their status as weak, ineffectual, or powerless. This is a "legacy of the male model of heroism that dichotomizes independence and relatedness, promotes autonomy at the expense of intimacy and connection, and extols the virtue of stoic isolation while ignoring its very real and debilitating consequences."[38] And where does the culture send fallen heroes? For women it is mental institutions, and for men it is penal institutions.[39] For a culture shaped by the mind/body split and its domination/submission control dynamic, this is a means of institutionalized inverse control of what is devalued in each sex: the mind for women, the body for men.

Often, a trauma patient does not trust the therapist until convinced the therapist can stand to hear the details of the trauma story. At the same time, the patient mistrusts the motives of a therapist who can listen, attributing to the therapist the motives of the perpetrator as exploitative or voyeuristic: "The dynamics of domination and submission are reenacted in all subsequent relationships, including therapy."[40]

The contrast between the mimetic explanations of Girard and those of Erikson describe the different fundamental relationships with the self and world, that of basic mistrust and basic trust. Girard's descriptions of the adult's perceived inadequacy, subsequent mimetic rivalry for objects of desire, and idealization of an omnipotent rescuer are contiguous with Erikson's description of the mistrusting adult and indicate trauma-related symptoms in violent rivalry. Navigating the signs of trauma in Girard's work, the following is a comparison of the theoretical discourses of the victimage mechanism and trauma treatment.

For Girard, desire that is given free rein inevitably will lead to conflict, which will eventually lead to a double bind of sharing the same desire. (This does not acknowledge the social mediation and development of desire and its expression since infancy.) The process of reciprocity between model and disciple eventually equalizes, and the antagonists are *"doubles."* The interchangeability between model and disciple paves the way for sacrificial substitution. The *monstrous* double is a hallucinatory imaging of the model as a double that serves to divert attention from the mimetic rivals. The doubles are substitutable and are given over to the "process of sacrificial substitution—to the polarization of violence onto a single victim who substitutes for all the others."[41] Hence, a surrogate victim or scapegoat is created.

Asymmetry and difference are introduced into what was a symmetrical identity of sameness. The rival doubles become "different" from the victim. The monstrous double gives the rivals a means to arrive at a compromise that includes "unanimity *minus* the victim of the generative expulsion."[42] The community members then know never again to do what the "victim" has "done." They know they must act "differently" than the victim. The community becomes "conscious" of the danger of mimesis through differentiation in the process of the victimage mechanism.[43]

The surrogate victim nullifies the conflict, reconciles the community, and provides it with a normative resolution for preventing future conflict. The victimage mechanism is a "spontaneous psychological mechanism" that operates as the transferral from the hallucinatory double of the model in the mimetic crisis to the surrogate victim.[44] The shift from acquisitive mimesis to conflictual mimesis in the inevitable mimetic crisis enacts the victimage mechanism and provides a reconciliatory outcome through ritual, particularly religion and law.[45]

The "damming of mimetic forces by means of prohibition and the diversion of these forces in the direction of ritual" are the only means of perpetuating the reconciliatory effect of the surrogate victim.[46] Desire as mimetic force is the "sin" or "flaw" that in actuality is "violence equally shared by all."[47] The human condition revealed by the role of the double is that "violence has always been inherent in man."[48]

Turning to trauma treatment, there are parallels in trauma transference discourse to Girard's victimage discourse. Girard's thematic
concept is 'violent mimetic desire' that develops into a rivalrous mimetic crisis between disciple and model resolved by sacrificial substitution. In trauma discourse, the parallel concept is 'traumatic
transference' reenacted in the relationship between patient and therapist, described below by Judith Lewis Herman. For heuristic purposes,
consider Girard's role of the model replaced by the therapist, and the
role of disciple replaced by the trauma patient.

The experience of terror deforms the trauma patient's emotional
responses to anyone in a position of authority. Traumatic transference
reactions have an intense, life-or-death quality to them. "A destructive
force appears to intrude repeatedly into the relationship between therapist and patient. This force, which was traditionally attributed to the
patient's innate aggression, can now be recognized as the violence of
the perpetrator."[49] The transference is triadic: "The terror is as though
a patient and therapist convene in the presence of yet another person.
The third image is the victimizer, who . . . demanded silence and whose
command is now being broken."[50]

This "third image" is Girard's "hallucinatory image" of the
model as monstrous double thought to arise in the disciple/model
relationship as a result of the disciple's inherent violence. It is possible that Girard's monstrous double is a symptom of intrusive trauma
thoughts activated by exposure to extreme situations resembling a
previous trauma. This is also suggested by Girard's claims that only
that which is "implacably indifferent or hostile," as divine attributes,
can elicit violent desire. This characterizes victimization where the
victim's life depends upon the distant, careless victimizer: "It's frightening because you can kill me with what you say . . . or by not caring
or [by] leaving," observed a patient. The therapist responded, "We
can see why you need me to be perfect."[51] Hence, Girardean mimetic
desire that is attracted to violence that is triumphant is actually a
form of identification with an absent aggressor that is transferred to
an idealized rescuer.

Trauma Transference and the Victimage Mechanism

The transference reflects the experience of terror and abandonment, creating the need for an "omnipotent rescuer." Because the patient
feels his or her life depends upon the rescuer, there is no room for
tolerance or human error. There is a displacement of rage from the
perpetrator to the caregiver, for the threat to life and loss of security

by the perpetrator. For Girard, this is the rage of the disciple whose very being depends upon the model, which the model cannot provide.

The patient cannot trust the therapist due to the experience of trauma. There is no confidence in the therapist's benign intentions. The therapist may eventually react to these hostile attributions in unaccustomed ways. "Drawn into the dynamics of dominance and submission, the therapist may inadvertently reenact aspects of the abusive relationship . . . Once again the perpetrator plays a shadow role in this type of interaction."[52] This dynamic has been attributed to the patient's defensive style of "projective identification." For Girard, this is the mimetic crisis. The victimage mechanism as a "spontaneous psychological mechanism" operates in the transferral of the double of the model to the surrogate victim. This psychological "mechanism" is the victim/patient's "projective identification" of the shadow perpetrator with the therapist, who now assumes the role of perpetrator for the victim.

Twinning Girard's claim that violence is "contagious," Herman states, "Trauma is contagious."[53] In the role of witness to disaster or atrocity, the therapist can be overwhelmed, experiencing to a lesser degree, "the same terror, rage and despair as the patient." This is known as "traumatic countertransference" or "vicarious traumatization."[54] The therapist may begin to experience symptoms of posttraumatic stress disorder.

Vicarious traumatization, also termed "secondary trauma," refers to the effects in people who care for, or are involved with, those who have been directly traumatized.[55] These secondary trauma victims are spouses or family members exposed to the trauma victim, resulting in "intergenerational transmission" of trauma.[56] In the empathic identification with the victim, caregivers may also become victims of the originary trauma.

Traumatic countertransference includes the therapist's emotional reactions to the victim and to the traumatic event itself. For Herman, this shows the shadow presence of the perpetrator in the patient-therapist relationship and traces countertransference, like transference, to the triadic original source outside of a simple dyadic relationship.

In the role of witness, the therapist may be caught in conflict between victim and perpetrator as being able to identify with the feelings of the perpetrator.[57] The therapist's own identification with the perpetrator, or aggressor, may have several forms. The therapist may doubt the patient's story or minimize or rationalize the abuse. The therapist may find the patient's behavior revolting or disgusting and become extremely judgmental. The therapist may feel contempt for the patient's helplessness or paranoid fear of the patient's vindictive rage. There may be "moments of frank hate and wish to be rid of the patient."[58]

For Girard, this is the moment of the mimetic crisis in the double bind when the model and the disciple share the same "desire" or posttraumatic symptoms. The process of reciprocity (the therapeutic relationship of traumatic transferrence) eventually equalizes and the model and the disciple as antagonists are "doubles." In the therapeutic relationship, this is the process of projective identification between therapist and patient. In identifying with the perpetrator, the therapist internalizes the perpetrator's hatred of the victim, and in identifying with the victim, the therapist internalizes the victim's rage and revenge toward the perpetrator. The patient also has these identifications, having internalized the perpetrator's hatred as self-hatred and rage toward the perpetrator. The patient and the therapist are now "doubles" for each other. However, contrary to Girard's analysis, this does not result from sharing the same *desire*, but from sharing the same *symptoms* of the shadow trauma of the perpetrator and the *expectations* of exploitation created by traumatic damage to trust (which may have occurred antecedent to the model/disciple relationship).

For Girard, the doubles now are substitutable and give over to the process of sacrificial substitution and the polarization of violence onto a single victim who substitutes for all the others. The victimizer/ victim dynamic has been internalized both by the therapist and by the patient. The therapist identifies with the aggressor and wishes to be rid of the patient, and the patient fantasizes revenge on the perpetrator, which is transferred to the therapist, and both have internalized self-hatred as victims. As rivalrous equals in exploitive relation, they can cancel each other out. They are facing a *death* end.

Hence, there arises a need for a diversion to avoid death. For Girard, the hallucinatory double of the model (the shadow image of the perpetrator) is introduced and transferred to a surrogate victim to differentiate the rivals in the double bind. The rivals become "different" from the surrogate victim. The monstrous double facilitates a compromise that provides a "unanimity *minus* the victim of the generative expulsion."

Yet, consider the double bind as the enmeshed identification both of the therapist and of the patient with the aggressor and the victim. It is important to remember that the relationship between the therapist and the patient is not a dyad; it is a *triad* that includes the shadow of the perpetrator. The "spontaneous psychological mechanism" of victimage is the associative intrusion of the absent presence of the perpetrator into the therapist/patient relationship. Moving from the helplessness and loss of control while within the victimizer/victim dynamic, the trauma victim may attempt to restore power and control by role reversal and assume the role of victimizer, and may attempt or fantasize the attempt to victimize the victimizer. As an attempt to exit the double bind, this reversed dynamic is reenacted in the therapist/ patient, model/disciple projective identification of the *shadow perpetrator/monstrous double* with a third party victim, the surrogate victim.

Thus the stage is set for the sacrifice of the surrogate victim. We have seen how the reversal of the victim in the role of aggressor permits this victimization to take place. However, the victim as aggressor still harbors the self-hatred characteristic of the victim role. It is the self-hatred of oneself and one's kind that allows vengeance upon one's own kind as the internalized aggressor's gaze directed toward one's own. Thus the therapist/patient, model/disciple in both roles of aggressor and victim displace the victimized state from the original victim to a communal representation of the original victim. This permits the *communal* (as unanimity) projective identificaton of the perpetrator/monstrous double to the surrogate victim. The selection of a surrogate victim who "substitutes for all others" implies that any community member could be a victim.

Subject to the dominance/submission dynamic, the community would enact the identification with the aggressor and displace its rage of helplessness toward the aggressor onto the surrogate victim. This characterizes Girard's assessment of the community as rejecting the victim and vowing not to do as the victim has done. However, contrary to Girard's analysis, this is less an avowal to act differently than it is an affirmation of submissive loyalty, in reality or symbolically, to the dominating aggressor to avoid further victimization or retaliation in response to victim resistance. Hence, the originary trauma is transferred through the internalized symbolic re-presentation of the perpetrator in a perpetual cycle of victim/victimizer relational reenactments.

For Girard, desire as mimetic force is the "sin" or "flaw" that in actuality is "violence equally shared by all."[59] The human condition revealed by the role of the double (shadow perpetrator) is that "violence has always been inherent in man."[60] However, these claims to the universality of violence inherent to humans look differently when seen from the perspective of trauma transferrence. The identification with the aggressor and victim in countertransference is played out by displacing responsibility for the trauma to another, as hatred of the aggressor and of one's own. *All* of one's own then become possible victims, and in displaced blame, *all* also become responsible for violence as projected perpetrators. This then repeats the cycle of violence by making the victim the victimizer of another, without confronting the originating trauma. By avoiding holding the aggressor accountable, or processing the symptoms of the trauma of origin, untreated victims protect themselves from reliving the life-or-death issues of the original trauma, while inadvertently retaining the pathology for reenacting and perpetuating the trauma transferrence dynamic.

The perpetual and cyclical nature of the pathological trauma triad is reflected in Girard's discourse as a "desire radically disruptive of human relations" that cannot be posited without positing the "means of keeping this desire in check."[61] The biological braking mechanism that works for animals is paralleled in humans by the cultural transmission of the surrogate victim institutionalized in religion and in law.[62] "*The sacred is violence*," and the worship of the sacred is meant to ensure peace.[63]

For Girard, the transferral from monstrous double to surrogate victim is the shift from acquisitive mimesis to conflictual mimesis. This shift activates the victimage mechanism and provides a reconciliatory outcome through rituals of religion and law. These rituals enable the "damming of mimetic forces by means of prohibition and the diversion of these forces." Ritual is mimetic, just like its model, the mimetic crisis. However, the mood is much different. This is a result of the terror and suffering (trauma) caused by the crisis. Ritual is "motivated by the desire to avoid further fighting and renew the benefits of unanimous victimage."[64] The crisis symbolized in ritual and its resolution now become a positive model of imitation and counterimitation.

Considering Michelangelo's *Pietá*, I am struck not by the obvious magnificent artistry in rendering imagery in stone, but by what it would mean for sheer collective survival. The second generation will not survive the first; the offspring will not survive the parent. The offspring of a trust relationship of faith and hope is killed by a culture of war and mistrust, and his disciples are traumatized at their loss and its meaning. Literally, the culture of trust cannot survive in the collective space of the body, but in re-presenting him as an omnipotent rescuer, can survive from generation to generation in individual spirit, by worshiping him in the space of the mind.

The clash of the world of trust with the nascent predominance of the world of mistrust is reflected in early hero narrative. The confusion that results from trauma transference is depicted acutely in the Oedipus incest. The private family relations of caregivers are disrupted and confused (shattered) in mistaken identity when as adults they

become public antagonisms of perpetrators and heroes. Oedipus realizes he has killed his caregiver father, a source of trust, through the
ritual mistrust of perpetrators in war. He epitomizes the psychic agony
of trauma transference, where his caregiver/rescuer is one and the
same as the antagonist perpetrator. In the shattering of his inner understanding, he withdraws from the world by putting his eyes out, for
he no longer "sees." He cannot assimilate or restore the contradictory
trauma images and assumes a victimized state. Subsequent heroes
wear masked armor, show no pain, and become ruthless, to avoid the
pain of processing traumatic experience, and inadvertently, the possibility of restoring trust. It has been said that adversity builds character; it has also been said to make people blind and bitter.

Sacrifice as Rite of Collective Trust/Mistrust

Religion provides the myths and rituals for resisting and resolving
the mimetic crisis. In myth, the victimage mechanism effects a mythic
structure that dissolves the differences between rivals and emphasizes
unity and commonality. The flaw attributed solely to the victim thus is
transformed into a common human flaw. Violence thus becomes violence that is "in the past, the future, and above all the present, a violence
shared by all."[65] This is the trauma triad chronology: the shadow perpetrator of violence in the past, its idealized rescuer double that secures
the future through violence, and the victim of violence in the present.
Girard's version obscures the mistrust dynamic of damaged interdependency underneath the trauma event and its transference. His version
describes the internalization of the aggressor, the resulting expectation
of exploitation in future relationships, and the reenactment of the domi-
nation/submission dynamic as violence.

The two fundamental orientations to the world, basic trust and
basic mistrust, are reflected in Mihai Spariosu's division of the history
of Western thought into "two basic sets of values: an archaic one . . . and
a 'median' one."[66] He describes the archaic as based on the principle
of "might makes right" evident in traditional communities, and the
median as an attempt to separate might from right evident in demo-
cratic societies. He writes that "what Nietzsche disparagingly calls a
'slave ethics' can neutrally be called a median morality, the aim of
which is to restrain and moderate the often self-destructive, violent
competitiveness of warlike communities."[67] It appears that Spariousu
has offered a suitable description of the dynamics of violent trauma
transference and collective attempts at restoration of trust in the hero
mythology of the West.

For Girard, all are implicated in the structures of myth whose imbalance between the unanimity of the doubles and the specificity of the victim is "designed to stimulate our own aggression."[68] This "stimulation" of "our" "aggression" is not aggression. It is the PTSD phenomenon of hyperarousal repetition at work. Hyperarousal is a means to reliving the traumatic event through a sensation-seeking syndrome. High-risk events induce this syndrome as a compulsion to repeat the psychological state in a different environment (the process of the victimage mechanism). Hyperarousal also requires accelerated information processing, which has as its consequence a sense of ego mastery over the challenge, which enhances a sense of self as competent and alive. It serves to recreate the survivor mode of adaptation and block the cognitive processing or integration of unassimilated trauma memories into the self-structure. For Girard, myths that evoke mimetic desire are part of the inevitable process of the victimage mechanism that eventually reveals normative "reconciliation" or, from the perspective of the trauma triad, the survivor mode of maladaptation.

Hence, the victimage mechanism is the symbolic trauma transference between communal trauma victim to communal member as the domination/submission dynamic repeats itself in new relationships. This is the tendency to repeat the representation of contents of unassimilated traumatic experiences stored in memory[69] at the individual level now symbolically reenacted at the communal level. The unassimilated behavior, experiences, and images of the testimonial discourse in individual trauma transference and countertransference are re-presented in the cultural imagination as the symbolic discourse of collective trauma transference and countertransference.

Girard's sacrificial victimage mechanism has been companioned with Freudian psychoanalysis to explain how culture prevails against death. Elisabeth Bronfen describes how "only sacrifice can eliminate the threat posed by uncanny difference within a system and bring about the acquiescent, unambiguous definition . . . of canny Otherness."[70] Following Freud, she restates that the death drive is located in "two psychic registers, in the murderous desires of the unconscious and in the harsh, punishing superego."

Bronfen continues, "The explicit representation of sacrificial violence can be used to provoke guilt as a cultural form of self-protection. Culture allows life to prevail against death by employing internalized violence against externalized violence."[71] In other words, culture is able to control/deter the violent individual through manipulating guilt that represses the violent desires of the unconscious. She quotes Ricoeur,

"Its supreme ruse is to make death work against death." In this scenario, violence deters violence.

However, violence is the symptomatology of the problem in the violence mythos. Violence is the symptom of trauma. Trauma is the problem in the violence mythos. The two psychic registers, the "murderous" unconscious and the "punishing" superego are the trauma triad doubles, the mediated psychic re-presentations of the victim's experience of trauma. These are the shadow perpetrator and the idealized rescuer images. The shadow perpetrator is an unassimilated trauma memory trace of the aggressor, and the idealized rescuer is the victim's idealization of memory traces of protective relationships. The *doubles*, or here the "psychic registers" themselves are the victim's form of self-protection from the exploitive internalization of the aggressor. Through the reenacted repetition of the exploitive trauma dynamic, the victim attempts to heal by restoring an earlier efficacy and power destroyed in the trauma. According to Ricoeur, the death instinct, or "the tendency 'to restore an earlier state of things,'" was "introduced precisely in order to account for the instinctual character of the compulsion to repeat."[72]

Hence the "death drive" is itself driven by the compulsion to repeat. This repetitive compulsion is in turn the result of unassimilated trauma traces in the victim's memory whereby the victim spontaneously reenacts the trauma dynamic to attempt to restore efficacy in the trauma event. All relationships are subsequently viewed through extremity, for no ordinary relationship has the intensity of the pathological bond with the aggressor.[73] The rage and rescue revenge scenario becomes normative of the victim's unsuccessful attempts to regain control over a life-threatening event superimposed on the present. Through reenacting the trauma, the victim attempts to *restore life*, the life-sustaining trust and connections with the world that trauma destroys.

Consider the case of H. H., a forty-six-year-old white male who suffered from posttraumatic stress disorder after returning from his second tour of duty in Vietnam.[74] Reared in an extremely abusive home, he was predisposed to PTSD. His father had had anal and vaginal intercourse with his sister and forced him to watch. He was sodomized by his father and forced to perform fellatio. If he attempted to protect himself or his sister, he was severely beaten and threatened with castration. His mother beat him with a broom or a hard object. In Vietnam, H. H. reenacted his abusive childhood in his father's role by cutting off prisoners' genitalia and discharging his M-16 weapon into the vaginas and anuses of Vietnamese women and children. In his mother's role, he clubbed Vietnamese women to death. These behaviors are congruent with Terr's Type II PTSD, following from long exposure to extremely traumatic events.

The psychic images are re-presentations of external events experienced by the victim. The so-called murderous desires of the unconscious are the internalized aggressor as the shadow perpetrator toward whom the victim directs desperate rage at the helpless inability to mediate needs for survival. The "punishing superego" is the internalization of caregivers as idealized rescuer the victim was dependent upon for survival.

In the event of aggression, the other's hostile gaze is redirected by the self toward oneself as a defense against the devaluation (self's life as less valuable, and hence expendable by the aggressor) undergone as an object of the hostile gaze. The self has an illusory sense of control as the object of the devaluing gaze, and simultaneously its own powerful spectator (internalized aggressor) observing and judging oneself. The self feels in control when, as the object of the *aggressor's* control, it gains the aggressor's approval, and when the self, as internal aggressor and observer of self, feels satisfied the commands are being followed. As maladapted unresolved trauma, this can lead to a victimized state of acquiescence and helplessness.

In a trauma event, the highly visual and sensory form of memory appropriate to young children appears to be activated. The linguistic encoding of memory is inactivated, and the central nervous system reverts to childhood sensory and iconic forms of memory.[75] The visual memory imprint of the child is a lasting imprint of what is "exemplary," as necessary for survival, and revived in extreme situations as an adult. The primary role of the face in early childhood development is prior to language in the communication between parent and child. There are facial behaviors specific to each emotion, and these relationships are invariant across cultures. Social conditioning influences the expectations and behavior of the interchange between caregiver and child. The sensory and iconic forms of memory record the language of somatic interchange in the caregiver's face and action responses to establish the child's fundamental orientation with the world, as basic trust or basic mistrust. It is these orientations to which the adult reverts in extreme states or situations.

The child's iconic memory of the caregiver and the collective's archetypal memory of the exemplary both use categories instead of events, and images instead of historical persons. Hence, collective rituals likely re-present the basic orientations of trust or mistrust.

Sacrificial ritual is a collective symbolic reenactment of an act believed to have been performed at the beginning of time by a god, a hero, or an ancestor. In this way, a historical act becomes real, or "meaningful" through repetition. To be preserved in the collective memory, the historical event approaches a mythic model and is the last, not the first, stage in the development of a hero. The mechanism of the transformation of human into archetype through repetition is reflected in how extensively collective memory preserves the memory of a historic event. The memory of historical events is altered so it can enter the archaic mentality, which cannot accept what is individual and preserves only what is exemplary. Collective memory uses categories instead of events, and archetypes instead of historical persons. Mythic archetype thus transforms history into nature.

Sacrificial ritual is a reenactment of this somatic interchange between self and other. Sacrificial ritual hence reflects a historical event. The nature of sacrifice is to give up something for something else. Sacrifice is about risking a loss, often in the effort of offering in the wish to be accepted by the other, who may or may not do so. Loss, or rejection, is intrinsic to giving. This is the basis for the trust process. Trust can be established in the following sequence of steps: (1) one person acts first and chooses the ambiguous path which exposes him to the risk of personal loss; (2) The other person then responds by choosing the alternative in which she forgoes a personal gain and the first person does not incur a loss. They are then able to establish their intention not to harm the other and continue to build trust. Sacrificial ritual is a reenactment of this process, the negotiation of giving, acceptance, and reciprocity of mutual need. The reenactment will depict the outcome of this process as establishing either trust or mistrust.

This process can reflect basic trust, whereby the archetype of this process reflects mutual respect and successful need negotiation that results in communal bonding, such as the tradition of Santa Claus and his historical atavist, St. Nicholas, and the ritual of annual reciprocal gift giving.

This process also can reflect basic mistrust, such as war. The ritual of war is the ritual of mistrust and exploitation. It is the dynamic of domination and submission. Intrapsychically, the aggressor becomes the shadow perpetrator and the caregiver becomes the ideal rescuer from a trauma event. Extrapsychically in the collective archetype, the shadow perpetrator becomes the "bad" and the ideal rescuer becomes the "good." These situations are devoid of trust, and loyalty is determined by allegiance to who is most likely to survive and dominate. As a life-threatening ritual, it is a trauma ritual based on terror and abandonment.

Hence, Bronfen's "representation of sacrificial violence" used to "provoke guilt as cultural self-protection" can be seen as a reinforcement of the internalization of the aggressor in exploitive trauma transference that provokes acquiescent submission. It does not deter individual violence; it legitimates the collective violence of unresolved collective trauma. Culture allows death to prevail against life by employing externalized violence against internalized violence perpetuated in trauma transgenerational transference. This is a dehumanization that systematically invades and breaks down the self's image of the body, internalized images of caring others, and values that provide a sense of coherence and purpose.[76] It is the divide and rule strategy of a culture of control unable to collectively process and integrate psychic and bodily pain. The compulsion to repeat will continue as long as shame and guilt are used as a guise to manipulate the nameless victim in the trauma triad who has little or no cultural acceptance, means, understanding, or support to assimilate trauma traces and restore trust in social connection.

In turning to the role of the community in the victimage mechanism, there is a third role identification made by the trauma therapist. In addition to identification with the victim and the perpetrator, the therapist's emotional reactions include the role of the unharmed bystander, as a form of witness guilt.[77] The therapist may feel guilt at having been spared the suffering the patient had to endure. He or she may have difficulty enjoying the comforts and pleasures of ordinary life and become self-critical, judging his or her own actions faulty or inadequate. Harsh self-judgment for lack of social commitment may provoke a "limitless dedication" to attempt to compensate for his or her shortcomings.

For Girard, the role of myth and ritual is to evoke mimetic desire, to stimulate universal aggression in the process of the victimage mechanism leading to reconciliation. Rather, the community in the role of unharmed bystanders outside a dynamic of domination and submission may experience witness guilt in a form of vicarious trauma and identify with the victim's suffering. This is contrary to Girard's assessment of projecting aggression onto a surrogate victim.

The community's commitment to act "differently" than the victim may come from an attempt to compensate for self-perceived shortcomings in being spared the victim's suffering. The reconciliatory outcome Girard attributes to the prohibitive rituals of religion and law may not serve as a "damming of mimetic forces" within his paradigm of mistrust. Rather, social institutions may be a means to provide persons with "collective reassurances" in regard to anxieties of mistrust accrued from an infantile past.[78] For Erikson, this may result in a collective restitution of trust that provides mature adults a combination of faith and realism. Religion may restore a new sense of wholeness, of things rebound.[79] Girard's view normalizes traumatic rage as aggression within the collective in the exploitive trauma triad of perpetrator, victim, rescuer. Affirming safety, integrating unresolved trauma traces, and empathic sharing of collective pain restore the interdependent reciprocal trust triad of survivor, caregiver, and community.

The triad of the original trauma—the shadow perpetrator, victim, and idealized rescuer—is replaced by the cultural roles of unknown perpetrator, life-threatened victim, and invulnerable hero. Without collective institutions to understand and resolve trauma, the cycle of domination/submission then can be repeated indefinitely as cultural expectations adjust and normalize this dynamic. Based on the mistrust dynamic of exploitation, community members suspect each other of the shadow "evil" of the perpetrator and only trust those who live up to the survival role of hero. The interdependent collective is dis-integrated into isolation individualism and divided into the public and private spheres: the combat zone of the hero and perpetrator, and the private, protected sphere of the life-threatened victim.

The human internalizes these roles and as invulnerable hero triumphs over the trauma experience of overwhelming raging violence of the perpetrator and the helplessness of the victim by exerting absolute control both over the feelings of anger and terror—the central emotions in the exploitation dynamic—and over bodily pain—the somatic signifier that life is threatened. The hero must do this alone, for he cannot trust anyone to *not* be a shadow villain. This creates a denial shield of invulnerability for public acceptance and approval that signifies that *life is not threatened* and the community *will survive*. The indefatigable hero ethic was echoed in Winston Churchill's 1940 Dunkirk declaration that wars were not won by evacuation, and promised that England would "fight on . . . never surrender."[80] A short five years later such sentiments induced images of global nuclear suicide.

Life, signified by the reproductive process of women and their offspring, was thus protected, rescued, and secured. The individual testimony of the triadic trauma event is reinterpreted as the symbolic cultural metanarrative of triadic drama. The public sphere becomes a male battleground for isolated survival between the hero and the perpetrator, and the private sphere becomes the sequestered sphere of the helpless, women and children. The hero's home is his castle. The heroic cultural survival behavioral paradigm is set.

Trauma Doubles: The Shadow Perpetrator and the Ideal Hero

Often dramatic characters in the roles of perpetrator and hero wear masks. This reinforces their faceless, identityless, interchangeable, unintegrated, and unassimilated symbolic dimension as psychic images in the victim's drama of trauma.[81] This also is what happens with the hero at home, in the domestic duplication of the triad. This is the sphere of generating human life, of vulnerability and mutuality, varied intensities of the feelings of the body and emotions, creativity, trust as reciprocity, sexual pleasure and reproduction, intimate relationships. This is not the sphere of the hero: sacrificial death on the battlefield.

The hero expects himself and is expected by the victim/woman to remain an idealized rescuer at home. The human hero is not to be the traumatized veteran of battle with posttraumatic stress disorder that he *is*, wounded and vulnerable and interdependent. The idealized rescuer hero cannot take off his armor because he has no human skin: he cannot be cut. His covering *is* his armor. He is not human. He is the psychological double of the shadow perpetrator.

In the transition from public to private sphere, there is a reversal from the collective trauma triad back to the individual trauma triad, and the dominance/submission dynamic is transferred and reenacted once more. The roles change as the human hero is now the victim of battle and the female the rescuer waiting for him in the refuge of his castle. The human hero/perpetrator displaces his rage and rescue on the woman at being victimized by the woman as family and collective into denying his humanity in the role of sacrificial hero required for collective survival. This creates the roles of whore/shadow perpetrator and madonna/idealized rescuer for the woman in the human hero's trauma transference.

Yet the human hero is not allowed to have a rescuer, especially not the victim he is supposed to be protecting from the perpetrators of the world. To remain a hero, the human hero's rescuer must be himself. This is the double standard of the hero myth. He can rescue the world, but the world cannot rescue him. As an interdependent human, he simply has to live with his pain if he is to be accepted and loved by the other members of the trust triad of life—caregiver (women) and community (fellow invulnerable heroes)—or die.

Priscilla Beaulieu Presley describes her life with Elvis: "In many ways, he was a victim, destroyed by the very people who catered to his every want and need. He was a victim, too, of his image. His public wanted him to be perfect while the press mercilessly exaggerated his faults. He never had the chance to be human."[82] Reflecting on the day their daughter was born and their joys of new parenthood, she confides, "The man in my hospital room that day was the man I loved, and always will love. He didn't have to try to be strong and decisive or sexy, he wasn't afraid to show his warmth and vulnerability. He didn't have to act the part of Elvis Presley, superstar. He was just a man, my husband."[83] In nearly six years they were to be divorced, and within another four, Elvis dead. Cognizant of his temperamental outbursts, means of control, manipulation, and use of drugs, her epitaph reflects his complexity as superstar human: "I don't think anyone can begin to capture the magic, sensitivity, vulnerability, charm, generosity, and greatness of this man who influenced and contributed so much to our culture through his art and music . . . He was a man, a very special man."[84]

The impossible emotional dilemma of the hero role and the human man is straightforwardly described by Aaron Kipnis: "We *are* angry: some at our fathers, some at our mothers, some at others, both close and distant. Mostly we are pissed off about the double standards our society holds for men. When unexpressed, this feeling gets internalized, and repetitive patterns of self-abuse emerge."[85] Hence, the hero turns the victimizer/victim dynamic on himself. However, the hero cannot be the perpetrator or the victim; he cannot allow himself to be overwhelmed and remain a hero. In order to survive, he must exert absolute control, or he will shatter. "When the system doesn't have a means for ridding itself of stresses a little at a time, they build up to the point of blowing apart. So we (men) have a fear of our anger."[86]

The human hero cannot survive in isolation. He needs his family and community to survive, but he is not to express this. His duty is the physical realization of the idealized rescuer role in the trauma triad. The hero, as idealized rescuer and psychological image, is the double of the shadow perpetrator, and the shadow perpetrator is the unintegrated memory trace of a victim's traumatic experience. The human hero as veteran at home has come full circle in the trauma victim role. Because his trauma is unresolved, he will reenact the trauma dynamic in transference with whomever he interacts.

At home, the hero is the victim without a rescuer. That means he is left with the shadow perpetrator and the domination/submission dynamic. At home, the human hero displaces the traumatic rage and rescue onto the woman. The woman as victim cannot possibility rescue him. If she tried, *she* would be the hero and he would be the victim. He can not be the victim because he is the idealized rescuer who rescues real victims from their shadow perpetrators. The idealized rescuer can not leave the symbolic stage and enter reality to assume a human identity as victim. He can only identify with his psychic double, the shadow perpetrator. The *human* hero *is* a victim, but the hero myth tells him he cannot be; he must be a hero. He is trapped between the human and the psychic worlds, unassimilated in either, with no resolution in sight except a dual to the death with the shadow perpetrator.

To prevent this psychic death, there is a role reversal with the shadow perpetrator. He then becomes a perpetrator in human (private) life in congruence with the shadow perpetrator in psychic life. The outer world and the inner world unite, and his identity is resolved in reenacting the trauma dynamic in relationship with the woman/victim. This is his perpetrator identity within the private sphere, that in the public sphere reverses back to his hero identity, with both grounded in the trauma triad of the victim.

Still, the *human* hero is a real human *victim*. That means he has within *his* mind the psychological resources to create the idealized rescuer role in order to survive. The idealized rescuer role is derived from the collective, where all of the collective experiences of trust are compounded as the single memory trace of the primary caregiver as rescuer. This memory is idealized to a role that can successfully counter the perpetrator and provide the means to reestablish a continuity between inner and outer worlds.

Even if he has been socialized out of awareness of his connectedness with others, these psychological resources are still in place in the isolated human hero. The human condition is associative and reciprocal, it is the way our minds work and our bodies interact as elements of the same integral whole called a "human being." It is the way we survive in our world. The human always exists in the interdependent triadic relationships of self, other, world. The health, well-being and likelihood of survival in this context stabilizes with increases in degrees of trust. The psychological images/roles of shadow perpetrator and idealized rescuer in the trauma victim are traumatized signs of this interconnectedness and dependence of the victim, as abuser target and rescued refugee, upon others for survival.

The human hero as victim has a rescuer: the idealized rescuer in his mind. The rescuer of the hero can exist only in the inner world of his mind. He cannot have a rescuer in the outer world. His hero outer world of family and collective, in "the unmistakable language of somatic interchange," the social interactions of his body, cannot accept his inner world identity as victim in need of rescuer. They need him as interchangeable hero and perpetrator, for the culture is based upon the mistrust dynamic of the victim that replays the triumph of hero over perpetrator. The human hero as victim must be able to create an identity that incorporates his own trauma triad with his double life as hero and perpetrator in the outer world.

His human victimization is a result of the injury suffered from the expectations from his somatic interchange with the world of his family and collective to be something he is not: their ideal hero. They disrespect his reality for their own purposes. The somatic interchange with the world of his family and collective is exploitive. He mistrusts the life-threatening "perpetrator" bodies/body of the world to meet his needs as a human and a victim.

His survival depends upon his withdrawal from the somatic, or bodily interchange, with the outer world that has assumed the dynamic of domination/submission. For the human hero as hero/perpetrator, this is the dynamic of exploitation to be overcome in the public world and reenacted in the private world. Because he is expected to be invulnerable and not need help or rescuing, the human hero as victim can play out the dynamics of victimization only in his inner world.

For the human hero to survive, his idealized rescuer must overcome the shadow perpetrator in his mind. The "body" of the family and collective is internalized and re-presented in the mind of the victim hero as the shadow perpetrator. The idealized rescuer in the mind is the double of the shadow perpetrator from real life. The idealized rescuer thus takes on the character of the "body" of the family and collective as trustworthy inside the mind. The rescuer that can exist only in his mind overcomes the shadow perpetrator by making the mind the trustworthy "body" of the family and collective. The mind becomes the idealized body of the rescuer that cannot exist in reality. The exploitive somatic interchange as trauma dynamic between the body of the victim and the "body" of the outer world as perpetrator is "contained" by the mind as rescuer to prevent the mind from shattering from this trauma. The mind of the hero cannot shatter if the family and collective are to survive. The survival of the mind, and hence the human hero, thus requires the absolute control of the body (of self, other, and world) as shattering trauma threat between the human hero and the world. The body, and hence world, has been rationalized.

Public War, Private Battle

The human hero thus develops a schemata in his inner world that corresponds to and unites with his hero/perpetrator role in the outer world. The successful control by his mind as rescuer over its double, the "body" of the world (family and community) as perpetrator, corresponds to and is mutually dependent upon his hero role in the public sphere successfully controlling his perpetrator role in the private sphere. In order to secure this self-contained and isolated human hero identity, his mind/body dualism is externalized in the outer world to create a denial shield of invulnerability for public acceptance and approval that signifies that life is not threatened and the community will survive while shadowing the silent threat to that same life and its survival in the private sphere. Exposing the private perpetrator in the public sphere of the hero would be forbidden, for this would shatter the human hero, destroy the hero myth, and the world. The human hero rationalizes the double (hero/perpetrator) standard expected of him by the world and reverses it as a double (mind/body) standard that replaces rescue with control. He can control (rescue) the world, but the world cannot control (rescue) him.

The human hero's dual identity creates a sense of continuity and sameness between self and world that is a sense of something between trust and mistrust: persistent anxiety. This is Girard's disciple's "lack of being." He is apprehensive toward somatic interchanges with the world that can no longer be reciprocally gratifying, only controlling or exploitive. He has a constant, pervasive, elusive sense of alterity and dis-connection. This is a dissociation from "full" awareness, from being whole with the world, a separation from the center of somatic interchange: his interdependence with the world. He can only rely on his own affirmation and validation of himself in his role as hero. He cannot trust the evaluations of others in an ease between self, family, and community. He has become dis-eased in himself. As Vic Seidler observes, "As boys, we have to be constantly on the alert to either confront or avoid physical violence. We have to be alert to defend ourselves . . . Masculinity is never something we can feel at ease with. It is always something we have to be ready to prove or defend."[87]

Life, now signified by the controlling process of the mind over the body, is thus protected, rescued, and secured according to the human hero's dis-eased needs, and his needs only. Interactions with the world alternate between the control dynamic of the hero and the exploitation dynamic of the perpetrator. Both are characterized by violence as means to instrument the needs of the hero/perpetrator. Violence becomes internalized in the human hero as hero (mind) violence needed to control perpetrator (body) violence. Violence thus becomes identified with divinity (mind) and anger (body). This rationalization is externalized as the law of legitimate (hero/mind/divine) violence in the public sphere to control the violence of the illegitimate (perpetrator/body/anger) violence in the private sphere. Both constructs deny the caregiver-taker reciprocity marginalized to silence in the privacy (abuse) of domesticity: the interdependent victim/self/need in community. In a not-so-humorous attempt at humor, Erma Bombeck writes of this confusing male duplicity: "Was it my imagination, or was I developing a nun wish? Sometimes my husband could be the kindest man in the world. Other times he made me feel like I was lobotomized by domesticity."[88] The conspiracy of silence is brutal. In a Canadian Violence against Women Survey, 22 percent of women assaulted by their spouse never told family, friends, police, or anyone else about the abuse, and 18 percent (111,000) of these women were injured.[89] In the United States, in marriage "many states grant a permanent and absolute prerogative for sexual access, and any degree of force is legally permitted."[90] Indeed, the legal system is designed to protect men from the superior power of the state, but not protect the women and children from the superior power of men.[91] The illusion of the unquestionable legitimate power of the hero in the public sphere obscures his double life in the illegitimate brutality of the perpetrator in the private sphere.

The outer world is divided into private and public to control the illegitimate violence of the perpetrator. This is doubled in the outer-world division into domestic and foreign fields of security by the legitimate violence of the hero. The perpetrator has his crimes and victims, and the hero has his sacrifices and casualties. The legitimation of posttraumatic stress disorder after 1980, through the efforts of combat veterans, revealed that the psychological syndrome seen in survivors of rape, domestic battery, and incest was essentially the same as the syndrome of veterans.[92] "The implications of this insight are as horrifying in the present as they were a century ago: the subordinate condition of women is maintained and enforced by the hidden violence of men. There is a war between the sexes ... The hysteria of women and the combat neurosis of men are one."[93] As well, the effects of trauma during normative identity formation, adolescence, may become integral to identity. Both combat and rape are primarily experiences of adolescence and early adult life. Military service in the United States and other countries begins in the late teens, and the period of highest risk for rape is late adolescence. "Rape and combat might thus be considered complementary social rites of initiation into the coercive violence at the foundation of society. They are the paradigmatic forms of trauma for women and men respectively."[94]

The silent violence in the domestic sphere to buttress the hero in his foreign conquests was reflected in the industrial war effort in the United States during World War II. "Workers endured speed-ups, long hours, and a hazardous environment. Between 1940 and 1945, eighty-eight thousand workers were killed and over eleven million injured as a result of industrial accidents, eleven times the total U.S. casualties in combat."[95] As well, a 1988 study of Vietnam veteran suicides concluded that military service during the Vietnam War caused an increase in subsequent deaths from suicides and motor-vehicle accidents. The most important implication, according to this study, was that "before sending young men to war, especially one in which they have experiences similar to those of Vietnam veterans, those who make the decision should weigh all costs. The casualties of forced military service may not be limited to those that are counted on the battlefield."[96]

This observation resonates with the words of a World War II Estonian political refugee written in December 1945 in Berlin:

We are foreigners.

Russian girls dance with French labourers. My next room neighbour Ian too. And his sister. Not we. Loss of homeland the biggest sorrow.

Bigger than loss of family.

We feel a longing for our homeland. Wife cries. Savagely.

Little man. Already standing on his own feet. Looks at mummy. Seriousness in his blue eyes. Why is mom crying?

Coming from my shift. He beats his hands. Like a squirrel.

His whole world is in mummy. Daddy. Food and sleep.

New Year of 1945.

What will it bring?

End of Big War? Sure.

Fall of Germany? Very sure.

End of communism? No.

Free homeland? Very doubtful.

It's tragic for small nations. God himself forgets them.

Great Powers do that on purpose. Still their conscience.

They forget our rights for life.

Our fate—

Families destroyed. Dispersed. Deported. Some working in Siberia. In slave camps. Some killed. Some fallen for holy homeland. Some fled. To Sweden. To Germany. Are without homes.

Anglo-American air raids.

Thousands of bombers paralyse Berlin. Railways at standstill.

Orannienburg is a pile of rubble. Can't find that aircraft factory. Thank God! I didn't get job there.

Alarm telephone gives messages.

Three hundred bombers. Six hundred. Eight hundred. Thousand.

Over the west border. Over Bremen. Hamburg. Course south-east.

Every day. Every night.[97]

The human hero's experience of the triadic trauma event of self, family, and community as world is reinterpreted as the symbolic cultural metanarrative of the triadic drama as a dualism of mind (self) over body (family and world). Once normalized, the transgenerational unresolved traumatic content of self, other, and world as victim, shadow perpetrator and rescuer hero can repeat indefinitely as a dialectical dualism of mistrust of mind over body based on the transferrence of the exploitive dynamic of domination and submission in isolated relationships. The hero's armor and the perpetrator's cloak of death and mistrust, of denial, isolation, and violent control in the battle of doubles, smothers and brutalizes the sparkles of life and of mutual needs, interdependency, and reciprocal negotiation in the trust triad of integrated self, caregiver, and community.

Men may adapt to this constrictive process by rejecting the private sphere and treat/threaten the world with heroic endeavors. The conflict between the public and the private spheres and the adaptation/addiction to the hyperarousal of extremity in violence and conflict in the hero role is depicted in the resistance to "domestication." It extends into science, and not even the world of virology is immune, where the denial of the domestic is reinterpreted as a heroic battlefield:

Infectious disease is one of the few genuine adventures left in the world. The dragons are all dead and the lance grows rusty in the chimney corner . . . About the only sporting proposition that remains unimpaired by the relentless domestication of a once free-living human species is the war against those ferocious little fellow creatures, which lurk in the dark corners and stalk us in the bodies of rats, mice, and all kinds of domestic animals; which fly and crawl with the insects, and waylay us in our food and drink and even in our love.[98]

These words were written in 1935, a decade previous to the detonation of the first nuclear bomb. Perhaps the author would have reconsidered the value of heroic warlike endeavors that succeeded in leaving cockroaches as the only free and living species. Perhaps he would have concurred with Vannevar Bush, the Director of the Office of Scientific Research and Development responsible for coordinating the activities of six thousand scientists in the development of nuclear fission and the Manhattan Project, the birthplace of the nuclear bomb dropped on the people of Hiroshima on August 6, 1945, that left 200,000 dead, 60,000 buildings destroyed, and the rubble in an inferno:[99] "The applications of science have built man a well-supplied house, and are teaching him to live healthily therein. They have enabled him to throw masses of people against another with cruel weapons. They may yet allow him truly to encompass the great record and to grow in the wisdom of race experience. He may perish in conflict before he learns to wield that record for his true good."[100]

Bush's observation is astute. Over half of all nations have taken part in at least one war in the twentieth century.[101] There have been an estimated three hundred wars since 1945, with no single day free of war since that time.[102]

The human interdependent male as ideal invulnerable hero is expected to live a role that is destructive to his life as a living human. He is expected to deny his humanity and remain human at the same time. He is to deny that his body hurts when he is wounded, be indifferent to rejection, calm in the face of terror, inexpressive of uniqueness, stoic in the pain of loss or failure. The hero has no limits. Hence he has no boundaries, and no growth, and hence *no identification with life*. He stays the Same, and we never see him die (like all psychic content, he appears and dis-appears). He lives on from generation to generation. He does so because he is the re-presentation of a natural human psychological response to life-threatening abandonment and loss, and the need to survive. Trapped as he is in the toxic trauma of the mind, the human man as hero is a shadow of the natural vital man he could be in the life world with others.

The hero human is told his anger is dangerous: "Men's anger, when it finally does emerge, is often expressed violently. This has given anger a bad name."[103] Girard's analysis of desire normalizes the mythology of the controlled violence of the hero (divinity) and the uncontrolled violence of the perpetrator (desire). Desire is attracted to violence that is triumphant and seeks to "incarnate" its "irresistible force." "Desire clings to violence and stalks it like a shadow because violence is the cherished being, the signifier of divinity."[104] Only that which seems "implacably indifferent or hostile . . . can awaken this desire."[105] The quality possessed by the deity, "blessed self-sufficiency," is the unattainable object sought by mimetic desire. For Girard, only through renunciation of this desire enacted by the victim is humanity able to curb the mimetic process leading to violence. In other words, only through controlling his violent behavior as a result of the angry denial of his need to be human, to trust and be trusted, to rely on his fellow humans and the world to reciprocally respect and meet his needs, can humanity survive.

In the parallel discourses of mimetic violence and trauma treatment, it has become apparent that rather than an "innate aggression" or "inherent violent desire," it is the pathology of the trauma triad, the relationship dynamic of domination and submission, that characterizes mimetic rivalry. This rivalry is a reenactment of a shadow relationship with a perpetrator of trauma that has created some degree of basic mistrust in the victim. This basic mistrust creates a "lack" of wholeness, or inability to trust, and prevents the integration of the inner and outer worlds in a sense of continuity and sameness. Girard's "lack of being" stems from this damaged sense or lack of social connectivity and affirmation from the outer world.

The primary effect of trauma is the shattering of basic trust, a firm sense of personal trustworthiness within a trusted framework of a community's lifestyle.[106] This changes the victim, where "behavior is then altered to be functional in a world that is based on an expectation of exploitation rather than a sense of basic trust."[107] Hence, for Girard, only that which is indifferent or hostile can awaken *the desire that seeks* (the expectation of) violence. Similarly, abused children mistake abuse for caring simply because that is what they imprinted in their dependent primary experiences. They often enter into abusive relationships in adulthood in futile attempts to gain the long-sought validation missing since early life. They also profoundly mistrust the sincere care of others, because they do not know what to expect from, or how to behave in, caring relationships.

The Lone Hero as Interdependent Human

Myth and ritual may serve the symbolic narrative function of telling and showing the story of trauma and the means to restore the trauma victim to communal connection. For instance, native American healing and purification rituals prepare men for battle and for return from it.[108] Within some native American tribes, war is regarded as an abnormal condition and an aberration of the harmonious order of the universe:[109]

The men who become warriors must of necessity assume a changed psychological state in order to kill the enemy and win victory so as to restore harmony and balance in nature. After the battle the community recognizes the need to return the warrior to a new role and identity in the culture. To do so the culture honors the warrior's acts of bravery and provides rituals to purge, purify, and heal the physical and psychological wounds of war. In addition to providing a supportive and caring milieu for the warrior, there is an awareness, often tacit and intrinsic to the group, that the warrior identity must be transformed into a new identity that demands maturity and responsibility. The failure to achieve this transformation of the warrior identity may lead to alienation and the assumption of a victimized state with debilitating psychological behaviors (e.g., alcoholism, depression, and self-destructiveness).

Within this world view, the warrior-to-be must be prepared for the psychological consequences of a certain type of *overwhelming experience*: life-threatening trauma. The collective experience of the tribe has developed a tradition that copes with the disintegrative effects of trauma that disrupt the natural lifecycles and relationships in the community and its wholeness. The community understands the effects of the terror of trauma to create profound mistrust by shattering the warrior's sense of self and social trust.

The overwhelming nature of trauma damages the integrated boundaries the self has grown to unite the inner and the outer worlds. Trauma dramatically exposes the limitations of the self to effectively interact with the world in order to appropriately mediate its needs, and the self's dependence upon the world to mediate its needs. In effect, trauma shows that the self's needs will *not* be met and hence robs the self of power and control. This is the cause of mistrust in the self to be able to survive. The boundaries between the inner and the outer worlds have been violated inappropriately and overwhelmed, and hence disintegrate. In trauma, the lack of boundary between the inner and the outer worlds creates a fusion and enmeshment between these worlds, and the self identifies with the overwhelming trauma perpetrator in an attempt to survive. This is the internalization of the aggressor and the hatred of the self for not being able to secure its means to live by maintaining the integrity of its boundaries appropriately.

In recoiling from and not exposing itself to the trauma, the self withdraws. It cannot update its boundaries without interaction with the world, cannot express its needs or get them met. The self no longer "fits" in the world. It becomes alienated and feels like it does not belong. It can no longer "feed" itself the information for survival, and turning from living to dying, becomes self-destructive. In the overwhelming threat to its life, the self thus loses its sense of safety, disintegrates its boundaries, and enters into mistrustful isolation from the outside world. The trauma event wounds, and may even destroy irrevocably, the sense of self, grown in the self's interaction with the world since birth.

We have carried this tragic cultural knowledge of posttraumatic stress disorder implicitly in an astute depiction of the wall, or protective shield, and the hero shell concealing the fragile human in a nursery rhyme about an egg, the container of life: Humpty Dumpty sat on a wall, Humpty Dumpty had a great fall; all the king's horses and all the king's men, couldn't put Humpty together again. The tens of thousands of suicides of Vietnam veterans pay silent homage to this folk wisdom, as do those of violated women.[110]

The tribal community prepares the warrior for terror in the disparity between the overwhelming power of the event and his own limited power, and that this trauma may kill him, and he may need to kill in order to prevent this. This is a psychological and a moral shock, for the warrior likely knows that the act of killing his own is a profound disrespect for life and a threat to its continuance. Yet he is being asked by his community to risk his life for them. All life is interdependent and valuable, and killing one's kind is an abhorrent contradiction to this belief. Prior to war, the warrior must be prepared as much as possible to have his integral trust in himself, his community, and his world challenged, and to defend it to the point of self-contradiction and self-disintegration. He must be prepared to *sacrifice* his life for his community's life, a contradiction of the psychological mindset of trust he has experienced in his community to *ensure* his life. He must be psychologically prepared for the abnormality of exploitation, the use and abuse in disrespect for life, while attempting to ensure respect for life.

After war, the community attempts to restore his trusting mindset and disintegrated boundaries by honoring him. This is an acceptance of him in his wounded condition that validates his morally appropriate and safe place as a member of the community. Like a collective therapist, this acceptance says, "We are sorry this happened, and we are glad you were not killed. It was not your fault." He is re-integrated into a whole network of trusting relationships that are large enough to process the effects of trauma without further risk of loss to life, his or theirs. The community that understands trauma effects then will be able to renegotiate the damaged boundaries of the warrior and restore trust. The community may reassure him that he will not be exploited within these relationships and intervene to prevent his identification with the aggressor (so he will not turn away from life toward self and other destructive death) by his re-identifying with the previously internalized wholesome identification with trusted caregivers and the world.

The re-identification and integration from warrior to community member demands responsibility and maturity. Indeed, the war experience is one of brutal disrespect and denial of personhood and the interdependency between persons. Taking responsibility for one's actions means acknowledging the effects of one's actions on others. It means recognizing that what one wants and what the other wants are not the same, simply because each has a distinct life history. It may be painful to learn this. The pain means there is a boundary that has been tested and that there is a need imbalance between each person and the world that requires adjustment. Since survival depends upon successfully meeting one's needs with the assistance of others, this negotiation signifies social interdependence. One must pay attention and sincerely respect the other person's needs as well as one's own and negotiate a balance so both can be satisfied and survive. Successful negotiation results in trustful social harmony, conciliation, and continuity.

Refusal, the signal that needs are not being met appropriately in the social give-and-take, results in social disruption and threatens the life of self and community by leaving the needs of the members unmet. If this resistance is not respected, trust is damaged and may turn to mistrust if enough painful experiences accrue that demonstrate survival is jeopardized. Social interactions turn hostile as members become angry at experiencing the need for things to change to stop the pain and enable their needs to be met. They become rageful when they feel ineffective to enact such change with uncooperative others. These signs of helplessness may try to find compensation by an attempt at over-control, or domination, enacted in attempts to make others submit to satisfying the dominator's needs. That which shows them the pleasures of life, usually realized through trustful endeavors, is devalued and rejected, because for them, in their mistrustful experience, life is not pleasurable or satisfying, affirmed or validated, and that which is life affirming is a lie. Destructive exploitation is their truth. This marginalization and devaluation largely have been the fate of unscientific, playful creativity in Western culture.

Because the boundaries in hostile social interactions are imbalanced through unsuccessful need negotiation, members may try to meet their needs inappropriately, in behaviors that are damaging to themselves, others, and the community as a whole. These behaviors, called "violent" because they violate or threaten the integral relationships between self and world required for survival, result in suicide, rape, assault, murder, and war. The culture staggers on with its walking wounded dodging death. These behaviors signify that the interdependent community is dying; the needs of its members are not being met, and life is not being affirmed, validated, or supported. Some simply stop trying and die.

The war veteran may gain maturity from the experience of the horrific implications of needs imbalance and may learn that life relies upon mutual dependence in appropriately and respectfully meeting each other's needs. He may learn that life depends upon him as much as he depends upon life. Paula Gunn Allen describes cosmic cycles as related to life processes on earth and within the universe because of natural relationship. "They are aimed toward forces far bigger than the community or the individual, though each is inescapably dependent on the other, 'circles within circles' as Lame Deer says, 'with no beginning and no end.'"[111] This describes the cyclic nature of reciprocity within the trust triad.

The perpetrators of destruction or trauma may be people who have suffered the neglect or inability to ensure the integrity of self with others and the abuse resulting from inappropriate need negotiation. In their own unbalanced and mistrustful behavior, they may ignore the boundaries of others in desperate attempts to satisfy their needs for survival. The degree of violence and the degree of the need for social control of community members reflects the degree to which the society has not successfully negotiated respect for needs and their collective fulfillment in order to generate trust in social relationships.

Re-identification of the warrior from war victim to war veteran may restore control and a sense of the responsibility for the effects of his powers, now that he has been exposed to the new possibilities for destructive behavior in the trauma event. Through re-integration with the community the ex-warrior may be able to develop a new set of behavioral expectations for himself and his community that reaffirm their mutual dependency, trust, and good will in meeting each other's needs. A "failure to achieve this transformation of the warrior identity may lead to alienation and the assumption of a victimized state"[112] of mistrust and self-destruction.

This process is reflected in Mardi Horowitz's description of how trauma shatters the inner schemata of the mind's ability to process new information to update the inner schemata of self and world. "Unassimilated traumatic experiences are stored in an active memory which has an intrinsic tendency to repeat the representation of contents. The trauma is resolved only when the survivor develops a new mental 'schema' for understanding what has happened."[113] The compulsion to repeat represents spontaneous unsuccessful attempts at healing, in trying to restore efficacy and power.[114] The eternal return the eternal return the eternal return . . . of a traumatized will to empowerment, not a will to power.

In the population of Vietnam veterans there is a strong adherence to the warrior role because that was the core identity that developed during a critical stage of life.[115] At deep levels of consciousness these veterans fear letting go of being Vietnam veterans because they feel "they will have nothing left of their souls." Indeed, recall that to give up the survivor mode functioning of hyperarousal and alertness to danger is often experienced as death anxiety because of the unconscious belief that without it the individual self will die or be injured. Posttraumatic stress disorder may be much more than a reactive transformation, by becoming an integral part of intrapsychic development,[116] with long-lasting effects.

One ritual used to enact the psychological transformation from warrior to ex-warrior and re-integrate with the community is the sweat lodge. There are three primary dimensions to the sweat-lodge treatment for war veterans with posttraumatic stress disorder. These include (1) transforming the warrior identity to a more generative mode; (2) establishing individual and cultural continuity; and (3) promoting self-disclosure while physically and emotionally bonded to others in an environment of intense heat, sensory deprivation, and shared collective pain.[117] Through this ritual, trauma transferrence occurs within the supportive recovery structures of basic trust: safety, remembrance and mourning, and reconnection with ordinary life.[118] Transference is a process of symbolic rebonding necessary for developing deeper levels of trust needed to work through the most painful and unresolved aspects of the war stress.[119] The rebonding process counteracts purposeful distanciation and psychic numbing. The binding feature of re-integration into the community is not violence common to all, but the common interdependent need to have each other's needs respected and reciprocally met to maintain and continually generate a sense of trust and wholeness with the world.

This native American tradition acknowledges what only since World War II have become known as the two principles of military psychiatry: (1) men of unquestioned bravery can succumb to overwhelming fear; and (2) the most effective motivation to overcome that fear is something stronger than patriotism, abstract principle, or hatred of the enemy—love of soldiers for one another.[120] These principles are a direct contradiction to the idealized values of indifference and self-sufficiency symbolized in the hero mythology created to deny the pain and vulnerability of victims of violence.

In contrast to the native American tradition, consider the testimony of Michael Norman, a marine Vietnam veteran and a product of the Western tradition of the socialized warrior and war system that normalizes and glorifies those who participate in war:

Family and friends wondered why we were so angry. What are you crying about? they would ask. Why are you so ill-tempered and disaffected. Our fathers and grandfathers had gone off to war, done their duty, and came home and got on with it. What made our generation so different? As it turns out, nothing. No difference at all. When the old soldiers from "good" wars are dragged from behind the curtain of myth and sentiment and brought into the light, they too seem to smolder with choler and alienation . . . So we were angry. Our anger was old, atavistic. We were angry as all civilized men who have ever been sent to make murder in the name of virtue are angry.[121]

From Mimetic Desire to Interdependent Need

The victimage mechanism depicted by Girard seems to have described something less than the means to normative reconciliation. It seems to show the exploitive perpetuation of unresolved collective trauma content. The thematic concepts of Girard's work parallel the symptomatology of trauma transference. The mimetic triangle of disciple, model, and object of desire is the unintegrated trauma triad converse of the trust triad of self, other, and world. The process of the victimage mechanism in the shift from acquisitive to conflictual mimesis is trauma transference and countertransference. Mimetic desire based on violence is the mistrustful social interaction of the dominance/submission dynamic. This leads to the "conflictual mimesis" of countertransference in the reenactment of unresolved trauma psychological content. The monstrous double is the projective identification of the shadow perpetrator onto a third party, the surrogate victim. The surrogate victim is the symbolic transference of the trauma dynamic of displaced rage and rescue to the community. The shadow perpetrator's double is the ideal hero. The shadow perpetrator is life destroying and the ideal hero is life ensuring. The ritual reenactment of trauma transference creates the evil perpetrator role and the hero rescuer role. This effectively identifies uncontrolled rage or anger with violent death as natural, and stoic infallibility with life-defending sacrifice. This places the perpetrator and hero roles in archetypal hostile opposition in order to perpetuate the dominance/submission dynamic culturally.

The idealized, invulnerable hero is created to counter the actual shadow perpetrator in a cultural re-creation of the trauma triad of shadow perpetrator, victim, and imagined rescuer in the repetition of transgenerational trauma transference. The hero must tightly control feelings, for this could render him vulnerable to rage and terror, the extreme emotions of trauma and their shattering effect on integrated identity and social bonds. Hence, he must not have social bonds that could be shattered. He must be a "he" to protect the life-producing source, "she." If he shows emotion, it is rage, and that only to control the overwhelming perpetrator. He must therefore be emotionless—except for rage—self-sufficient, and a dutiful martyr with the strength to overcome the traumatic event. In order for life to be rescued and continue, the hero must win. The cultural life crisis is solved, and life can continue *under the protection of the hero*, not the "mother" or caregiver/community. Neither the caregiver nor the community can be trusted, for they "betray" the victim in "abandoning" the victim to/in the trauma event. Traditionally, the roles of victim, perpetrator, and hero have had gender specifications, but as roles in human traumatology, are interchangeable. Without re-integration and resolution of the trauma experience by the individual and the community, a cultural mythology of mistrust develops with the idealized hero myth at the center.

The only catch is, the hero is not human. The hero only exists in the unresolved trauma content of the cultural imagination. Male humans *do* feel emotional and physical pleasure and pain in *vulnerable* bodies; they do *need* other people; they *change and grow* with their environment; and *they want to affirm life and live*, too. If we create collective forms for reintegrating trauma victims into trusting collective frameworks, we will no longer need the hero, or to reenact the paradigmatic extremes of toxic violence and victimization and vindication. We can let the Superstar Hero rest in peace. We can appreciate our local heroes and their unique, ordinary lives like ours. We will no longer expect our male humans to perform like courageous forbidding Warriors, or treat them with contempt if they do not. We will not expect our female human damsels in distress, as victims, to be submissive and helpless, and fear them if they are not. We will not treat our (usually male) perpetrators as inherently violent aggressors, and deny them the appropriate attention they probably need. It is time to realize, with Herb Goldberg, that behavior that is abusive to the self and the other is not symptomatic of the chauvinistic "bad boy" behavior of the inherently "evil" man. Rather, it is indicative of "the frustrated, trapped male,"[122] such as the human hero trapped in his suffocating armor.

The hero myth and the transgenerational transference of the trauma triad make victims of us all, to varying degrees, by misrepresenting what we are: humans interdependent with the world. Restoring our collective connections with our selves and others will integrate the terror of the shadow perpetrator and fantasized dependence upon the idealized rescuer and restore the victim as survivor with personal accountability and responsibility within social relationships of trust, reliability, and shared experience.

Girard states as "fact" that "the dynamism of mimetic desire has always been oriented towards madness and death."[123] Its antidote of trauma triad detoxification through trust is oriented toward integrity and life.

We can turn off the cutting torch and put the scrap armor in the recycling now. Among other things, my dad was a water well driller and a welder. When I was a kid, I would visit him at the drilling rig wherever it was on the plains of eastern Montana between the sagebrush and the rattlesnakes. I would listen to the clashing kerklunk of the mud-slipped bit sounding in the casing and of steel on steel as the hole was drilled and the pipe driven into the ground. He would drill for hundreds of feet and then run the baler from the tower of cables, and "whoosh!" like magic, water would rush in soft miniature foamy waves over the firm dry ground and around our feet. I learned that sometimes you have to go deep to find what you need.

When he was turning a bit on the big metal lathe at the farm, I would find a box pedestal and peer over his shoulder at the sharp metal curling in tiny even, delicate blue-silver tendrils dropping on the shop floor. The transformation from the block of iron to the sculpted tool and pile of shiny spirals was fascinating. When he was welding, he gave me a big, rectangular, medievalesque, black eye-plated, gray hood that was half as big as I was to don. He would turn on the acetylene tank, scratch the little black metal cup, and "whoosh!" ignite the torch. There we were, all three of us, dynamic duo and de longue durée; trusting child, parent, and generations, watching the showers of rainbow sparks spray all over us as the blue fire flashed from the cutting torch as he put together and took apart molded pieces of metal to let life gush from the earth. He was an aqua armor artist, and the hero armor histrionics simply do not cut/get it: the vitality of life forged in trust.

While our human heroes are testing out their tender skin, the rest of us may politely turn our attention from the victim traumatology of Girard to the deferred dissociative deconstruction of Derrida.

FIGURE 8

Pagoda and G.I.s on Patrol, Chu Lai, Vietnam, 1969

Photographer: Clinton C. Whitmer, U.S. Army Spec 4 Medic during
September 1968 through October 1969 Tour of Duty, Chu Lai, Vietnam.

6

Derrida and the Heroic Arché

The discourses of testimony, analysis, theory, and symbol were used to describe trauma and mimesis. These discourses described the dynamics of interpersonal relationships of trauma transference. This dynamic was archetypally symbolized as paradigmatic for the community. Interpersonal expectations of exploitation largely result in exploitive relationships when dealing with unresolved trauma. The effect of unresolved trauma in the mind, and its theoretical discourse generated in culture, is the focus of the comparison between the psychological symptoms of trauma dissociation and Derrida's philosophical discourse of deconstruction.

The previous discussion of trauma and the human hero centered around the idea of an acute trauma event, the victim's reenactment of that trauma in subsequent relationships, and its collective symbolization. What happens when the event turns into a kind of normalcy, a chronic trauma without end, such as prolonged wars of attrition? Let us consider Algeria as a case in point.

Passive Resistance and Differing Deferral

In the late 1800s, Napoleon III depicted Algeria as an Arab kingdom, a European colony, and a French camp.[1] The Algerian war extended from 1954 to 1962. It was conceived as an unresolvable war arising from a climate of hate between European colonials and Moslims. After World War II and the winning of independence by several Asian colonies, Africans asked why they also should not be free of the bonds of colonialism.[2] The innovations brought about by wartime expansion and the impact of returning veterans from abroad engendered a political awakening toward self-government. Winston Churchill responded in 1945 by saying that the freedoms in the Atlantic Charter only applied to victims of Axis aggression, and the French decreed in 1944 that the initiation, "even in the far-off future, of self-government in the colonies is out of the question."[3] The Algerian war was seven years of armed rebellion, terror, and counterterror, and a French army revolt.

Correspondent John Phillips, born and raised in Algeria, wrote about the hopelessness of finding a final military solution to the Algerian problem.[4] The problem was encapsulated for Phillips in the interchange between a Moslem prisoner and his Foreign Legion captors attempting to obtain information about his army's arsenal. A French officer announced, "The prisoner spoke of his own free will," and he was brought in for questioning. "The passive resistance of this single Arab suddenly became the passive resistance of all the Arabs I have known since childhood . . . it was his slyness that struck me . . . the more he smiled and degraded himself, the more I became convinced that the French would get nowhere in Algeria with force." Finally the colonel thundered, "Why did you take so long to tell us this? I'll tell you why. So you could give your pals time to move the stuff, that's why." And it was. Phillips recalled that in the French Resistance it was said that a man had to hold out four days to protect his friends; among the Moslem *fellagha*, apparently three days was enough.

The description of this somatic interchange looks very much like the philosophical dynamics of deconstruction. Holding out from a discourse of war, and maintaining an absent presence between alterities in a differing deferral/passive resistance in the intersection of force and meaning, means survival. This is the zone between domination and submission that succeeds in failing to achieve a submission to the aggressor. It is continuously deferred.

Here the site of trust is silence, a silence that ensures the life of one's own against the pervasive, intrusive wounding violence/discourse of the outer world. There is no space in the discourse of force that respects the discourse of the other. Breaking the silence and engaging in the discourse of force risks the betrayal of one's own, a collaboration with the perpetrator. The discourse of force does not allow one to name the violence: it *is* violence. The perpetrator is unnameable and remains a pervasive shadow, an absent presence signified in the traces of discourse. The discourse of force does not allow one to name the rescuer either. The rescuer must remain an elusive possibility. Following a rule of war, "Be unpredictable—it's safer,"[5] the resulting dynamic with the world is distrust, sly somatics, and collective attrition. Shifting sands of austere dunes give over to a perpetual state of resignation, re-signing the exhaustion of delayed recovery following trauma.[6]

The linearity of trauma reenactment in the violating dynamics of domination and submission, the heroic arché, is disrupted in the refusal to submit, to allow it to "progress," or, exploit.

Différance and Signification

In contrast to Ricoeur's hermeneutic of the meaning of meaning, or symbolically constituted expressive subjectivity, Jacques Derrida describes the fallacy of the origin of the subject, or presence, "behind" expressivity. The preoccupation with presence in Western metaphysics is a history of meaning, of subjectivity that is the referent, or signified of the signifiers in language. Traditionally, metaphysics has inscribed subjectivity with creativity, origin, expressivity, intention, and self-presence in speech. Such presence that is a value or a meaning is thus antecedent to the system of signs through which it expresses itself, a meaning that exceeds and governs the composite of differences that makes up subjectivity. This presence is called the "transcendental signified."[7]

Derrida substitutes "text" for "speech" in order to move from a subjectivity that enounces, expresses, speaks, *means*, to the inscription of writing that is a play of differences, of different signs that constitute a would-be subject as intertextual interiority. The inside is the outside, as they are both within the same system of differing signs. There is no subject that transcends this system of signs. The "subject" always is inscribed within the system of signs. Hence, the person is contextualized within the linguistic system of culture, and for our purposes, within the violence mythos.

Derrida substitutes the word *différance* for the word *sign*, as 'sign' has traditionally referred to a subjectivity that signifies, to indicate the absence of subjectivity as referent. "Nothing—no present and in-*different* being—thus precedes *différance* and spacing. There is no subject who is agent, author, and master of *différance*, who eventually and empirically would be overtaken by *différance*."[8] *Différance* is an attempt to refute the reduction of writing to speech, to an expressive subject. Writing simultaneously presents and erases speech. That there is no purely phonetic writing is evident in the necessary spacing of signs, punctuation, intervals. This difference between speech and writing introduces the principle of difference that does not privilege one substance, the phonetic or temporal, to the exclusion of another, the graphic or spatial. Every process of signification is a formal play of differences, or traces.[9] The interplay of phoneme and grapheme is the means whereby the subject is "divided from itself, in becoming space, in temporizing, in deferral."[10] The subject is an effect of *différance*, the differing deferral of signification.

The expressivity of the subject is already surpassed; it is already a text, "a network of referrals to *other* texts," where "the presumed interiority of meaning is already worked upon by its own exteriority."[11] Because the text of subjectivity is already intertextual, its so-called expressivity is in actuality a nonexpressivity of meaning, because the *meaning*, or rather *a* meaning, is no longer anterior, but inscribed in the text. Only nonexpressivity can signify, because signification can occur only within a text. Such is the nature of passive resistance, the double entendre of intertextual signification.

Meaning becomes a "meaning-to-say-nothing," a nothing that has no present, as in-*different* being that precedes *différance* and spacing. The signification of nothing is dissemination, or "seminal *différance*" that cannot be conceptualized because "the force and form of its disruption *explode* the semantic horizon."[12] To deconstruct philosophy is to mark "an erasure which allows what it obliterates to be read, violently inscribing within the text that which tried to govern it from without."[13] The interplay of *différance* is able to determine what is unnameable by philosophy through its history of repression. The texts of our culture are treated as "symptoms" of "something that *could not be presented* in the history of philosophy, and which, moreover, is *nowhere present*" as to do so would put into question the "meaning of Being as *presence*."[14] For Derrida, the history of Western philosophy is a history of the repression and deferral of the question of presence. Hence, the signification of presence becomes a question of the detection of deliberate silences deferred in discourse.

Différance divides the text from itself, in becoming space, in temporizing, in deferral. Philosophy "opens history" in a "violent way" by "opposing itself to nonphilosophy."[15] Said differently, "Discourse is originally violent," for in the philosophical logos, peace may be declared only because it is "inhabited by war."[16] "Nonviolence could be the telos, and not the essence of discourse."[17] The unresolved silent war of attrition continues intertextually despite a feigned phonetics of presence. The alter of hero as perpetrator is disguised in deliberate public discourse, and so is the submission of the resistant victim. Derrida disrupts the heroic arché with the elusive patois of psychological warfare traced in texts.

Husserlian Intentionality

The logos that attempts accessibility to the other is thwarted on the inner and outer fronts of alterity, an alterity reinterpreted from Husserl's intentional phenomenality.[18] For Husserl, outer perception gives us a "primordial experience of physical things," but not an experience of another's inner mental life. We have "primordial experience of ourselves and our states of consciousness, in the so-called inner or self-perception, but not of others in their vital experiences in and through 'empathy.'"[19] We are able to perceive the experiences of the other "through the perception of their bodily behavior," a primordial act, and can only intuit their mental life through empathy, which is no longer a primordial act. The other and its psychic life are apprehended as being "there in person, and in union with his body, but unlike the body, it is not given to our consciousness as primordial."[20]

According to Alfred Schutz, mental life is not given originarily, yet the body is. "For this reason the possibility that any other consciousness posited by me in empathic experience does *not* in fact exist cannot be compellingly refuted by any experience of mine."[21] However, because only one's own empathic experience is given originarily, empathic evidence excludes, in principle, originary verification of the existence of the other. One's understanding of the mental life of the other as existent is conjectural, yet potentially true due to the verifiability of the existence of the body through one's primordial experience.

Derrida interprets Husserl as agreeing that "Bodies, transcendent and natural things, are others in general for my consciousness."[22] Bodies are "outside and their transcendence is the sign of an already irreducible alterity." Another "sign" of this alterity in general is that something inside them as well is "always hidden, and is indicated only by anticipation, analogy, and appresentation."[23] The possibility of presentation of the other as "transcendent thing," or physical object is "always open, in principle, and a priori."

However, such a possibility is "absolutely rejected in the case of Others." The alterity of the transcendent thing is so only by the "indefinite incompleteness of my original perceptions." The alterity of things cannot be compared to the alterity of Others because the latter adds a "more profound dimension of nonoriginality—the radical impossibility of going round to see things from the other side."[24] The "system of these two alterities," where one is "inscribed in the other," needs to be thought together as "the alterity of Others, therefore, by a double power of indefiniteness." The original experience of the stranger is infinitely and always inaccessible as an original experience "*proper* to me."

For Derrida, Husserl "gives himself the *right to speak*" of the infinitely other because he acknowledges the infinitely other as appearing as such. Derrida castigates Emmanuel Levinas by asking, "What authorizes him to say 'infinitely other' if the infinitely other does not appear as such within the zone he calls the same, and which is the neutral level of transcendental description?"[25] For Derrida, Levinas does not acknowledge the infinite alterity of the other but rather names the other within the same and thus excludes the other from appearance, and hence does violence to the other.

The "distinction between discourse and violence will always be an inaccessible horizon."[26] The intentional phenomenon of the apprehension of the other that "lends itself to language, *to every possible language*," may be to give "oneself over to violence," or to make oneself its accomplice, and "to acquiesce—in the critical sense—to the violence of the fact."[27] The violence of the fact is an allusion to an "irreducible zone of factuality," a "transcendental violence, previous to every ethical choice, even supposed by ethical nonviolence."[28] If such transcendental "violence" is "tied to phenomenality itself, and to the possibility of language, then it would be embedded in the root of meaning and logos, before the latter had to be determined as rhetoric, psychagogy, demagogy, etc."[29]

Because of the inaccessibility of the other, "there is war only after the opening of discourse, and war dies out only at the end of discourse."[30] "Entering into war—and war there is— . . . it gains access to the other as an other (self)."[31] "War . . . is the very emergence of speech and of appearing."[32]

There is a shift in language, a language that distances, in Derrida's rendition of Husserl's intentional phenomena. To illustrate, consider a juxtaposition of Derrida's text presented in quotes, and Husserl's in parenthesis.[33] Bodies are "outside and their transcendence is the sign of an already irreducible alterity." (The other is apprehended as there in person.) The possibility of presentation of the other as transcendent thing, or physical object is "always open, in principle, and a priori." (The lived experience of the other is perceived through the perception of their bodily behavior.)

However, such a possibility is "absolutely rejected in the case of Others." Another "sign" of alterity is the "radical impossibility" of perceiving the "profound dimension of nonoriginality" of the other. The alterity of the transcendent thing is so only by the "indefinite incompleteness of my original perceptions." (The other and its psychic life is beheld empathically in union with its body, but, unlike the body, is not given to our consciousness as primordial.) The "system of two alterities," where one is "inscribed in the other," needs to be brought together as "the alterity of Others, therefore, by a double power of indefiniteness." (The other and its psychic life is apprehended as in union with its body.)

Deconstruction and Dissociation

Through this phenomenological refusal, Derrida does not signify the alterity of the other or the inability of our experience to perceive the other. He simply denies the somatic interchange between the body of either, the realm of feeling, of affect, of empathy, of relationship. He leaves our experience of the other as an abstraction of alterity. This is the methodological source of the "waning of affect," a decline in authentic emotion and depthlessness of postmodernism acknowledged by Frederic Jameson.[34] This distancing has a double effect, first as a protective form of philosophical distanciation that numbs one's feelings and casts one's environment as intrusive, and second as a subtle dehumanization required to distance an enemy as other, alien, and killable. Indeed, the purpose of war is to *destroy bodies*. By disembodying the other, the other is moved *away*, as absent, from the sight/site, as presence, of a perceptual outside that for Derrida, attempts to rule an inside. Derrida is closer to Nietzsche than to Husserl: "He lives most splendidly who pays no heed to existence."[35] Nor, in affect, to others. This is the precedence of the passive victim as perpetrator, as passive aggressor.

Derrida has the other cloistered away in the indefiniteness of the power of life, the indecision of *différance* that erupts in the monumental history of the same (Nietzsche's fundamental thought of the faith in humanity as eternal), the ontotheological logocentrism of philosophy. The double play of *différance* includes respecting, along the lines of Freud, the structured geneology of philosophy's concepts while at the same time attempting to determine "what this history has been able to dissimulate or forbid, making itself into a history by means of this somewhere motivated repression."[36]

There is a parallel to this absent anonymous power in the shadow perpetrator of PTSD treatment, where a destructive force appears to intrude repeatedly into the therapeutic relationship. Traditionally attributed to the patient's innate aggression, it is recognized as the violence of the perpetrator.[37] In working through the terror of the trauma, it is as though "the victim and therapist convene in the presence of yet another person. The third image is the victimizer, who . . . demanded silence and whose command is now being broken."[38]

In Derridean terms, this absent presence is *"nowhere present"* in a trauma discourse that is "originally violent." The traumatic transference to the therapeutic relationship reflects the experience of terror and also the experience of helplessness.[39] At the moment of trauma, the victim is utterly helpless, unable to defend himself. Unheeded cries for help result in feelings of total abandonment. "The memory of this experience pervades all subsequent relationships."[40] As well, the greater the conviction of helplessness and abandonment, the more desperate is the need for an omnipotent rescuer. If the therapist fails to live up to the idealized expectations of the victim to be rescued, the patient often is overcome with rage.[41] The terror at the source of the patient's demand for rescue shows how frightening it is "to need someone so much and not be able to control them," where for the patient, "It's frightening because you can kill me with what you say . . . or by not caring or [by] leaving."

Rather than a discourse of phallic dominance aggressively irrupting in the semantic horizons of rational discourse, Derridean deconstruction signifies the distrustful discourse of the heroic arché, the dynamics of perpetrator and victim: the absent presence of the omnipotent (heroic) perpetrator; the threat of the irruption of violence in the exclusive commands of silence by the perpetrator, making discourse itself violent as an act of repetitive intrusion by the perpetrator and of resistance by the victim.

The shattering of basic trust destroys a firm sense of personal trustworthiness within a trusted framework of a community's lifestyle.[42] The victim's behavior is altered to be functional in a world based on an expectation of exploitation rather than a sense of trust.[43] Indeed, a passive resistant war of attrition in the cultural effects of deconstructive discourse in postmodernism is reflected in Mihai Spariosu's observation that "the relation between postmodern authors and readers is no longer based on a shared code of communicating deriving from a traditional hermeneutics centered on allegorical and hierarchical modes of reading, but on an arbitrary and unruly power game of distrust, (dis)simulation, and oneupmanship."[44]

For Derrida, consciousness as thought "means nothing" and is the "effect of a *différance* of forces, the illusory autonomy of a discourse of consciousness whose causality is to be analyzed."[45] The effect of decentering from the center of consciousness with its "transcendental violence" has its parallel in the phenomenon of traumatic dissociation, defined as "the separation of an idea of thought process from the main stream of consciousness."[46]

Dissociation is a normal process, and usually takes the form of daydreaming. Bennett Braun describes dissociation as the farthest distance from "full" awareness, farther away than suppression, denial, and repression. However, used as a coping mechanism in response to trauma, "it may evolve into a maladapted, pathological activity."[47]

Dissociative behavior distances "behavior, affect, sensation and knowledge from the integrated flow of mental activity." Dissociation marginalizes, in deconstructive terms. This "dis-integration is a characteristic of dissociative symptomatology."[48]

Dissociation and the Decentered Self

The essential feature of a dissociative disorder is the "disturbance or alteration in the normally integrative functions of identity and memory. It can be seen as an insertion or a withdrawal from the ongoing flow of consciousness."[49] This is similar to the "violence" of discourse described by Derrida. The intrusive symptoms of PTSD, such as intrusive thoughts of the trauma, nightmares, hypervigilance, episodes of strong emotion, and denial symptoms (inattention, amnesia, constriction of thought processes, emotional numbing), can be seen as opposite sides of dissociation. Intrusive symptoms are seen as the breakdowns of the protective mechanisms of denial and amnesia.[50] Here "irrupts" the "violence" of "phenomenality of itself" in deconstruction. The link between trauma and dissociation is the defensive mobilization of dissociation to contain and distribute the psychic residue (Derrida's traces) of trauma.[51] "The price of this defense is often subsequent psychic fragmentation manifested as dissociative symptoms."[52] This is the differing deferral of decentered subjectivity.

Sherry Turkle comments on the fragmented self presented by patients with psychological disorders and theories that stress the decentered subject. Contemporary psychology now must "confront what is left out of theories of the unitary self" and ask, "What is the self when it functions as a society?" and "What is the self when it divides its labors among its constituent 'alters'?"[53] She observes that "those burdened by posttraumatic stress disorders suffer these questions," and in her discussion of Internet cyberspace, she suggests that "inhabitants of virtual communities play with them."[54]

Turkle indicates the proximity of psychological disorder and the philosophy of deconstruction. However, there is more to this juxtapositon than proximity. They are methodologically distinct theoretical descriptions of the same phenomenon. As two sides of the same coin, both the pathology of posttraumatic stress disorder and the philosophy of deconstructive postmodernism describe the symptomatology of traumatic dissociation within the violence mythos.

Deconstruction can be seen as a disintegrative philosophy of basic mistrust. The shattering effect of trauma and the philosophy of mistrust/deconstruction with its radical indeterminate incompleteness and transcendental violence come together in Arthur Cohen's comments on the inability of historical description and analysis to encompass the Holocaust as one of the primary reasons for the incommensurability of the Holocaust to thought: The Holocaust "cannot be thought because it cannot be exhausted by historical narration. It remains elusive, uncontained, a putative mystery because the categories by which such immensities are grasped seem inadequate and trivial."[55] This includes Foucault's analysis of the discourses of anonymous power in repressive histories of thought, where one's point of reference is shifted from language to that of "war and battle," as relations of power, not relations of meaning.[56]

It seems Foucault offers support for Derrida's claim that war is the very emergence of speech and the appearing of the other. It also seems he is describing war as the definitive instance of somatic interchange of the self, who relies on imagery and interaction for communication prior to language. A child "at war" with its caregiver develops mistrust as its primary orientation toward life. This may influence the symbolic representation of the hero myth and war in the violence mythos to configure cultural understanding to present war as definitive of the constitution of events and self-understanding to the exclusion of other possible constitutions of reality. This could contribute to the exploitive trauma triad transference as paradigmatic for social behavior in Western culture at the expense of the reciprocity of the trust triad. Deconstruction may be seen as a coping mechanism to deal with experience in the culture of the violence mythos that has evolved into a maladapted, pathological activity of mistrust in postmodernism.

Inscription and Maladaption

Turkle offers an anecdotal account of an Internet user who feels part of something far larger than himself.[57] The user describes the Internet as a "giant brain . . . It's developing on its own. And people and computers are its neural net." For him, this idea "felt like an epiphany." Turkle comments that in an era of feeling like fragmented individuals, "it is not surprising to see the emergence of popular mythologies that try to put the world back together again."[58]

There are elements of restoration of self with others and community in an attempt at healing our fragmented selves in this integrative anecdote. This is not mythology. It reflects the way our minds deal with our experiences in the world. Our memory system is dynamic and integrative.[59] We learn through an active interaction with our environment, not a passive build-up of stimulus responses. "This mode of operation pervades all of our experiences and is fundamental to the way we deal with the world we encounter."[60] Our mind is associative. "With one item in its grasp, it snaps instantly to the next that is suggested by the association of thoughts . . . trails that are not frequently followed are prone to fade, items are not fully permanent, memory is transitory. Yet the speed of action, the intricacy of trails, the detail of mental pictures, is awe-inspiring beyond all else in nature."[61] As we develop and mature, more information about the world is accumulated, and our understanding continues to grow and become elaborated as we update with new information. "As an automatic by-product of this changing structure, our knowledge continually changes."[62] We seek to understand our experiences, to integrate them into ourselves, and ourselves into the world.

Deconstruction gave us new information about the arché-ic assumptions we used to understand the world and ourselves by disintegrating those assumptions, and in effect, ourselves. It created an alterity to sustain a rhetoric of passive resistance to the somatic interchange with the world based on distrust. This information describes *one* dimension of the phenomena of human experience that has been repressed in the central tradition of domination/submission in Western culture: the exploitive events of a perpetrator's use of force to gain submission through heroic rhetoric, and the dissociated resistance to that force. Deconstruction disclosed the discourse of the hero/perpetrator and the victim in philosophy. Yet to treat this discourse as culturally prototypical is inaccurate. The *lasting* effects of this conceptualization is to enframe us all as heroes/perpetrators or victims, within a violent system of mistrust that casts the shadow absent perpetrator presence over all discourse and somatic interchange. The dynamic of exclusion is one of exclusion of and exclusion to; it is a boundary that if successfully negotiated provides protection and instills respect and trust, and if unsuccessfully negotiated exposes to abuse and instills disrespect and mistrust.

Mark C. Taylor describes self-assertion that aims at self-identity as mediated by "the domination or even the destruction of the other. Violence, however, is inextricably related to eros . . . Successful aggression not only masters but actually consumes the other."[63] The so-called "regressive character of instincts" (the primary masochism of Freud's destructive death instinct) has its basis in "observed material—namely on the facts of the compulsion to repeat."[64] Within this framework, there is no alternative way for our selves or the other to appear than in war, in relationships of hostility that produce "differences" resulting from compulsive repetition driven by violent instincts. Yet from the perspective of PTSD, what Taylor is describing is the regressive, repetitive mode, not of violent instincts, but of trauma experiences and exploitation.

If we dwell in deconstruction as a coping mechanism to explain our world, we become helpless to name our experience, to *integrate* it into our self-understanding because we are informed that we do not *have* a "self" that assimilates understanding without violence, and hence promotes a demoralizing illusion of self as linguistic violence. We are informed that naming is violent, framing is violent, discourse is violent. Even with the acknowledgement of the diversity and multidimensionality of the self, those who *do* attempt to name their experience, to delimit and set boundaries, are held in suspicion, as perpetrators of exclusionary violence, or as committing the violence of resistance to the discourse of the perpetrator. Radical decentering denies the integrative psychoneurological functioning of human linguistic/somatic survival functioning. So goes the violence mythos and its repetitive trauma transference.

As a culture of the violence mythos, we have directly and indirectly experienced the shatter effects, the decentering fragmentation of dissociation derived from trauma events. These effects were conceptualized and disseminated through deconstructive philosophy that, in describing the machinations of the controlling mindset of the heroic arché, indicated the profound underside of the cultural trauma wrought by millenia of domination and exploitation. Deconstruction dismantled the conceptual dominance of homogeneous conclusivity with elusive differing deferral. Its form of passive resistance still engages the domination/submission dynamic and shifts it from overt to covert violence. It does not give up the ghost/shadow of trauma and allow a resolution to reform in the inner schemata to restore the self with others and the world.

Those who live in perpetually hostile environments suffer this ongoing trauma. This changes the body. Those who suffer from a combination of generalized anxiety and fears do not have a normal baseline level of alert but relaxed attention.[65] Rather, they have an elevated baseline of arousal: their bodies are on the alert for danger. Traumatic events appear to recondition the human nervous system.[66] Our experience is inscribed in the text-ure of the somatic interchanges of our bodies. We update our inner and outer associations in our changing understanding of the world in relation to our intrapsychic identity formations. The difference between each other is *literal* and needs to be respected. That it is mutual needs to be acknowledged. When it is trophic, it is adaptive. When it is traumatic, it is tragic.

To deactivate the exploitive dynamic, the perpetrator must stop hedging his or her position with implicit conditions and attempts to retain secret agreements for the victim to give up autonomy. Unless the abuser relinquishes the demand for dominance, the threat of violence is still present and the victim cannot speak freely without the risk of violence.[67] Resolution is moot until the pattern of dominance and coercion is broken, for both parties, overtly and covertly.

Within philosophy, Ricoeur articulates a curiously heroic battle fatigue in his description of the task of Heideggerian deconstruction. It must "take on Nietzschean geneology, Freudian psychoanalysis, the Marxist critique of ideology, the weapons of the hermeneutics of suspicion. Armed in this way, the critique is capable of unmasking the unthought conjunction of hidden metaphysics and worn-out metaphor."[68]

All three of these theoretical discourses of suspicion have the repetition of unresolved trauma transference at their core in their abstraction of the spontaneous attempt of a victim to master the traumatic event and restore efficacy and power over a perpetrator: Nietzsche's will to power, Freud's death instinct, and Marx's class conflict. Derrida depicts the exploitive dynamic in reverse, by withholding power from the perpetrator in the differing deferral of passive resistance. His is an invasive/evasive dynamic of intrusion and exclusion. For the most part, these masters of mistrust signify the open wound within Western culture: the unresolved pain and anger of disconnected use and abuse in disrespectful somatic interchanges among self, other, and world.

Rather than confirming the priority of violence or the elusiveness of mysticism, as symptom description, deconstruction dis-mantles, decenters, and un-authorizes the legitimacy of the aggressor and the identification with the aggressor. Though it does not go beyond the dynamic of domination, for as deconstruction it cannot be constructive, it delegitimates it and activates the reorganization of experience. This creates the liminal space of transition, a moment of passage when new cultural symbols and meanings can emerge.[69]

To describe the symptomatology of the dynamics of sly *différance* is not enough. As dynamic and integrative, our memory systems will create a new self-understanding of our world, whether it is based on a maladapted pathology of mistrust or a restoration of trust that heals both self and social connection. Acknowledging the chronic trauma of those whose ordinary lives are incised by war, no matter how much the violence mythos would have us believe to the contrary, trauma and violence do not encompass all of human experience. In contrast to basic mistrust, basic trust is the first developmental bond in the social world, the foundation upon which all subsequent integrated, positive developmental accomplishments rest.[70] In the trust triad, the link between infantile trust and adult integrity ensures "healthy children will not fear life if their elders have integrity enough not to fear death."[71] As Judith Lewis Herman observes,

> Integrity is the capacity to affirm the value of life in the face of death, to be reconciled with the finite limits of one's own life and the tragic limitations of the human condition, and to accept these realities without despair. Integrity is the foundation upon which trust in relationships is originally formed, and upon which shattered trust may be restored. The interlocking of integrity and trust in caretaking relationships completes the cycle of generations and regenerates the sense of human community which trauma destroys.[72]

Home Free

She told me the war
Was so long ago
But the chaplain
Never knocked on her door;
When she looked at his picture
She kept him alive
In her heart
And the bracelet she wore . . .

Chorus: His memory is home free
And she can't forget
The truths that he lived by
And the love that he left;
His memory will live free
'Til they bring him home
And she kisses him each morning
Or weeps alone.

His letters are wrapped
With ribbons she saved
From his flowers
When they danced one last time;

When she touched every postmark
She prayed he'll come back
From the jungle
That never says he survived . . .

Chorus: His memory is home free
And she can't forget
The truths that he lived by
And the love that he left;
His memory will live free
'Til they bring him home
And she kisses him each morning
Or weeps alone.

Refrain: Their memories are home free
And we can't forget
The truths that they lived by
And the love that they left;
Their memories will live free
'Til we bring them home
And we greet them each morning
Or weep . . . alone.

—Rita Whitmer, © 1994

PART III

THE INTERDEPENDENT MYTHOS

FIGURE 9

Life Lariat

Photographer: Clinton C. Whitmer

FIGURE 10

Vietnamese Woman, Chu Lai, Vietnam, 1969

Photographer: Clinton C. Whitmer, U.S. Army Spec 4 Medic during
September 1968 through October 1969 Tour of Duty, Chu Lai, Vietnam.

7

Restoration and Trust

Rumor has it that Columbus started his journey with four ships. But one went over the edge so he arrived in the new world with only three. When he landed, one native American turned to another and said, 'Well, there goes the neighborhood.'[1]

The subordination of other histories is a violence that is the subsumption of difference and otherness into the same, or universality. It is attempted through the elimination of difference, as in war; the medieval burning of "witches," homosexuals, and heretics during the Inquisition; racist genocide; and sexual violence. The eradication and subordination of difference occurs under a legitimating sheepskin of progressive universal humanism, or logocentrism, worn by the wolf of the gender-biased hierarchical dualism of mind and body.

In part 1, violence in culture was explored by contrasting discourses of innate and acquired violence in a history of legitimation and tradition. In part 2, the work of several theorists was examined to show the influence of the tradition of trauma transference in the violence mythos in cultural understanding. We now turn to an alternative to the violence mythos, the interdependent mythos focused upon restoring trust in healthy relationships of the self, other, and community.

Expanding the Emotion Lexicon

The postmodern critique focuses predominantly upon desire and is silent in regard to emotion. This is understandable, as desire is central to the public discourse of the hero and the system that seeks to control "violent" desire and emotion in the discourse of the private sphere of the victim. Traditionally, desire signified lack in its wish for something other than itself, as addition, rather than the need to develop itself. The hero myth translates this as ownership, control, the exponential power of possession. However, this also implies vulnerability and dependency, as well as the risk of rejection, nonsatisfaction, betrayal, disappointment and pain in attempts to acquire from others and the world. These are elements of the human condition of interdependency negotiated in somatic interchange. These are the possible emotional consequences of the unsuccessful attempts to fulfill desire that may lead to mistrust. They contradict the Western prototype of heroic stoic self-sufficiency and invulnerable individualism. They imply a "weakness" in desire, the "fallible" element of humans. If not controlled by the rational mind, desire would invite chaos (emotion, female attribution) to disrupt the legitimated rational dominance control in culture.

Translated into a wholistic interdependent mythos, desire signifies the opportunity for the fulfillment of need, as interdependence with one's environment. This translates into the wish for belonging, acceptance, care, and simultaneously freedom for growth and expansion. The satisfaction of these needs occurs within the parameters of what is learned as socially acceptable and expected behaviors. Vulnerability, in a supportive environment, is an impetus for growth. A world tinged with the symbolization of purposeful distanciation in the violence mythos cannot tolerate the valuation of vulnerability. It has attempted to obliterate the expectation of interdependency and the responsibility between social participants to respond to one another with respect, trust, affection, and acceptance, that satisfy desire. To value relation and emotion in a praxis of desire positions one in the integrated wholism of the interdependent mythos.

The subtle and lifelong social negotiations required to achieve emotional fulfillment and social bonds, a task traditionally assigned to ritual, are denied and devalued in a culture lacerated by an addiction to violence. As mirrors of each other, the more extreme the violence, the more difficult the restoration of social bonding, for violence is a wound to the social body. Those plagued with despair at the annihilation and futility of establishing and restoring social bonds and growth may turn on themselves. They internalize the rejection without to rejection within and attempt to stop the pain of denied desire in self-destructive behavior. Such was the enslavement and mutilation of Arawak aboriginals in 1495 by Columbus. He described them as having "as much lovingness as though they would give their hearts . . . they remained so much our friends that it was a marvel." This island people resorted to mass suicide and by 1540 had vanished from the earth.[2]

Denise Ackermann points to the impoverishment of "faith language," the language of emotional life and trust relationships in Western culture, where language has been "stripped of holism and empathy, truncated and one-dimensional."[3] The enrichment of this language comes with taking "the emotions, the faith, the characteristics and hopes of all humanity seriously."[4] Such an exercise in enrichment for violent situations could be defusing in its appeal to pay attention, to listen closely to others and oneself, and healing as well, as it is committed to communication and not concerned with alienation but reconcilation.[5]

The discourse of imagery around the emotions of intimacy and sex reveals a lack of terminology for love, intimacy, tenderness, and erotic pleasure.[6] The terms men use to describe women's anatomy are predominantly hard, monosyllabic, and degrading, as well as obscene and scientific. Other cultures have a diverse lexicon to describe a different attitude toward sexuality and emotional bonding as natural, mutual, and reciprocally pleasurable.

Within the hero context, men are introduced to sex as a rite of passage to prove their manhood.[7] Women's sexuality is socially presented as more desirable than men's, and men are to compete to win attention and affection. The focus of sexual relations becomes shifted from the intimacy of mutuality between man and woman to the heroic battlefield between men. The trauma triad shifts into gear again, as the woman simultaneously is idealized and degraded, and the competing heroes displace their unexpressable anger and resentment on her and become their double, the silent perpetrators with feelings of resentment, objectification, contempt, and brutal behavior. "Perhaps degrading the feminine image made us feel more equal."[8] The debilitating dynamic of dominance and submission in the hero myth does nothing but degrade both women and men. When women internalize these abusive somatic interchanges of men and media as self-hatred, they can alter their self-perceptions into anything from ataxic anorexia to satanic succubi.

The significance of anger, or rage, is not its destructiveness, but rather its "work" as an emotion to indicate an obstacle in relationship and that something needs to change. There is no *necessity* for the expression of aggression. Rather, it is the case that the destructive expression of rage, anger or aggression in intimate relationship is the way culture has *sanctioned* the expression of male rage, anger, and aggression in accordance with a paradigm of behavioral expectation.

If women and children were perceived culturally as persons deserving of respect, consideration and empowerment on par with men, and men were accustomed to the awareness of their emotions and were expected to be responsible for them in a nondestructive manner, then the dynamic of victimizer-victim could be altered. Perhaps it would be better to consider taking seriously the vulnerability of humanity, and viewing it as a strength instead of a weakness. A sincere acceptance of marginalized emotional life in the realm of the perpetrator and victim would enable a realistic integration with the heroic rational life idolized by Western culture. This would procure an enriched ability to communicate the pain, fear of loss, anger, and need for somatic connectedness behind the raging facade of rationality.

Disengaging from Dominance and Submission

So how does one identify the patterns of trauma transference and begin to learn how to disengage from them? The three elements of safety, remembrance and mourning, and social reconnenction are required in appropriate stages to restore trust and connection destroyed by trauma.[9] For those involved with trauma victims, there are four main patterns of trauma engagement: exploiter/exploited, allies/enemies, aggressor/aggressee, and rescuer/rescuee.[10] In the instance of trauma patient and therapist, the therapist who engages in these patterns will experience secondary trauma through an increase in affect, and will alternate between periods of numbing and withdrawal, the symptoms of posttraumatic stress disorder. As discussed earlier, the families of trauma victims, those emotionally close to the victim, and those family members born after the trauma events occurred also are susceptible to secondary trauma. The process of healing the trauma patterns begins with validating the affect or feelings of the person involved, identifying the trauma pattern, and proposing healthy alternative patterns that restore trust.[11]

Generating healthy patterns requires cooperation, not exploitation, the underlying dynamic of all four trauma patterns.[12] For the exploiter/exploited pattern, this means shifting the focus to non-exploitation, in looking out for the best interests of both parties and including others. In the ally/enemy pattern, this means using direct and open communication. In the aggressive pattern, include others in the community who are not directly threatened to reinforce boundary limitations. In the rescue pattern, helplessness is replaced by prediction and planning to restore a sense of control. For all healthy patterns, the restoration of a sense of safety and control and strengthening social networks is essential to healing.

Without freedom from exploitation, there can be no safety or recovery.[13] For victims of trauma, freedom may come with an extremely high price. Survivors may have to give up almost everything else and compound the trauma with more loss. Battered women may lose their homes, friends, livelihoods. Survivors of childhood abuse may lose their families. Political refugees may lose their homes and their homeland. These are the silent sacrifices that are rarely recognized and accommodated within the violence mythos. Indeed, they are expected to be borne with stoic self-sufficiency or displaced blame to the victim as cause of their plight, in order to maintain the hero myth.

It is important to remember that trauma is a dynamic between a victimizer and a victim. Within a culture that has adapted the domination/submission as its pervasive mode of interaction, it has required the diplacement of blame to the victim in order to legitimate itself. This transferrence is especially noticeable in studies of wife beating. A survey of these studies reveals that "the search for characteristics of women that contribute to their own victimization is futile. It is sometimes forgotten that men's violence is men's behavior. As such, it is not surprising that the more fruitful efforts to explain this behavior have focused on male characteristics. What is surprising is the enormous effort to explain male behavior by examining characteristics of women."[14]

The hero's armor extends to the cultural mindset that protects him as invulnerable and unquestionable while rationalizing his perpetrator brutality behind his private castle walls. This is because the culture thinks it needs the hero to survive. It does not. It needs a strong sensitivity to social needs between its members, and the understanding of how to meet them. It is time the hero is held accountable as a human being for his debilitating actions that affect all of us, including denying him his humanity. As a symbol, a collective memory chip of acceptable behavior to emulate, women are as vulnerable to the destructive behaviors of the hero myth as men, and are capable of enacting the trauma triad that continues the abuse.

The core experiences of psychological trauma are disempowerment and disconnection from others.[15] Recovery relies upon empowerment and restoring lost social connections. Because the damage of trauma occurs in the context of relationships among the self, other, and community, healing only can occur in the trust triad of self, other, and community. It cannot happen in isolation, for this is counter to the human condition of interdependency.

Within the context of relationships, autonomy can be reaffirmed as a sense of separateness within the flexibility of connectedness.[16] With healing comes a self-possession capable of defining one's self-interest and making decisions. Empowerment comes from the convergence of mutual support with individual autonomy. The inner and outer views of the world become integrated into an updated understanding of the self, others, and the world.

The recovery from trauma includes the secondary trauma experienced by the families and caregivers of trauma victims. Intergenerational transmission of trauma may result from genetic predisposition or from the child's identification with the parents and/or dysfunctional family structure.[17] This analysis is based on family systems theory with three main assumptions: (1) the family is a complex system of interlocking parts engaged in patterned interaction and seen as a unit; (2) individuals influence each other through their interaction; what affects one part affects the others in the system, with concerns not needing to be openly shared to be deeply felt; and (3) interactions are hierarchically organized, with each generation playing a different role in respect to the others. Hence, the interactive patterns between parents are, or ought to be, quite different from those between parents and children.[18]

A family system affected by trauma exhibits three patterns of interaction: enmeshment viewed as a challenge to authority or another loss, disengagement as withdrawal or dissociation, and impulsivity and parental violence.[19] The problems resulting from these patterns include difficulties in communication, intimacy, problem-sharing abilities, and the presence of substance abuse and/or violence.[20] Not limited to war, trauma may include the loss of a child, from which parents do not recover and create dysfunction within the survivors in the family system. Children of Vietnam veterans with PTSD show impaired self-esteem, poor reality testing, hyperactivity, aggressive behavior, and problems coping with their own feelings, especially fear, rage, guilt, and mistrust.[21] The victims of secondary trauma themselves develop posttraumatic stress disorder and require their own recovery process.

There are three stages of successful recovery from trauma.[22] The first is establishing a sense of safety, of moving from the trauma experience of unpredictable danger to reliable safety, the first stage of restoring trust. The second stage is psychologically working through the dissociative trauma memory traces to an assimilation of acknowledged memory. This stage usually involves working closely with a caregiver where the trauma transference can be reenacted in a nonexploitive interaction. Within this relationship, transference is a process of symbolic rebonding.[23] The rebonding process is required to develop deeper levels of trust that are necessary to work through the most painful and unresolved aspects of the trauma stress. Rebonding counteracts purposeful distanciation and psychic numbing.[24] This is accompanied by mourning, the grief of acknowledging the pain and loss associated with the event. The third stage is moving out of the stigmatized isolation of the trauma event into restored social connection.

The effects of trauma during normative identity formation, adolescence, may become integral to identity. Both combat and rape are primarily experiences of adolescence and early adult life. This is the transition to adulthood when the individual needs to establish a coherent and reasonably stable sense of identity and self-esteem.[25] The tasks of this transition include separating from parents; formulation of a career plan; developing patterns of interdependence with others that are congruent with personal dynamics; making commitments to career and lifestyle choices; forming a broad sense of perspectives for political, moral, and social issues; and integrating all of these into an identity structure with a "sense of continuity and self-sameness through time" where future aspirations, hopes, and dreams seem reachable.[26]

Trauma disrupts this transition that is a continuation of basic trust and healthy development. The stressors of war for men and of rape for women negatively affect the task of identity formation. This disruption includes delayed career plans; instead of interdependence, social interaction is characterized by mistrust, fear of closeness, purposeful distanciation, psychic numbing, and emotional constriction; commitments to self, others, and career are difficult because of a confusion in values; and the sense of continuity of self is profoundly altered by the trauma experience.[27] In this respect, posttraumatic stress disorder may become an integral part of longterm intrapsychic development and identity formation.[28] As alterations to core identity structures, treatment requires focusing on the development of a healthy self-concept that can encompass the old self, the trauma self, and the newly integrated self.[29] This process facilitates healing, growth, and the restoration of human integrity and dignity.[30]

The prevention of transgenerational trauma transference requires acknowledging the impact of war and rape on men and women as identity transforming socialization rituals into the mistrust dynamic of the violence mythos. Disrupting trust and relations of respect and interdependency, left unhealed, these experiences perpetuate themselves in isolationist relationships of social interaction. This reinforces the expectations of exploitation and violence for social behavior, and hence normalizes mistrust and violence in the dynamic of victimizers and victims. Violence is reified as natural, the trauma triad is replicated in transference directly and vicariously, and the trust triad is eclipsed in a conspiracy of mythical silence as the absent presence of a lost time or a distant telos.

Yet violence is a behavior, one possible behavior, one form of somatic language that finds its counter in the somatic language of trusting behavior in the risk of exposure that brings restoration. Distancing difference dissolves in the acknowledgement of respectful interdependence and compassion. We affect each other, whether we admit it or deny/defer it.

The three stages of restoration—establishing safety, remembrance and mourning, and reconnection—focus on the biological, psychological, and social components of human experience that are shattered in trauma and require healing to integrate the person's understanding of self and world in order to be able to function as a healthy human being. Healing may include participation in groups where there is solace in being present with those who have endured similar ordeals. There is a sense of being understood, and with this understanding, a sense of acceptance of one's feelings and limitations without judgment. An incest survivor talks of breaking through the isolation weighing on her all of her life: "I have a group of six women from whom I have *no secrets*. For the first time in my life I really *belong* to something. I feel accepted for what I really am, not my façade."[31] In a men's group, one member in his forties recalled that when his father died when he was nine years old, he started to weep uncontrollably at the funeral. His grandmother told him to stand up straight and stop sniveling. She said, "You're the man of the family and now it is time to start acting like one." The night he shared his story with the group, he let go of his numbness and wept, completing the interrupted grieving process for his father almost forty years previous. His frequent, irrational attacks of rage began to stop thereafter.[32]

The façade, the numbness required to be invulnerable heroes in the violence mythos suffocates us, confines us, constricts us. This is the pervasive need for social control in a culture based on mistrust. It is the panoptic eye that searches for inconsistencies between what one says and what one does because its somatic language is based on mistrust; it expects exploitation and hence creates it. It generates quiet desperation that dares not expose itself for fear of exploitation and indifference that deepens the accumulation of wounds.

Where individuals cannot enjoy the full range of experience, they live vicariously through others. Instead of a rich common language to signify the subtleties of emotional experience and personal accomplishments, the heroes do it for us. We celebrate superstar performers that are allowed to express the ordinary in extraordinary events that can be collectively controlled and witnessed publicly. They feel it, they do it for us, instead of us feeling it and doing it for ourselves, and they pay for it. The ability to have effective control in one's life becomes the ability to control others and their lives, because one's own life is not enough. The mirror of the outside world does not reflect our image back to us. Our image is only human, it is not heroic. Through the smoke of greater and lesser, of exploitation, the image gets distorted, and the faces of our caregivers-takers and the world reflect a heroic image, an idealized image that demands and expects us to be something less than we are: half human. The hero as half human half god is the split between the body and the mind in trauma. To stay a hero, the hero is not allowed to integrate body and mind, to heal, to become wholly human. And that is the true trauma of the violence mythos.

The limitations of the violence mythos for cultural integrity and unity are reflected in the aspiration toward a different kind of model of justice and freedom described by Gustavo Gutierrez: "The poor countries are not interested in modeling themselves after the rich countries, among other reasons because they are increasingly more convinced that the status of the latter is the fruit of injustice and coercion. It is true that the poor countries are attempting to overcome material insufficiency and misery, but it is in order to achieve a more human society."[33]

Prejudice and Tradition

Restoration encompasses personal and cultural healing as our understanding changes through time. We attempt to understand ourselves and our world and integrate ourselves as belonging in the world. In this process, what is important is the awareness of one's own bias; of one's own fore-meanings and prejudices so the other "may present itself in all its newness and thus be able to assert its own truth against one's own fore-meanings."[34] There is an opening between given and possible; between the past and the possible, between prejudice and the possible undergirded by a fundamental respect for otherness. This is what gives historical hermeneutics its significance. The idea of prejudice in Hans-Georg Gadamer's hermeneutics is not that of the enlightenment where the belief in legitimate knowledge was perfect knowledge freed from prejudice by reason as the "prejudice against prejudice."

Gadamer redefines prejudice as our history of pre-judgments that give rise to our beliefs up to the present time. Judgments made in the present may alter these beliefs, and hence become new pre-judgments we bring to future situations. It is our history of prejudice as prejudgments that illuminates the face of finitude from within our concrete experience. Prejudice is not subject to corrective measures of reason that seek to perfect humanity. But rather, reason and prejudice mesh in an acceptance of the unpredictability of continually developing historical being. Reason does an about-face, so to speak. Instead of working to discredit prejudice under the illusion of absolute knowledge, "reason exists for us only in concrete, historical terms, i.e., it is not its own master, but remains constantly dependent on the given circumstances in which it operates."[35] We belong to history, it does not belong to us. Self-understanding is accomplished in a context, in a family, a society, a state in which we live. Individuality is only a parcel of the larger experience of historical life. The prejudices of the individual, far more than one's judgments, constitute the historical reality of one's being.

Reason in history is important for the idea of prejudice in respect to authority and tradition. Authority is an acquisition of knowledge as a broader perspective that can be presented by a person as well as substantiated by "solid grounds offered by reason."[36]

This notion of authority as acquired knowledge gives rise to the concept of 'tradition as a form of authority.' Gadamer calls tradition a brand of authority that is "nameless." Our finite historical being is characterized by the fact that "the authority of what has been transmitted—and not only what is clearly grounded—has power over our attitudes and behavior."[37] He cites the validity of morals as a case in point. Morals are "freely taken over, but by no means created by a free insight or justified by themselves. This is precisely what we call tradition: the ground of their validity."[38] These are the indirect assumptions that are learned and reinforced in the willingness to engage in a social practice. For good or for bad, the past may influence the present, yet also only to the degree that one chooses to accept the authority of the past once that authority has been brought into awareness and enters the utopian world of possibility where it may be replaced by the authority of new experience. This is the renewal arising from letting go and forgetting, not excluding and silencing.

Gadamer refutes the romanticist bias that sees tradition as equated with nature and opposed to reason. Tradition is not an unquestioned part of our conditioning. Tradition incorporates freedom and history in the act of preservation, the act of reason, because tradition needs to be "affirmed, embraced, cultivated. It is, essentially, preservation such as is active in all historical change . . . preservation is as much a freely chosen action as revolution and renewal."[39]

In contradistinction to the idealist position that designates self-understanding as a result of reflection, we stand always within tradition, and this is no objectifying process. We do not conceive of what tradition says as something other, something alien. It is always part of us, a model of exemplar, a recognition of ourselves, which our later historical judgment would hardly see as a kind of knowledge, but as the simplest preservation of tradition.[40] Such is the hero mythology, as an examplar of social behavior that persons willingly model as social practice. Such a model may have had collective survival value and hence been authoritative in the early centuries of discriminate warfare in the Western tradition. In the contemporary world of indiscriminate warfare, the hero mythology is inadequate for providing a symbolic model for collective cooperation and conflict resolution in a diverse global community.

Understanding is an opening that allows tradition a voice in determining the meaning of what we are examining. It is through this continual process of bringing to bear the authority of tradition or reasoned preservation upon the act of understanding that creates a proving ground for the validity of what is true and hence creates the possibility for historical knowledge.[41] In this respect, the tradition of the subordination of women is a historical reality, and so is women's assertion of empowerment, as in the suffrage movement of the nineteenth century, and the feminist movement of the twentieth, which created a new tradition, ground of validity, and authority. The fusion of past and present in tradition from which meaning can spring is understanding's claim to objective validity, "which is not a mysterious communion of souls, but a sharing of a common meaning."[42]

The Concept of 'Play'

Gadamer's concept of 'play' is critical for historical understanding because of its diminution of the importance of the knowing subject, by involving persons in that which is more than them. It is a model of the risk involved in the trust process and interdependent somatic interchange. "Play fulfills its purpose only if the player loses himself in his play. The mode of being of play does not allow the player to behave towards play as if it were an object."[43] The intention of play is the "to and fro movement which is not tied to any goal which would bring it to an end."[44] The definition of a game relies upon this movement. Play is this movement of the game.

The involvement of the player is that of deciding amongst the possibilities realized in the play. The freedom of decision carries with it the element of risk in the game itself that could prove dangerous. "One can only play with serious possibilities. This means that one may become so engrossed in them that they outplay and prevail over one . . . all playing is a being-played."[45] The lure of the game is its engagement of the players. In the game, the player is spellbound, being drawn into play and kept there. The enjoyment of play is dependent upon the "freedom of playing himself out," whereby the player is transforming the aims of behavior into mere tasks of the game. Hence, the purpose of the game lies not in the solution of the task, but rather in "the ordering and shaping of the improvement of the game itself."[46]

There is no longer a gap between participants but a clearing where the reciprocity between the meanings of texts or persons is "played out." A hermeneutics of interdependence demonstrates "the effectivity of history within understanding itself," or effective history,[47] in the story told by each person, in the language that gives rise to meaning. This effective history bears in it the commitments of tradition that have been preserved by reason and body in understanding and the emotional associations of experience. Thus, authority is manifested in understanding as the "having been" of the person's experience, and by implication supports the "to be" that is the possible meaning that is disclosed in the "playing out" of discourse. What is described here as play, but is not articulated by Gadamer, is a philosophical rendition of the trust process.

Recognition and Trust

We have described already the dimensions of basic trust and mistrust articulated by Erik Erikson. We focused on the maladaptive process of mistrust in the repetition of trauma transference and its collective symbolization in the hero myth. Restoring the human from the exploitive dynamics of trauma requires a reengagement in the trust process. Trauma victim testimonies repeatedly attest to a moment when a sense of connection is restored by another person's unaffected display of generosity.[48] Something in the victim that she or he believes to be irretrievably destroyed—faith, courage, decency—is reawakened by an act of common altruism.[49] Mirrored in the actions of others, the survivor recognizes and reclaims a lost part of the self and rejoins human commonality. This is the opening of the trust process and the invisible bonds of interdependency generated from mutual attention and care, the reciprocal play of life.

The openness to the newness of the other is a precondition for the establishment of the trust relationship. In a situation where two people are interdependent, trusting behavior is defined as "choosing to take an ambiguous path that can lead to a beneficial event or a harmful event depending upon the behavior of the other person—where the harmful event is more punishing than the beneficial event is rewarding."[50]

In order for both participants to experience the beneficial event, both must make a trusting choice. If either instead makes a nontrusting choice, the other will experience a harmful event. There is an implicit assumption or expectation that one person will not deliberately hurt the other to satisfy his/her own needs.[51] What is investigated here is the actual process of the establishment of the trust relationship, distinct from the conditions under which trust will be found.[52] There are certain steps two people must go through to move from a state of expectations in which "they make nontrusting choices to the state in which they make trusting choices." There is a commitment period where the two people expose more and more of their "selves" to each other in their initial communication from which they coordinate their choices: "If the response is disapproval or rejection, the relationship freezes at that point, is terminated, or testing begins anew. If each exposure is met with acceptance, there is continual build up of trust, a growing confidence that they will not hurt each other intentionally. The process is mutually reinforcing, since when one person trusts enough to make himself vulnerable by exposing himself, trust is generated in the other person."[53]

The person who exposes herself makes a statement and asks a question in signaling the wish to make a trusting choice and asking if the other is willing to do so. A response of acceptance by the other signals that she also wishes to make trusting choices and coordination is achieved. If the response is nonacceptance, the other neither trusts nor expects trust of the other. The success of the communication depends upon the ability of the participants to expose themselves (if they cannot expose themselves, they cannot signal) as well as on their willingness to do so and their "ability to recognize the meaning communicated by doing so."[54]

There are two presumptions that make the coordination of trust more explicit. First, if the responding person makes the choice that does not hurt the first, he foregoes a personal gain. If the respondent was personally indifferent to the available responses, he could not contribute to the relationship by his choice. There would not be an exposure of self on his part, and the first person would not know whether or not the respondent had made a commitment to trust. Second, the outcomes of the interaction do not give immediate extra reward to the participants for exposing themselves instead of not exposing themselves.

Thus trust can be established in the following sequences of steps: (1) one person acts first and chooses the ambiguous path which exposes her to the risk of personal loss; (2) the other person then responds by choosing the alternative in which he forgoes a personal gain and the first person does not incur a loss.

These two steps, which must be carried out in this order, should establish a degree of trust. After a certain level of trust has been reached through this sequential process, participants may expect trusting behavior from each other over a test period of simultaneously making trusting choices in instances where the risks and payoffs are large.

In the event that the respondent does not forgo a personal gain, then he must subsequently expose himself and have the other respond with acceptance, thus taking four steps instead of two.

In sum, it could be said that it is "necessary that *both* participants give something to the relationship before trust was established."[55] What is more important, previous to being cast into a situation where they are compelled to choose between trusting and not trusting, participants need to be given the opportunity to signal their desires: "Whether it be in interpersonal relations or international relations, the participants cannot be expected ever to trust each other in critical moments if these constitute their only opportunity to act. They need a period in which they can carry out the coordinating process of exposure and acceptance."[56]

The process of establishing trust, where one person initiates by signaling her desire to trust through the exposure of self and the choice to trust at the risk of personal loss and the second person responds by forgoing personal gain that did not cause a loss to the first, is a parallel to Gadamer's concept of the 'play of risk' in self-understanding with another.

The preconditions for trust include the ability to expose the self and signal one's willingness to make trusting choices and ask if the other is willing to do so. Once trust is established, the participants will be able to present themselves in the newness of their own meanings without fear of injury from the other. A buildup of trust based upon respect creates bonds of loyalty and belonging and enables greater risk taking for the future.

In one's own vulnerability, the truster sees the means whereby the trust relationship may be created. The ability to expose oneself contains within it the "original trust" of infancy that offers one the possibility of presenting it as a norm that one's trust is not to be disappointed and thus bring the other over to one's side.[57] Here we have an alternative understanding of persuasion as vulnerability, confidence, and choice in historical interpersonality rather than the disrespect and betrayal by violence, coercion, and authoritarianism of manipulation and control of persons as social objects used as instruments for each other.

To open ourselves to the other, and hence signal a willingness to trust, is the opening of the horizon of our experience with the other. Our horizon is the finite flux of our experience. It is recognition of what is that has been substantiated with what was as well as the possibility of what might be. The experience of the horizon is a testing ground for our prejudices. Understanding "is always the fusion of these horizons which we imagine to exist by themselves."[58] This is the integrative reciprocity between the other and the world in the present. The movement of horizon as simultaneous projection and removal in understanding hence shows the problem of applying prejudice, or prejudgments to understand a new situation.

The significance of prejudice is to be aware of one's own bias. This allows the newness and possible meanings of the text or other person to assert its own truth against one's own foremeanings. It provides an openness to the other, without which there can be no genuine human relationship. In prelinguistic experience the trust process is somatic and remains so with the development of language, even though it may be devalued and unrecognized in a cultural paradigm that favors the linguistic mind. A violation of this openness is the false claim to understanding the other in advance, a denial of the validity of the other's expression, or a betrayal of previous trust, and thus distances her. This becomes a means of "mastering the pact" and ultimately the other person. The other person is denied a voice. The splintering of such dogmatic presuppositions comes with silence and the withdrawal of the other from participation as an absent presence or with "the question" by which the other initiates the trust process anew.

In a conversation between persons who are open to what the other is saying, questioning becomes a testing, where questions are not suppressed by the dominant opinion. The give and take, or play, of questioning and answering becomes meaningful. Faithful to the hermeneutic method, "the possibility of its truth remains unsettled, this is the real and basic nature of a question, namely to make things indeterminate."[59]

Persons who are engaged in conversation, somatic or linguistic, are involved in the hermeneutic situation where communication of meaning is the common goal. It is the purpose of language to perform this exchange of meaning. Language is the common milieu of persons seeking to understand. "To reach an understanding with one's partner in dialogue is not merely a matter of total self-expression and the successful assertion of one's own point of view, but a transformation into a communion, in which we do not remain what we were.[60]

Authority as Preservation of Belief

The opening between self and other becomes the opening between the given and the possible, past and the possible, and prejudice and the possible. Prejudgments are the history of prior judgments that inform one's decision making. Prejudice is the "covering" between the gaps in the constancy of self that gives the self a structure of meaning. This preserves the structure of meaning as forestructures and expectations that orient the self in its historical context of becoming self. It is the prejudgments of historical reason that allow the self to recognize and orient itself in new encounters and situations in everyday life.

The receptivity of the self to the meaning of the other includes the possibility of reciprocity between self and other. The recognition of shared meaning and agreement to mutual cooperation by making trusting choices creates the context for establishing trust and expectations of trusting behavior. Objective knowledge as such shared agreements becomes possible, as does a meaningful relationship with the other. Through the play of language, new thought and action may alter tradition and institutions while replacing previous self-understandings and become realizable on the basis of new commitments between self and other.

Language, then, is "the game of interpretation that we all are engaged in everyday."[61] In linguistic or somatic language, everyone participates as equals. There are none that are endowed with superior knowledge or hold a position of objectivity separate from the historical process. Rather, all are playing the game of expressing, of interpreting, of understanding, "especially when we see through prejudices or tear away the pretenses that hide reality."[62] Understanding as "seeing through" something odd or unintelligible is understanding that "solves" a difficulty.

Acceptance or acknowledgment by choosing to accept one's own authority or the authority of another is the key to relationships of authority. Granted, acceptance can express "a yielding of the powerless to the one holding power rather than true acceptance," but this is not true obedience, because it is not founded upon authority but rather upon force. Belief is the fulcrum of acceptance or nonacceptance. "Authority can rule only because it is freely recognized and accepted. The obedience that belongs to true authority is neither blind nor slavish."[63] The process of risking one's prejudices in the play of authoritative claims to acceptance requires a linguistic description of new meaning to incorporate it into one's horizon. This is the task of metaphor.

Metaphor as Similarity

For Gadamer, the unity of the word and the object, the use of metaphor, is a *proximal* unity that remains distinct from the object as a *similar* reality, not the *same* reality. The attempt by metaphor to name the other, the object, remains a metaphorical name that stands in the stead of the other as a signifier of that reality, and does not "capture" or replace that reality. Instead of Ricoeur's "loving struggle" between metaphor and other, there is a respectful acknowledgment by metaphor of the existence of the other without claiming to have appropriated the other. It is the way our inner schemata organizes the continually changing perceptions of the outside world with existing cognitive frameworks, to create a unity between inner and outer worlds to allow us to survive.

What we have in the meeting of two existents is a socially desiring self constituted through shared symbolic and somatic discourse through metaphor that allows each to approximate the other's reality. Recognition is a proximal unity of knowledge of each other's meaning. In mutually appearing similar, they remain different. Here metaphor is not the captor of meaning, but the bridge between coexistent different meanings.

Without the unity of sameness, the mimetic recognition of desires, with its attendant necessary attitude of hostility and repression, and ultimately death of the other, literal or symbolic, albeit as a defense of threatened respect, is disabled.

Recognition redefined as a proximal unity of meaning attends to the uncertainty of relation between existents, one where hostility remains a possibility, but is not a necessity. Acceptance and mutual pleasure are also possibilities. The outcome of the relation cannot already be decided, because of the ambiguous nature of the relation. The ambiguous path leads to the possibility of a "bridge" between social existents and allows for another kind of relationship, the continual reciprocity of the trust relationship.

Social rites are the basis for social protocols and what are called "manners" in the West.[64] These rites of social grace are used to signify degrees of socioeconomic hierarchy and the divisions among social participants, as well as social groupings and shared cultural intercourse, degrees of trust and mistrust, a network of ways of relationship between humans and other beings acquired through tradition, practiced and refined in the everyday. The terms *please* and *thank you* are signifiers of autonomy and respect for the other, and seldom heard in the discourse of war.

Gadamer's concept of 'effective history' depicts how experience shapes history in a process of social praxis that at once appropriates tradition (providing the context for interchange) and alters tradition, in the integration of previous and new experience. In the shift from the prejudices of the violence mythos to the interdependent mythos, violent desire and devalued emotion are replaced with interdependent negotiation of needs, boundaries, and integrated emotion in the trust process. This shift is further facilitated by the change from the discourse of innate violence to the discourse of attachment theory elaborated in the next chapter.

FIGURE 11

Montana Vietnam Veterans Memorial, 1988

Photographer: Clinton C. Whitmer, U.S. Army Spec 4 Medic during September 1968 through October 1969 Tour of Duty, Chu Lai, Vietnam.

8

Attachment and Actualization

The discourse of internal individualized violence mistakenly identifies anger and desire with violent behavior. This discourse shifts to the discourse of differentiation between anger the emotion and violent behavior enacted in relationship. The quasi-ontological status of violence associated with the medieval tradition and the legacy of the hero is replaced with a relational, interdependent mythos.

Social interchange will be discussed in this chapter in attachment theory, and in the last chapter, will segue into a discussion of cultural relationships and technology. Technology has been a product of and has helped to produce the tradition of culturally sanctioned violence. Technology has been developed in association with militarism, in the form of instruments of war, and in association with exploitive industrialism. The cultural representations of technology lend themselves to destruction and domination, and hence these associations promote a cultural unease and fear of technology and its consequences. Through its military tradition, technology has associations with violence and anger, the rage of rebellion and injustice against the perpetrator, and war cry of the hero. These conflictive associations proliferate in video games and the promotion of new technologies as hero helpers: faster, tougher, stronger, the better to annihilate the competition. As an extension of the human, technologies have reflected the mind/body dualism in rational instrumentalism and complex technologies of administration and surveillance of the body. Understandably, one of the overriding concerns of the technologies of distributed computing and videoconferencing is privacy, and conversely, intrusive surveillance.

The possibilities for integrating technologies as instruments of trust and not intrusion are introduced alongside the expected critiques of technologies of cyberspace by hyperrealists warning about the virtualization of existence into a frenetic consumerism and a faux reality. This is a valid concern given the exploitive tradition of technological development in the West. However, as an extension of human creativity, the plasticity of the appropriate development of technologies needs to be viewed from the perspective of social choices which direct how we want technologies to proceed. This dimension of the social responsibility for technological implementation and development will become more significant as our decisions about technological applications become more deliberate and public, as they increasingly affect nearly everyone on our interdependent planet. To effect this consciousness of considerateness, we turn now to attachment theory.

Separation and Loss

In attachment theory, John Bowlby attempts to recast psychoanalysis without the concepts of 'psychic energy' and 'drive.' He accounts for the lack of explanation for separation anxiety in traditional psychoanalysis by shifting from an intrapsychic model to an interpersonal model of development.

Erikson's concept of 'identity development' also relies upon the interpersonal relationship between child and caregiver. For Erikson, the child receives from the parents, and from the world through the parents' sense of stability in the world, a firm sense of personal trustworthiness within a trusted framework of the community's lifestyle.[1] As well, parents also communicate a deep, almost somatic conviction that there is meaning to what they are doing.[2] This creates a sense of basic trust, the first and basic wholeness where the inside and the outside can be experienced as an interrelated goodness.[3] The converse, basic mistrust, is the unsuccessful integration of the child-caregiver somatic interchanges, with a sense of conflict underlying experiences that is sustained as an adult.[4]

According to Bowlby, traditional psychoanalysis assumes that fear is aroused in a mentally healthy person only in situations that would be perceived as intrinsically painful or potentially dangerous, or that they are perceived as so because a person has become conditioned to them. Fear of separation and loss does not fit this explanation and is usually considered fear of some other situation or a result of biochemical maladjustment.

For Bowlby, the problem disappears when one considers that humans, like animals, respond with fear to uncertain situations not because of the "*high* risk of pain or danger, but because they signal an *increase* of risk."[5] Many species, including humans, are disposed to respond with fear to sudden movement or to a marked change in the level of sound or light, because to do so has survival value. The human responds to separation from a caregiving figure for the same reasons.

The concept of a 'mother' or 'mother substitute' is central for providing a child with a secure base from which to explore. The proximity-keeping behavior of a child in attachment and exploration cannot be explained as a build-up of psychic energy which is then discharged. Rather, it is the activation of a set of behavioral systems due to the receipt of certain signals of internal/external origin. Its cessation is due to the receipt of other signals, also of internal/external origin. Changes in the organization of this attachment behavior are thought to result from raising its threshold for activation and in the increased sophistication of control systems. This is done partly through the incorporation of representational models from the environment and significant people in one's own experience.

In contrast, the dynamic between mother and child is described by Dorothy Dinnerstein where "woman is the will's first, overwhelming adversary." Such a war of the wills rests upon the Freudian dynamics of force, where "inside the toddler who hugs the woman's knees—living cheerfully within the framework of each day as she defines it . . . some center of the will is suspended, tensed for necessary confrontation."[6] Here, the "core of voluntariness in the self is still violated." Thus, the development of the child is foremost a result of intrapsychic forces, in which relation is merely a (violent) means of making conscious the process of self-actualization as separation in rage directed toward the adversary.

Dinnerstein's project to restructure "the rigid forms of symbiosis, of fixed psychological complementarity, which have so far dominated relations between men and women"[7] is a project to restructure the objects of rage both as men and as women. "The early core of human rage can no longer vent itself on the mystical figure of the early mother, when we all take on ourselves the blame for the damage we do each other and the responsibility for stopping it."[8] Dinnerstein's project of reconstructing rage as something for which both men and women are responsible is a feminist version of drive theory's inevitability of violence which can only be prevented through altered forms of discharge (venting) in relation to more equitable repressive forms of authority to inhibit/restrain the supposed innate rage/violence.

The interchange between child and caregiver relies upon the care and support the caregiver receives from his or her environment. In Erikson's view, the caregiver must feel a certain wholesome relation between him and the community.[9] A mother who is not supported by a loving and present mate may start to resent her child.[10] If the caregiver lacks the calmness and ability to cope with her own pain and loneliness, she may invade the infant with excessive needs or neglect it. This is traumatic for the infant, who may develop feelings of smothering and be overwhelmed by the caregiver's attention, or frustrated by neglect. "As a result he can develop an attachment to an inner state of minimal excitation or deadness, which the onslaughts of the outer world, perceived as disturbing or hostile, cannot penetrate."[11] Narcissism may result, a form of self-involvement that excludes intimate relationships with the world.

These types of caregiver-child relationships may occur as a means to overcompensate for the absence of the caregiver's partner, traditionally, the father. For Kipnis, the sons of overly involved mothers become preoccupied with careers, needs for validation, self-gratification, and other interests that exclude intimacy with others and responsibility to the world in general. A major factor in substance abuse was that it supported the user's need to feel special and separate, insulated from the world around him. Hence, parents who are insecure communicate this to their children in the subtleties and complexities of somatic interchange. "When a child's world lacks secure parents, it is a dangerous world."[12] In the case of the absent father, adolescent males may search for some sort of masculine identity and male community wherever they can find it, even if that means violent gangs.[13]

In one study, psychiatric symptoms were observed in children suffering major losses and continued family distress during development.[14] The comparison of "controlled" or daily stress allowing the child to learn and respond appropriately to stress with uncontrollable, nonscheduled stressors shows significant differences in development.

> An infant who is allowed to have an 'optimal' degree of frustration, one who can control, during reproach, his or her own optimal degree of "tension anxiety" (i.e., stress) and return to mother for comfort, is one whose developing CNS (central nervous system) is establishing an appropriate neurochemical milieu for the development of a flexible, maximally adaptive physiologic apparatus for responding to future stressors. A child who is reared in an inconsistent, unpredictable environment will likely have evoked in his or her developing CNS a milieu that will result in a poorly homeostatic, dysregulated stress neurochemistry.[15]

Thus, neurological developmental pathways result from genetic endowment and environment interaction during successive stages of development. The effects of such pathways on development are evident in one's world view and expectations of potential attachment figures. These are derived from representational models of caretakers in childhood. The persistence of these models at an unconscious level thus allows neurotic or other aberrant behavior to be viewed as due to interactions that have already occurred, and that may still be occurring between the development level of an individual's personality and the current situation of the individual.[16]

A therapeutic change in aberrant behavior may come from affectional bonding and human informational processing. Bowlby gives the example of a woman who as a young child repeatedly had her desire for love and care frustrated. The behavioral systems that governed attachment behavior in the child had become deactivated and remained so into adulthood. The desires, thoughts, and emotions that are part of attachment behavior thus were excluded from her awareness due to the selective exclusion from processing any information that would lead to the activation of the system.

Selective exclusion is within the capabilities of our cognitive apparatus, and is termed "defensive exclusion" by Bowlby. Defensive exclusion requires constant cognitive activity at the unconscious level. "The fact that behavioral systems remain intact and capable in principle of being activated, and so may on occasion show brief or incipient activation, manifested in behavioral and/or cognitive and/or affective ways, can account for all those phenomena that led Freud to his ideas about a dynamic unconscious and repression."[17] Indeed, *defensive exclusion* is another name for repression as *repression in the context of relationship*, and not an intrapsychic agency, within the conceptual framework of attachment theory.

Therapeutic change may occur when information that was previously excluded is allowed by the patient, or caregiver to be processed because of the now secure trust base provided by an analyst. This includes information derived from the present situation and information stored in memory. The result is a chain in which information from the present is linked with information from the past. Once the relevant information is accepted, attachment behavior is reactivated, with the accompanying urges, desires, thoughts, and emotions that go with it. In traditional Freudian terms, "the unconscious has been made conscious and the repressed urges and affects released."[18]

The selective exclusion of certain information from processing constitutes a self-censoring authority derived from one's own experience. It differentiates between acceptable and unacceptable information for cognition according to the developmental needs of the person within a specific environmental situation. Authority is the plastic principle of exclusion/acceptance that continually, and so historically, adapts to changes in internal/external events.

Assuming that cognitive, neurochemical and affective systems are interrelated, it has been argued that these cognitive schemas become activated in the case of depression and structure how a patient interprets experience. Negative interpretations then influence the patient's mood and motivation.

For Dana Jack, such negative interpretations associated with female depression are reflections of patterns of beliefs about how women "should" act in relationships in order to secure intimacy.[19] Social beliefs (e.g., marriage is forever and the woman is responsible for maintenance of the relationship) get translated into moral values,[20] and the achievement of these values serves as a symbolic model for feminine adulthood. Hence, the social sanction of beliefs shapes moral values which in turn influence behavioral response.

The Relational Self

For Jack, the separate self stems from the Western tradition of philosophical individualism and Freudian drive theory.[21] Philosophical individualism issues from the tradition of Cartesian egology, or subjectivity. Subjectivity, as a premise for cognition, is accompanied by the practical acting human subject in modern social and political theory.[22] The practical ego in individualism was autonomous, and society was viewed as a composite of the wills of the individuals who made it up.

In epistemological individualism, the autonomous human agent derived knowledge of the external world through the certainty of the individual's own existence. Originating with Descartes, the individual as "cogito, ergo sum" arrived at certain knowledge through transcendental reflection. Later, Kant held the categories for the conditions of possible knowledge as innate in the (abstract) individual. In the empiricist tradition, knowledge arises within the individual mind and the sensations it receives.[23] The cognitive character associated with individualism is articulated in the "abstract individual" who embodies "theoretically presupposed 'interest, wants, purposes, and needs' "[24]

As well, the predominant view in psychology is that of the self, "man," as intrinsically separate. The certainty of the feeling of self, or one's own ego, appears as autonomous and unitary, distinct from everything else. In Freud's drive theory, self-development "progresses from the infant's 'oceanic feeling' of unbounded connection to the delineated autonomy of mature adulthood."[25]

Relationships become important to autonomous individuals to the extent that assumed drives, such as sex and aggression, are satisfied by people, and "people become important emotionally as the objects of drives."[26] Relationships, or attachments to others, become secondary to the economics of drive theory as the means by which drives are satisfied. The developing child becomes less dependent upon "supplies" of "comfort, closeness, security, and self-esteem from another person" as these are internalized and become parts of the self, as introject, identifications, and superego. Thus, the developed mature self is defined as self-sufficient and autonomous, while immaturity is defined as a childlike dependence on others.[27]

Jack intertwines the ideology of capitalism, primarily articulated in Adam Smith's notion of self-interest and the invisible hand, with the cultural symbols of the lone cowboy, the hero, and the warrior as supportive of the concept of the 'separate self' that make it look "right." Within the paradigm of profit, the autonomous self makes use of relationships with people as long as they are profitable, and relationships are terminated when the interests or "needs" of the individual cease to be met. The individual's needs are given priority over the people with whom one has relationships, as people are replaceable by other objects of satisfaction. Relationships are thus functional, and are not "needed." "Objects can be replaced; therefore, relationships are not valuable in and of themselves, but only as they serve to satisfy basic drives or needs.[28] The loss of a particular relationship simply would necessitate its replacement with another relationship as easily as possible.

Jack outlines how Freud perceived depression as a failure of the self to remain within the bounds of the autonomous separate self whereby the self identifies with the lost object. Here the self is altered through identification with the object, and inner division and self-judgment result. Jack articulates two Freudian assumptions: first, that the healthy adult exists independent of and unaltered by current relationships; and second, that depression is produced by "an inability to detach from a lost relationship rather than by an inability to connect with a loved one."[29] For Freud the origins of depression reside with the individual personality and an unhealthy dependence upon another.

In contrast, the relational view of self for men and women depicts the self as part of a fundamentally social experience. There is no "self" in a psychologically significant sense that exists in isolation apart from a matrix of social relations. Attachments provide the context for self-development, mind, and behavior. "Striving for relatedness replaces sex and aggression as the motivation for behavior; attachments are the soil from which cognition, emotion, and behavior originate."[30] Researchers who have analyzed interactions between infants and caregivers report that "infants come into the world ready, eager, and equipped for social interaction."[31] From a relational perspective, the goal of infant behavior is to attach securely to the caretaker, not to

separate from symbiosis with her or him. Attachment is not a failure
to differentiate but rather is a success of psychic functioning. Further,
not only children but adults have this biosocial motivation for making
secure, intimate connection with others.[32]

On the relational view, the analysis of depression alters from the
intrapsychic to the interpersonal and the quality and nature of attachments. Where connectedness is of primary importance, it becomes
evident why a person would go to great lengths, including altering
the self, to maintain intimate ties. For "most forms of depressive disorder, including that of mourning, the principal issue about which a
person feels helpless is his (her) ability to make and to maintain
affectional relationships."[33]

Culturally, relationships are viewed differently for men and for
women. For boys and men, separation and individuation are linked to
gender identity because separation from the mother is valued as essential for the development of masculinity.[34] For girls and women,
feminine identity does not rely upon separation, but rather is defined
through attachment. Girls have an unbroken identification with the
primary caregiver and learn not to relinquish their earliest identifications with the mother. They also are socialized to be prepared to reenact the mother's nurturing role and "take on" the cultural devaluation
of female gender. "Male gender identity is threatened by intimacy
while female gender identity is threatened by separation."[35]

Self-development for women follows the path of forms of connection within relationships with others rather than separation and
individuation. Developing and actualizing "one's talents, abilities and
initiative within attachments" generates the formation of a complex,
mature self. The experience of "mutual empathy" gives rise to "empowerment, vitality and self-knowledge." Here empathy refers specifically to an emotional response. The empathic experience is the
simultaneous experience of one's own thoughts and feelings as well as
those of another, and the emotional interaction between the two. Differentiation is a specific way of being connected to others, and not a
distinct separateness. A person is "differentiated not by a separateness
that emphasizes *difference* from the other but by the assertion of one's
agency—one's needs, feelings, capabilities—within relationships."[36]

Moral Imperatives

A woman's assertion of agency within relationships has certain
moral imperatives in a tradition of male authority and the valuation
of autonomy where females are devalued as relationship dependent.

The standards by which women assess themselves, "should," "ought," "good," "bad," and "selfish," tend to be articulated through the traditional female role of compliant relatedness, self-sacrifice, and maternal nurturance. Jack sees the cultural norm of a man's unresponsive, more distant interactive style as anxiety provoking for a woman's style of self within connection. Compliance in relationship is one way a woman may ensure that a partner will be "accessible and potentially responsive" in times of need.

The internalized cultural standard, which Jack calls the "Over-Eye," rates women in their success or failure at relationship. The moral imperative gives a *vision* of self in relationship, guides *behavior* within the relationship, directs self-blaming *judgment* toward the self, incites *anger* but demands its repression, and directly affects *self-esteem*.[37]

Freud's emphasis upon separation and detachment appears to reflect cultural attitudes described by Foucault's concept of the panoptic gaze of conscious and permanent visibility. In what Focault calls "rituals of exclusion" and "disciplinary projects," the processes by which models of "exercising power over men, of controlling their relations, of separating out their dangerous mixtures" are formed.[38] The war experience for young men and the rape experience for young women are the somatic signifiers of exclusion and control by the hero/perpetrator behavioral models of the violence mythos. The panoptic gaze assures the automatic functioning of power, where "power produces; it produces reality; it produces domains of objects and rituals of truth. The individual and the knowledge that may be gained of him belong to this production."[39] The panoptic gaze has restrained men from behaviors deemed feminine, including the display of pain, emotional vulnerability, and the need for attachment, ritualized in war. Simultaneously, in the tradition that has been women's subordination, the panoptic gaze has been one which oversees their separation and discipline into a cultural constraint of subservience and exclusion from empowerment, ritualized in rape.

Jack gives the example of a woman who considers herself selfish if she estimates her needs to be as important as the needs of others. The moral standard of selfless subservience for women directs her vision of the hierarchy of needs within the relationship and directs her behavior by showing how she should choose when her needs are in conflict with those of others she loves. It provides a guide for harsh self-judgment if she chooses other than its dictates and arouses her anger when she places her needs second to those of others yet demands she repress that anger through the moral imperative of selflessness, as denial and suppression of her own needs. As well, it reinforces a woman's low self-esteem by affirming that she is not as worthy or important as others and legitimates the historical view of woman's nature as self-sacrificing. It was learned in a research group of battered women that when the husband uses force and/or emotional cruelty, "women blame themselves for not being loving enough, or in the right ways. Anger becomes a club that is used against the self and traps a woman in a damaging relationship."[40]

In contrast, the point of anger is to signal an obstacle. In intimate relationship, anger is aroused when there are obstacles that threaten the affectional bond, and its goals are to remove the obstacles to reunion and discourage further separation.[41] Anger toward a loved one often is accompanied by anxiety about the attachment, as these feelings are elicited in the same circumstances. When women suppress their anger, the bond is weakened if conflicts are not resolved but continually feed an accumulation of repressed rage.

Jack characterizes the "inner revolt," described by Freud as part of a depressed person's intrapsychic structure, as actually stemming from structures of relationship.[42] The "revolt" is an inner refusal to give any more which arises from anger about issues in the relationship. And yet, power imbalances within heterosexual relationships influence a woman's choice of compliant relatedness. As targets of male violence, women learn early in their lives that one defense against hostile male attention is "sweet compliance."[43]

In a culture where women are taught by their mothers and social matrix that compliance secures relationship, the invisible moral standards of subordination prevent women from claiming their own authority and asserting themselves within relationship. Within this mode of identification with the aggressor (of internalizing the values of male authority and turning them against oneself and isolating from other women) the depressed women had only their stories of resistance and refusal of the life most women lived and no one to tell what they had learned. "They would have been hard put to answer the inevitable question asked of unhappy women: What do you want?"[44]

The answer to such a question requires the language and power to image, to entertain alternatives, as well as the ability to meaningfully integrate repressed parts of the self and allow for risk, trust, commitment, and change within relationships.[45]

The dynamic of identification with the aggressor turns the self upon the self in self-hatred and reinforces isolation from others. This is exemplified in the mentality of compliant relatedness that perpetuates women's subordination in a culture of male valuation of separateness. Also, the valuation of male separateness includes a valuation of violence, because in order for the self to be actualized, it must place itself in violent opposition to and detachment from those from which it separates. This is the legacy of the hero myth. In contrast, interdependent differentiation within relationship can lead to self-actualization of an empathic, mature self that is connected with others. In order for violence against women and children to stop, male violence needs to be devalued and recontextualized in relationship and attachment.

The intrapsychic structures of self are fundamentally interpersonal. The person's relationships provide a context for the arousal of certain responses that in themselves are mediated through learned responses to environmental stimuli. This is Erikson's language of somatic interchange that establishes a sense of basic trust in the child with others and the world in the trust triad. The self is socially motivated. Rather than violence perceived as innate to the self, it is a behavioral symptom of a self that has cultural expectations for the appropriateness, as legitimate and illegitimate violence, of enacting learned violent behavior. In this respect, the aggressor is acting out culturally sanctioned, overtly or covertly, learned violent behavior.

The appropriate milieu for discussing violence is relationships, attachments, and transgenerational trauma triad transference. To delimit the factors in relationship that constitute a threat to disconnection—such as denial, detachment, neglect, and intrusion, the factors of abuse and exploitation—is to understand the mistrust dynamic behind the violence. Healing the wounds of unsuccessful needs negotiation requires trust, understanding of self and world through assimilating trauma memory traces, and reconnection with a social network that may anticipate and prepare for certain types of trauma, such as loss of loved ones, or life transitions, and restores accountability and engagement, where violence is secondary to a primary concordance of interdependency.

FIGURE 12

Pontoon Bridge, Temp Bridge, Blown Bridge,
Blown Railroad Bridge, Highway 1, Vietnam, 1969

Photographer: Clinton C. Whitmer, U.S. Army Spec 4 Medic during
September 1968 through October 1969 Tour of Duty, Chu Lai, Vietnam.

9

Technology and Interactivity

We turn now to a discussion of the linguistic/somatic context of the interdependent human extended in a technological setting. The ways, or techniques humans use to subsist, extend, and interact with others and their environment are technologies. Much of our relationship with the world is mediated through technology-produced mechanisms and images. These create virtual relationships with people, places, and things we do not encounter in our everyday activities and changes our sensibility of somatic relationships. Talking on the phone is a virtual mediation, as is viewing television, electronic mail, Internet commerce, or videoconferencing. The integration of absent presence as virtual presence in the language of somatic interchange, mediated by technology, compresses the trust triad into a simulation of two in the presence of one.

Raster Rasure

Indirect relationships mediated by technology can affect us as potently as our immediate experiences. They create virtual spaces for indirect vicarious participation without the response-ability of direct participation, such as television viewing. Television has its own unique language of somatic interchange. In 1970, Herbert Krugman decided to discover what happens physiologically in the brain of a person watching TV. He found that within thirty seconds, brain waves switched from predominantly beta waves, indicating alert and conscious attention, to predominantly alpha waves, indicating an unfocused, receptive lack of attention, the state of aimless fantasy and daydreaming below the threshold of consciousness.[1] Further research indicated that the brain's left hemisphere, which processes information logically and analytically, tunes out while the person is viewing TV. This tuning out allows the right hemisphere of the brain, which processes information emotionally and noncritically, to function unimpeded.[2] Krugman's conclusions were that "the mode of response to television is more or less constant and very different from the response to print. That is, the basic electrical response of the brain is clearly to the medium and not to content difference. . . (Television is) a communication medium that effortlessly transmits huge quantities of information not thought about at the time of exposure."[3]

The left hemisphere of the brain analyzes discrete parts to arrive at logical conclusions, while the right hemisphere recognizes faces and places and the completion of incomplete patterns (such as caricature recognition), and the response to archetypal or symbolic aspects of imagery. While the left hemisphere processes information analytically, the right hemisphere involves emotions, with previous experiences whose moods, sensations, and images have left a memory trace, sometimes not consciously remembered. "The individual's world-view, or basic feeling-orientation in the world, seems to be consolidated in the right hemisphere."[4]

The healthy adult uses both of these hemispheres to integrate and fully process information from the environment.[5] The right hemisphere, less verbally oriented than the left, requires the left hemisphere to articulate what it knows. As well, the left needs the right hemisphere to contextualize information in its analytical processes. To live "sanely" in the world, both hemispheres need to be engaged in experience, though one may predominate at times.

The television transmission process is unique. There is no actual image that is projected, as from a movie projector.[6] Videotape, audiotape, and television operate solely through electrical impulses. Television works through electronic scanning, or a raster scan. Tiny dots of light on the screen light up, one at a time, in a rapid succession of glowing dots across and down, in alternating lines, in a "sweep." There are 525 lines of dots on a TV screen. In each one-thirtieth of a second, the scanning process completes two full sweeps of a screen to create, through electrical impulse, the entire mosaic of an instant's image. We visually receive each dot of light, sending its impulse to the brain. The brain records this bit of information, recalls previous impulses, and expects future ones. "We 'see' an entire image because the brain fills in or completes 99.999 percent of the scanned pattern each fraction of a second, below our conscious awareness. The only picture that ever exists is the one we complete in our brains."[7]

This is different from the persistence of vision, the residual image anticipation that animation and film rely upon to make a movement appear smooth and complete in successive frames of moving pictures. The brain fills in the motion between frames. However, with television, the picture is never there. The brain is filling in both the motion and the picture. The brain is very busy, very involved, but only in the right hemisphere. The left hemisphere tunes out.[8]

Researchers suggest that the scanning process, or raster scan, of television is ideally suited to the right hemisphere's mode of processing information, namely the completion and recognition of patterns.[9] The left hemisphere tunes out because it quickly becomes habituated to the scanning dot, and lacking any need to respond critically or analytically, slows down into alpha. It may also become overloaded with trying to scan at electronic speeds, which permits direct access to the right hemisphere. Without the critical left hemisphere, the right hemisphere is "free to accept and act upon suggestions or commands, even nonsensical ones."[10] The raster scan has the physiological effect of rasure, of obliterating left brain critical activity, as raster rasure.

Television viewers may watch with a critical-analytical frame of mind, focusing on analysis of technique in production, such as soundtrack, camera angle, composition. However, this is not the usual viewing habit, which is more passive entertainment. McLuhan's observation may be more accurate: "The response to the medium may well be at the level of the nervous system, working its larger effect regardless of critical analysis on the part of the viewer."[11] This lends credence to the observation that technology is the knack of so ordering the world that we do not have to experience it.[12] Television viewers hence experience a rasure, an obliteration of critical awareness, through electronic rasterization on the television screen, that leaves them open to affective communication resonating with deeper feelings, beliefs, and symbolic expectations. Television advertising uses this to trigger an emotional association with a product or person.[13] A similar phenomenon may be at work with cases of Internet addiction to chat sessions, where the same process of raster scan bypasses critical thought and accesses affective thought in imaginative online engagement.

Viewer Vicarious Trauma

In a trauma event, the highly visual and sensory form of memory appropriate to young children appears to be activated. In states of high sympathetic nervous system arousal, the linguistic encoding of memory is inactivated, and the central nervous system reverts to the sensory and visual forms of memory that predominate in childhood.[14] The visual memory imprint of the child is a lasting imprint of what is "exemplary," as necessary for survival.

The somatic processing of information both in raster rasure in television viewing and in trauma experience is the same: they both overwhelm and bypass the critical, linguistic processes of the left brain hemisphere and access dissociative fantasy, emotional, symbolic, and visual image processes of the right brain hemisphere. In television viewing, emotional states may be uniquely manipulable by aligning cognitive processes, or expectations with the physiological state of alpha wave activity in the drone of raster rasure that allows affective access to environmental influences.[15]

Those exposed to televised violent or traumatic images or events are thus *psychoneurologically* primed to experience vicarious traumatization, including internalization of the aggressor, and develop the ensuing symptoms of posttraumatic stress disorder, including extreme dissociation, numbing, intrusive imaging, trauma transference, and reenactment. Children are especially vulnerable, as their memory is primarily visual and sensory. Within the culture of the hero/perpetrator, this means the trauma triad roles of hero, perpetrator, and victim depicted in programming may develop powerful emotional associations for modeling behavior and reinforce these roles in identity formation. The compression of the trust triad—self, other, world—into a violent simulation of two—the viewer and the virtual—reduces to the presence of one—the violated victim.

Laboratory and field studies in which young children and adolescents were repeatedly shown either violent or nonviolent images disclosed that exposure to filmed violence shapes the form of aggression and typically increases interpersonal aggressiveness in everyday life.[16] An elementary school teacher observes these effects every day in the schoolyard: "I haven't seen Red Rover or tag on the playground in years. The standard now is 'play-fighting,' often with kung-fu moves. But there is a real lowering of empathy—their standard line is, 'I was just joking and I kicked him.'"[17] These effects ripple through the classroom, for instance, when discussing violence in World War II. "There are always a few boys who will go, 'Yeah, right on.' There are kids in my class who will take delight in something a previous generation of students would have responded to with shock."[18] Conversely, programs that portray positive attitudes and social behavior foster cooperativeness, sharing, and reduce interpersonal aggressiveness.[19]

The 1972 Surgeon General of the United States Report stated, "At least under some circumstances exposure to televised aggression can lead children to accept what they have seen as a partial guide for their own actions. As a result, the present entertainment offerings of a television medium may be contributing in some measure, to the aggressive behaviour of many normal children."[20] Ten years later, a 1982 report by the National Institutes of Health in the United States sur-

veyed the research since the 1972 Surgeon General Report and concluded, "The consensus among most of the research community is
that violence on television does lead to aggressive behavior by children and teenagers who watch the programs. . . The research question
has moved from asking whether or not there is an affect to seeking an
explanation for the effect."[21]

Dr. Edward Donnerstein comments on these findings by saying,
"The interesting thing about that research, it's not only replicated in
the United States, it is replicated cross culturally. . . you find the same
pattern: that if you monitor early exposure to televised aggression and
follow children up one, two, three, how many years later, the best
predictor is going to be that early exposure to violence. And it's constant, and it's constant cross culturally."[22] What Dr. Donnerstein
is describing is secondary trauma transference repetition/replication
experienced through viewer vicarious trauma. As a human psychoneurological phenomenon, it is experientially the same interculturally.

Another ten years later, a study by the American Psychological
Association Task Force on Television Society reports "cross national
studies, supported the position that the viewing of televised aggression
leads to increases in subsequent aggression and that such behaviour can
become part of a lasting behavioural pattern."[23] From what we have
shown in previous chapters, these effects are consistent with PTSD
hyperarousal, the expectation of exploitation, and trauma transference.
Dr. Donnerstein submits, "Once the child is aggressive, the research
seems to suggest he/she searches out certain types of violent material,
or, if these types of children run across violent material: it reinforces
those beliefs and attitudes and values which they have."[24]

The content of a particular violent program is not the single
defining factor in vicarious traumatization: the language of somatic
interchange as raster rasure of televised viewing creates a unique
psychoneurological susceptibility to secondary traumatization that is
constant cross-culturally. The degree of traumatization likely will
correspond to the resonance with viewer previous experience, the
viewer's basic orientation toward the world (mistrust or trust), and
the identification with cultural role models for behavior, masculine
and feminine.

The erosion of basic trust becomes evident in the so-called mean-
world syndrome apparent in children exposed to television violence
as they develop a view of the world as more dangerous or sinister
than it really is, an effect also reported in adults, particularly the elderly.[25] A spin-off of viewer vicarious trauma is reflected in the video
game industry. Game makers rely on hyperarousal, a symptom of

trauma, to gauge the quality of its (predominantly violent) games. The encoding of hyperarousal symptoms in the somatic horizon between the real and the virtual is reenacted in the "twitch factor," or instantaneity of response, programmed into video game virtuality. As well, the neurotic compulsion of boys who play video games creates a "paranoiac environment" that dissolves any distinction between the doer and the viewer.[26] The structure of the video drives the players to constantly defend themselves from the entire universe of destructive forces. This play becomes a compulsive repeat of a life-and-death performance, or trauma transference.

The spontaneous repetition of trauma transference also may be reflected in copycat crimes modeled on media violence. Linked to more copycat killings than any film ever made, *Natural Born Killers* director Oliver Stone has been sued for negligence by John Grisham, whose friend was the victim of a copycat killing from the film.[27]

With this important precedent, the issues of freedom of artistic expression and social responsibility may need to be discussed and reformulated as we come to understand the impact of re-presenting violent trauma that may make viewers vicarious victims and perpetuate the cycle of violence. Men and boys are not enacting innate violence or aggression, they are engaging in violent behavior that a culture of the hero/perpetrator has deemed permissable and acceptable in the language of heroic masculine somatic interchange. If they present themselves "unheroically," by expressing pain and grief, they are afraid they will be rejected by "hero-loving women and men."[28] In other words, contrary to Freud, men are aggressive because it is expected of them in order to be loved. Such a model is toxic to women as much as men, where "the denial of feelings inherent in old male roles numbs women's souls just as readily as men's."[29]

Dr. Donnerstein lists several types of violence that seem to have more influence than other types.[30] First, *rewarding violence or lack of punishment for those who act aggressively*. This is consistent with the hero/perpetrator behavior and attitude association of using legitimate violence to contain violence. When the hero and perpetrator are doubles, to condemn the violence of one is to deprive the violence of other and nullify the dynamic, and hence nullify the hero myth. The dynamic, and hence the hero, can survive only if there is a covert and overt acceptance of violence as socially permissable and expected behavior. This leads to the second type, *strong identification with the aggressor* such as the hero and the level of violence in *Terminator I* and *II*. In traumatization, this is an internalization of the aggressor that permits trauma transference in subsequent relationships. Children habituated to violent television viewing may transfer their attitudes and expectations to film viewing and their real world relationships. The third type is *violence that is portrayed realistically or seen as a real event*. From the perspective of vicarious or secondary trauma, this allows the viewer to make emotional and imagistic associations that resonate with past experience and may be integrated into the viewer's inner schema as their own experience. The fourth is *portrayals that seem to please the viewer*. This is a tactic of resonance, or affective communication, that allows violence to be packaged in a way that is emotionally appealing. The brain in raster rasure processing is not critical of the content, but emotionally responsive to arousing content, especially in hyperarousal mode. The fifth type of violence is *when people are predisposed to act aggressively*. This is the viewer's foremeanings that have affective resonance with PTSD symptoms of identifying with the aggressor, expectation of exploitation, and trauma transference that repeat unresolved trauma. In the instance of viewers who have experienced trauma, vicarious trauma viewing may be a reliving of the trauma event in their past. For female victims of sexual assault, "sexual safety is so fragile for women it can be shattered each time the media spotlight a tragedy of random violence against women."[31]

These types of violence occupy a significant amount of viewer attention, between two to four hours per day. The child will see twenty thousand ads per year, and the average child between the ages of six and fourteen will have seen approximately 11,000 murders.[32] A *TV Guide* random sampling of eighteen hours of primetime programs showed an average of 102 violent (physical) acts per hour.[33] The George Gurbner violence index shows cartoons have the most violence, with 26 acts per hour, and MTV has 11 acts per hour, while violence has actual decreased on the three major American networks.[34]

The effects of viewing violence are revealed in the changes in perceptions of real violence. Researchers exposed healthy individuals to ten hours over two to three weeks of very graphic forms of violence, particularly violence against women, and then had them act as a juror in a rape trial and give evaluations of the real victim of violence. "They don't see as much injury, they don't see as much pain, they don't see as much suffering to a real victim of violence after exposure to media and fantasy violence: desensitization has occurred."[35] This study describes the process of dissociation in vicarious trauma and the symptoms of emotional numbing in the withdrawal from exposure to trauma representations.

The power of indirect and direct experience of trauma depends upon its cognitive and emotional value associations in the cultural belief system. For instance, in the culture of the hero, images of powerful, aggressive, invulnerable, triumphant men usually use violence to control or obtain control over their antagonist, usually another man, and get what they want. In this way, violence against men is entertainment.[36] The scenes of battle are replayed in violent films, television programming, and sports such as boxing, football, and hockey where men are wounded, maimed, or killed, or comedy such as "Abbott and Costello" or the "Three Stooges." The virtual reflects the real, and the real reflects the virtual where real men are victims of violence in 80 percent of homicides, 70 percent of robberies, and 70 percent of aggravated assaults.[37] And they displace their victim rage/rescue to women in wife assault, battering during pregnancy, femicide, and half of the homeless as women and children fleeing their violence.[38] This ripple effect is reflected in the economics of violence in costs to health care, legal, and welfare systems as well as work place absenteeism and unemployment.

Dissociated Simulation

The world captured in media images is a world dissociated from our immediate experience. For "McLuhan's children" who grew up with television and computer-mediated communications such as the Minitel in Paris and Internet MUDs, the boundaries of social and personal identity dissolve in *pretending to be somebody else*, or even several people simultaneously.[39] Kevin Robins notes how we can regulate our relationship with the images of suffering we see on the television screen, on video. It is a moment of exposure to and insulation from actual suffering.[40] He surmises that the image does not include us in the reciprocal relations necessary to sustain moral and compassionate existence. In an acute example of the Janus face of the hero in the violence mythos, he describes two instances of videotaped violence. One was a video taken by Gulf War Apache helicopter pilots, scanning Iraqui soldiers as they were ripped apart by helicopter fire. After viewing the footage upon return to their base, the pilots were slapping each other on the back because they thought they had "shot into a farm" because it looked like someone had "opened up a sheep pen."

The other example Robins gives is from the film *Henry: Portrait of a Serial Killer*. The film depicts Henry and his cohort, Otis, who have stolen a video camera and use it to record themselves torturing and murdering a suburban family. Afterward, they watch the replay and even fall asleep in front of it.

Robins queries how the sadistic acts of both instances are transformed into voyeurism that distances the killers from moral engagement. He explains the case of Henry and Otis as psychotic, because they are unable to distinguish reality from fantasy. But what of the Apache pilots? What makes their actions more acceptable to us? Robins considers these instances of "the institutionalized and normalized defiance of reality that increasingly characterizes the military-information society."[41] From the perspective of the violence mythos, it is the normalization of transgenerational trauma transference in the exploitive dynamic of the hero/perpetrator myth.

The pilots would not be labeled "psychopathic." They could dissociate themselves from the reality of the violence in which they participated. They could legitimate their actions as "punishing evil." Robins explains how the defense mechanisms of denial, disavowal, and repression preserve and protect "sanity within an insanely violent environment." This is the process of dissociation in posttraumatic stress disorder that is paralleled in what Robins calls "splitting," or the division of the self and disowning of a part of the self. Purposeful distanciation initiates the mind-body split that distances and denies emotional vulnerability. Through splitting, "individuals can manage to coexist both as killers and as apparently normal people."[42]

Robins extends his comparison of psychopaths and Apache pilots to everyday screen viewers and argues that the "ordinary" viewer or spectator of violence is close to the extreme, the fantastic, repulsive, and frightening. He quotes Ignacio Ramonet, who condemns the "necrophiliac perversion of television," as it takes nourishment from blood, violence, and death. Robins accurately notes that it is not so much that we live in the world of the image, but that there is "in our culture now, a kind of collective, social mechanism of splitting." The "spectator self" is morally disengaged and floats about in a vat of violent images. The "actor self" is part of a reality whose violence is overwhelming. This impetus for desensitization to violence and impotence to prevent it may be the trauma persona of the vicarious life of dissociated simulation rendered particularly acute in television generations raised in the violence mythos.

The testimony of the Apache pilots and the analysis by Robins reflect the symbolization of the trauma triad into the hero/perpetrator and mind/body split. At the level of cultural theory, the mind/body split was reflected in the work of C. P. Snow, who identified a polarity within Western culture between literary intellectuals and physical scientists, or the "two cultures" arising from the scientific revolution.[43]

From the perspective of the violence mythos, Snow's division indicates a cultural manifestation of the dualism of the mind/body prototype, in parallel with the shift from an organic to a mechanistic universe. Purposeful distanciation, the isolation of the individual from social interaction and responsibility, has its flip side in the flight to the mind, as dissociation in detached observation and manipulation without personal involvement, all prerequisites for science. Both may be reflected in the literary absorption in the tragic individual and scientific indulgence in the abstract. To bring these two together requires not only an integration of mind and body, but also a rethinking of the trauma triad of hero, perpetrator, and victim restored to the trust triad.

O. B. Hardison, Jr., critiques Snow's argument by saying that the idea of cultural fragmentation has its uses, but that it is misleading as a model for how people experience culture.[44] He argues that consciousness is not fragmented, but is a unified identity that is a product of all the influences that have shaped it, a result of everything that makes up culture. He argues that we inhabit our culture and that culture continues to shape us in ways we perceive and in ways of which we are largely unconscious.

There are helpful elements both in Snow and in Hardison. Snow points out an important divisiveness in experience (mind and body) that is culturally reinforced through respective institutionalized specializations in the arts and in the science communities. As a unified culture, we have exposure to the symbolic representations of both, as Hardison would suggest. However, the violence mythos is a symbolic patterning of basic mistrust reflected in cultural discourse in many dimensions of discourse. The violence mythos maintains the exploitive trauma dynamic in the assumption of the individual, other, and reality as violent that is reinforced in media image repetitions of trauma transference for vicarious consumption. This erodes existing trust and undermines the potential for trust in oneself, another, and world. Perpetuating the trauma triad prevents remedial action for restoring the interdependent human condition of trust and a fully integrated understanding of being human in responsible relationships with our environment.

Cyberbodies

In the virtual world of the screen there is the possibility of vicarious trauma and vicarious life. "The authenticity of human relationship is always in question in cyberspace, because of the masking and distancing of the medium, in a way that it is not in question in real life."[45] The discourse of cybernetics may be included here, defined as self-regulation in machines.[46] Central to the idea of cybernetics is the likeness between humans and machines. First is the likeness between the circular process of the central nervous system and the "feedback" of a cybernetic machine. Second, the firing of an organic neuron is "similar" to the "on-off" switches of electrical circuits and digital computers. Such a "hard-wire" theory of human neurology was expressed in the previous discussion of trophic theory. Cybor refers to "cybernetic" and "organic creatures who are part human and part machine." Distance from the human could become total as Hardison believes humans will "disappear through the skylight" as carbon-based humans are replaced by silicon-based creatures.[47]

Emily Martin critiques the apocalyptic tone of Hardison's work. She sees the proclamation of the doomed human body replaced by the machine as a "profound denial of the possibilities of human agency to sustain the potential for fundamental social and cultural change.[48] Such a vision, she claims, "denies the possibility of any form of human social life that is not voracious and destructive."[49] Rather, she sees scientific knowledge as one perspective among others. This knowledge is often able to pass for "natural fact," a "powerful means by which its vision of hierarchical human relationships is learned and internalized."[50]

Taking the idea of inevitable destructive technology and the disappearance of the body further, John Fiske elaborates a Foucauldian view of power and body. Fiske interprets Foucault as saying the social order depends upon the control of people's bodies and behaviors. "The body and its specific behavior is where the power system stops being abstract and becomes material."[51] The struggle for control thus takes place on the material terrain of the body and its immediate context.

The body is the physical limit of human existence. It is the boundary which distinguishes itself from other. Within the context of Western culture, the disintegration of the war experience into dissociative trauma transference, and subsequent reification and symbolization of the mind/body dualism into the hero/perpetrator mythology of the violence mythos, requires a disappearance of the body and its somatic language as a casualty of war. The discourse of virtual reality and cyber environments, which attempt to create integrated human and machine environments, is replete with the discourse of the mind, which "encodes data," "programs information," "systematically organizes sensory perceptions." The intolerable, imperfect body is lost in yet another discourse of the Western concept of mind's insatiable quest for heroic painless perfection. The incessant technological pressure to compile existence as instantaneity is a hyperarousal affective avoidance of somatic existence, the site of feeling, of limit, of interdependence, of pain, of fear. The heroic mind must master these in somatic simulation to create a safe place in a world perceived to be hostile. "As we grow up, we forge our identities by building on the last place in psychological development where we felt safe. As a result, many people come to define themselves in terms of competence, in terms of what they can control."[52] When mastery moves into mas(k)ery of fear, people can become trapped.[53]

Within the context of the violence mythos, it is the task of the mind to control and destroy the discourse of the body, with its feelings and emotions as well as its symbolic alternatives to a mind-centered world view. There is no diabolic force at work here; the cultural system simply is protecting itself in a manner which has been reinforced and reenacted for centuries in its adaptation for survival. The language of cyber environments talks about the body as encoding data and is an abstract attempt to interpret the body experience by the discourse of the mind. This takes away the body's own interpretation of its feeling experience and hence source of empowerment and trust of self and potentially another. This could pose an alternative to the discourse of the mind and disrupt the social configuration through alternative interpretations of symbolic discourse and action. Such was the objective of the claim to conscience by O'Brien in Orwell's *1984*, in his attempt to encompass and control Winston's unique experience through anticipation and manipulation of his fear of rats.

A friend's lament that it has been impossible to win at a computer game of solitaire reflects a similar ineffectual interaction with one's virtual environment. The programming of cynical values, however unconscious, into a piece of software is inaccurate. Sometimes we do win in life; sometimes we make a difference; sometimes we have quiet triumphs that are not sensational, yet are meaningful. When we acclimate ourselves in an everyday angst, perpetuated in a barrage of death-threat media images and conflict-ridden change, the subtlety of satisfaction veers into an addiction to increasingly trauma-inducing experiences, to confirm that the world is a dangerous place, and that escalating defense against it is at once futile and justified. This is the addiction to violence, fed by the violence mythos.

Howard Rheingold reflects on the electronic communication medium and its attraction to users to the point of obsession: "What is it about the way people are today, and the way we interact, that leaves so many people vulnerable to communication addiction . . . the questions are broad ones, addressing key ambivalences that people have about personal identity and interpersonal relationships in the information age."[54] Within the tradition of the violence mythos and transgenerational trauma transference, the development of technology has been directed toward the exploitive ends of surveillance, disinformation, control and destruction. It comes as no surprise that there has been a "manifest failure of technology to resolve pressing social issues over the last century."[55] Communication is the interdependent restorative antidote to toxic trauma, and people in the violence mythos crave technologies that provide its simulation of safe somatic connection. We need safe connections that allow us to experience our natural curiosity about the world and our need to play, to enjoy the world, and to grow. If our world of somatic interchange has become too hostile, we will resort to simulations to survive. It is the mind/body split all over again, in a media culture of vicarious traumatization. The vast popularity of the World Wide Web and its electronic linkage of 30 to 50 million users and rising globally attests to this simulation of interpersonal access both in corporate and in home markets.[56]

Marginalized Magic

Our culture has accepted the disintegrated community in the normalization of the trauma triad and the domination/submission dynamics that characterize social interaction. The community as safe context for growth has become marginalized. The unresolved, disintegrated trauma content from an extraordinary event is reenacted and becomes ordinary. In reversal, the integrated ordinary events of personal trustworthiness and a trusted community framework then become extraordinary. The events of a trustful or trusting world and the pleasure of living in it thus become "unreal" or "fantasy."

For instance, from the perspective of the trauma triad, the Walt Disney Company has shown the metanarrative of trauma in the stories of Western cultural experience and attempted to restore a trust triad. Consistently, in its animated feature films, the paradigm of mistrust begins with traumatic separation or threat of abandonment, with an evil woman (caregivers, usually female, symbolizing the perpetrator of mistrust in infancy), a young woman (threatened new life), and a male hero (rescuer and continued protection of life in mistrustful world), such as in *Snow White and the Seven Dwarfs*, *Cinderella*, and *Sleeping Beauty*. In *Pinocchio*, the caregiver is an old man. The animated features with a trusting mother role are of animals, and are themselves accurate portrayals of the emotional lives of animals.[57] However, the mother is usually traumatically separated from her offspring. These movies include *Bambi*, *Dumbo*, *101 Dalmations* (Cruella DeVil says it all), and *The Lion King*. There are orphan stories such as *The Jungle Book* and *The Rescuers* (Medusa is a child abuser). Since the feminist movement, the mother role has been left out and replaced by a nurturing father. These include *The Little Mermaid*, *Beauty and the Beast*, *Aladdin*, and *Pocahontas*. More recently, in a tentative manner, a trustworthy mother role appears, if only briefly, in the offstage mom in *Toy Story* and the introductory depiction of Quasimodo's protective mother in *The Hunchback of Notre Dame*. However, in this film, the mother role is quickly filled by an abusive man, and the trauma drama unfolds again.

Contrary to the rhetorics of corporate imperialism, simulation escapism, and misogyny, Disney is an affair of the heart. The films consistently attempt to show the process of sincerity, risk, trust, and growth in caring relationships. Western culture overall simply has not reconciled the trauma triad in real life and resists accepting the role of trustworthy caregiver, traditionally women, and hence trustworthy world. That would mean life is trustworthy, and for the most part, that is not what the culture believes. It is addicted to the hyperarousal of violence and rabid revenge. The culture believes only individual heroes are trustworthy in their violent domination of their abusive perpetrator double, perpetuating a victim hero addiction. The culture is cynical. Violence as the norm has been "known" for centuries because of the repetition and reinforcement of trauma transference. The culture has rarely, if at all, had the understanding or traditions to resolve the trauma triad successfully communally. Its safe places are rarely somatic: they have dissociated to the virtual world of television and computers to explore, relax, and play. They are disenchanted and distrustful of the traditional sanctuary of religious institutions as the infiltration of the violence mythos is revealed in the hypocracy of sublime belief and abusive practice. The virtual world itself is filled with trauma narratives that repeat and reinforce the dynamic through vicarious traumatization and dissociative image association. The culture fantasizes hero trauma resolution to counter the unresolved shadow trauma in its coded collective memory and media. That the culture has reduced the process of trust and those images, institutions, and persons associated with it to a heroic/superstar exploitive commodification is less a reflection of a consumer self-interest than it is a reflection of the erosion of flexible personalized trust replaced by a rigid mistrustful possessiveness fearful of loss and unacceptance.

Disney may have a cinematic formula for its success, but it also touches deep psychological and emotional chords of the trauma triad in the cultural imagination in its successfully integrated, joyful, restorative trust conclusions to stories of, for the most part, traumatic isolation and abandonment. Eric Sevareid, the noted newscaster, commented on Walt Disney's death in 1966: "By the conventional wisdom, mighty mice, flying elephants, Snow White and Happy, Grumpy, Sneezy, and Dopey—all these were fantasy, escapism from reality. It's a question of whether they are any less real, any more fantastic than intercontinental missiles, poisoned air, defoliated forests, and scrap iron on the moon. This is the age of fantasy, however you look at it, but Disney's fantasy wasn't lethal. People are saying we'll never see his like again."[58]

False Fortresses

A cultural inculcation of "paranoid rationality" is reflected in the observations of trend tracker Faith Popcorn. The first premise of her book *The Popcorn Report* is that "for the first time ever in the history of mankind, the wilderness is safer than 'civilization.' "[59] The wilderness does not have crack, carcinogens, street murders, or hi-tech wars. The trend increasingly will be to entrench ourselves in our homes, in the privacy of our own "fortresses." The purpose is to make people feel safe. What she calls "sophisticated distribution systems" (or what we have come to know as the "information highway" and its off-ramps) will stock and supply these fortresses, and shopping will become entertainment and diversion. The home fortress will be the center of production, security, and consumption. Under this scenario, we will work, feel safe, and consume in our banal bulwarks.

Politically, it is the task of the legitimization of violence to destroy the physical body in a manner acceptable to the abstracted social "body." It is part of the paternal mind-set whose policy, as evident in Vietnam, is to destroy the village in order to save it. Such is the case in violence against women, where male violence is legitimated by theories of innate violence, describing it as something natural and beyond self-control, and hence requires women to accommodate their behavior as non-provocation to the accusatory, so-called inalterable, male violence. The social control of the body may be couched in a scientific or anthropological narrative that ensures the continuance of the symbolic and enacted social order to such a degree that the body is virtually eliminated from the cultural symbolic discourse.

The popularized Freudian bondage between sex and violence is a destructive decoy created by the violence mythos to divert the cultural imagination away from the real issues: life survival and trauma. As long as the ersatz interpersonal dynamic of hostile sex and violence is perpetuated, the war between the sexes can be legitimated as "natural" between an "innately overtly aggressive male" and a "provocative covertly compliant female." The violence mythos can then perpetuate its hero/perpetrator paradigmatic initiation rites of millions of men and women to adulthood: war and rape. These unresolved trauma traces then can be repeated in self-reinforcing subsequent exploitive social and sexual relationships in maladapted cultural beliefs, attitudes, behaviors, and expectations.

To recontextualize the exploitive interpersonal dynamic as interdependent survival and trauma requires the risk of self-exposure in an openness to good will and trust. This is the assurance of safe somatic negotiation in relationships that respect mutual limitation, fallibility, and needs. The hero and perpetrator dissolve from unresolved psychic trauma images into assimilated experiences in an effective personal history. Ricoeur was right to a degree. The id, ego, and superego are roles in a personology.[60] However, they are not limited to the anonymous and suprapersonal in the individual's coming-to-be. They are the triadic roles of self, other, and world internalized as somatic interchanges of trust and of trauma, which result in basic trust or basic mistrust, respectively. Following Gadamer, the generation of life within the trust triad is no longer dependent upon repetition that links past knowledge with present in a progressive teleology, and within the violence mythos, a teleology of trauma transference as dialectical. Rather, understanding consciousness has a genuine opportunity to widen its horizon by a deeper dimension,[61] the wellspring of interdependency.

There are those who may say, nice thought, but in practice, real world competitive economics is cutthroat. Not everywhere. For instance, one company in America started in 1901 as a shoe store and expanded into a multifaceted retail merchant with seventy-two different stores. In the last ten years its net sales have climbed 345 percent and in fiscal year 1992 stood at $3.4 billion. It is the fourth-generation family company, Nordstrom. In the poor state of the economy over the last few years, the company has managed strong growth compared to moderate performance by the competition. The company attributes this to one of its competitive advantages: the Nordstrom culture. The company is a decentralized customer-focused system: "The customers and the front line employees are those that steer the direction of the company. . . [they] make immediate decisions that affect the way they interact with the customer . . . their number one rule is 'To use their own good judgment in all situations.' Few other rules apply. This explicit trust by management has created immense company loyalty among the employees,"[62] and economic success for the company as a whole.

Disembodied Technology

There are those who fret at the ruin technology would eventually bring to us, on the order of Hardison, Jacques Ellul, or Neil Postman.[63] It merely serves to alienate ourselves by seeing technology as some external force with which we wage a war of "loving resistance."[64] According to Postman, the so-called fight with technology is morally justified, for the "technology story, with its emphasis on progress without limits, rights without responsibilities and technology without cost . . . is without a moral center."[65] Indeed, this view of technology as a dehumanized product of culture is an echo of the Heideggerian warning that "the coming to presence of technology threatens reveal-ing [the truth of being], threatens it with the possibility that all reveal-ing will be consumed in ordering . . . Human activity can never directly counter this danger. Human achievement alone can never banish it."[66] However, Heidegger then adds that there was a time when it was not this threatening technology alone that bore the name *techné*. It is also the name for the arts and skills of the craftsperson and the arts of the mind and fine arts.[67] There was a time when bringing forth the true into the beautiful was called *"techné,"* and the *poiesis* of the fine arts also was called *"techné."*[68] Here Heidegger articulates a tradition long obscured in a cultural preoccupation with militarism and scientific progress, a tradition from which Snow's two cultures arose.

This tradition also is reflected in Marshal McLuhan's understand-ing of technology as extension of the human senses: "The power of technology to create its own world of demand is not independent of technology being first an extension of our own bodies and senses . . . As long as we adopt the Narcissus attitude of regarding extensions of our own bodies as really *out there* and really independent of us, we will meet all technological challenges" with a "banana-skin pirouette and collapse."[69] We can reconfigure the definition of technologies from their traditionally objectivated status as threatening inhuman tools, to re-sponsible augmentations of the senses that exist in the world.

To elaborate, Ursula Franklin describes the concept of 'technol-ogy as practice,' and as practice, it also defines the content.[70] She gives the example of listening or playing a particular piece of music in-tended as a spiritual plea for deliverance, that is not prayer. For Franklin, the technology of doing something also defines the activity itself, and thus "precludes the emergence of other ways of doing 'it', whatever 'it' may be."[71] Broadly, she describes the difference between holistic and prescriptive technologies. Holistic technologies are spe-cialization by product, where an artisan is in control of the productive process through situational decisions unique to the product. The op-posite specialization by process is prescriptive technology. Here, the production of something is broken down into clearly identifiable steps carried out by different workers through a division of labor.[72] She sees prescriptive technologies as designs for compliance, where "a workforce becomes acculturated into a milieu in which external control and internal compliance are seen as normal and necessary."[73]

Franklin acknowledges that prescriptive technologies have developed products that have raised the standard of living and increased well-being, while simultaneously instilling people with compliance and conformity. Prescriptive technologies as used in administration, government, and social services also have contributed to "diminished resistance to the programming of people."[74] Thus, the real world of technology seems to promote a dichotomy between people and machines and shift concern to "machine demography" and "machine population control" where there is "an inherent trust in machines and devices ("production is under control") and a basic apprehensiveness of people ("growth is chancy, one can never be sure of the outcome").[75]

The disembodiment of technology is part of the larger devaluation of the body and valuation of the mind, which also alienates emotion from a complete understanding of self. The observations of a medical doctor's diagnostic discourse with patients are helpful here. In effect, the disembodiment of unpleasant emotion construes them as external entities, that somehow "invade" the boundaries of the self. "We suffer from a 'panic *attack*,' an 'attack of nerves,' an 'attack of the Blues.'"[76] The emotions that are seen as "anti-social—like fear, rage, envy and hate—are the ones most often spoken of as if they were something separate, and somehow not part of the idealized self-image now common in the Western world," an ideal of a "paragon of self-care and self-control" with no place in society for the "the ill, the unhappy or the ugly."[77] The ideal hero is worshipped and the shadow perpetrator condemned, while the human being suffers in sanitized silence.

Technology and Interdependence

The association of anger or rage with the antisocial is evident in the text of the early Chinese military stategist Sun-tzu, where "killing the enemy is a matter of arousing the anger of our men."[78] The association of anger, hate, instrumenatal violence, and war shows military technology as an extension of violent behavior. Military technology from ancient times has been the weapon of warfare, alongside those technologies which were used to provide the foundation of a society's material life.[79] In Western culture, technology retains its associations with hostility and militarism, in popular attitudes wary of technology adoption and the memory traces of its intent to control and destroy.

Among the hostile and unpleasant byproducts of the cultural development of technology for military and other purposes, the factor least understood is interdependence.[80] Modern technology does not occur as isolated units, but as "complex systems that require widespread interactions and interdependence."[81] Insofar as telecommunications has been shown to be a medium of cooperation, history has given ample evidence to the contrary, in wars and espionage. The scientific revolution used technology to gain human power over nature, and in the twentieth century has shown the "power over nature can be transformed into the power of some people over others. In an era of conflicts, telecommunications has been both a weapon and a cause of national rivalries. Its history reflects the nature of its time."[82] The secrecy of warfare is not to be confused with national security. "In the age of information, less secrecy may well mean less fear of sudden surprise, and therefore more security."[83] In the open exchange of information, at all levels of human relationship, there may be hope, with Ferdinand de Lesseps, that "men, by knowing one another, will finally cease fighting."[84]

The prospect of humans knowing one another carries with it the indirect assumption that the honest exchange of information and the rites through which this information is exchanged will garner peaceful relationships of trust and respect. This is the opposite of the relationships of mistrust, conflict, fighting, and war, as "Warfare is the art (*tao*) of deceit."[85] The transience and tragedy of rage and of war are profoundly acknowledged by Sun-Tzu: "A person in a fit of rage can be restored to good cheer, but a state that has perished cannot be revived, and the dead cannot be brought back to life."[86]

The associations among anger, violence, and technology in the military tradition have as their effect a fear of anger and technology as violent, destructive, oppressive. Anger itself becomes something to fear, to suppress, to deny. In so doing, far less than with its appropriate uninjurious expression, anger serves to alienate oneself from one's experience and that of others. It becomes acted out in destructive antisocial behavior, reinforced through the transmission of the acceptance of the valuation of violence and devaluation of emotion and the body in trauma transference in the violence mythos. So, too, with technology. As an extension of the body, the history of technology mirrors the history of its culture.

The quandaries as to the blame or neutrality of technology are irrelevant, as technology is an extension of the tradition of cultural values of its time. It may serve as an indirect reflection of those values a society is reluctant to acknowledge. Like the body and other "illegitimate irrationals" marginalized by the mind/body dualism, technology may be scapegoated as antihuman and out of the bounds of legitimate morality, indeed, accused of being "without a moral center." In failing to take responsibility for the development of technologies in trauma transference, instead of appropriate to interdependent social life, we make technology not a straw, but a silicon tiger.

The nature of Western culture has been influenced by the valuation and sanction of violence and has developed technologies accordingly. In the shift from the industrial era to the information era, Alvin Toffler sees the primary struggle as not between capitalist democracy and totalitarianism, "but between 21st-century democracy and 11th-century darkness."[87] He sees xenophobic ethnicism, religious fundamentalism, and eco-medievalism linked together in a different brand of totalitarian universalism that is determined to impose rule over every aspect of human life and retract the freedoms of democracy.[88] Indeed, it was the medieval valuation of the intrinsic goodness of physical strength that gave violence cultural legitimacy, a legitimacy that the violence mythos has been wont to rescind when challenged. Yet the opportunities toward change present themselves and are uniquely exemplified in military sophistication as the possibility of conducting nonlethal warfare.[89]

With violent behavior placed in the arena of alternative socially appropriate behaviors, the persistence of human choice prevails. McLuhan quotes John Kenneth Galbraith on the implications of group decision making fostered by the interdependency of technology where nearly everyone's actions are known to others: "This acts to reinforce the code, and, more than incidentally, a high standard of personal honesty as well. The technostructure does not permit of the privacy that misfeasance and malfeasance require."[90] Indeed, it is the free flow of digital and electronic information on a global scale that renders technologies without boundaries accessible to particular individual users who replace the passive mass users of the industrial age with more vigorous interaction.[91] This does not necessarily mean the accessibility of information will lead to the democratization of power relationships. It may simply serve to reinforce existing organizational arrangements and power distributions in organizations.[92]

However, the validity of these arrangements can be called into question and exposed as based predominantly on the exploitive hierarchical representation of the mind/body dualism in the violence mythos. The cultural success of this model to provide societal survival has suffered. In the United States, in the absence of legitimate external foes and due to the loss of its cold war perpetrator/antagonist, the heroic war machine has had to fall back on the internalization of conflict in heroic domestic social wars of attrition.

The social consequences of the mind/body split have the opportunity to be altered in a new openness and exposure to alternative cultures, for instance those of the Orient, offered by the prospect of global access in the interactive age of digital convergence and customization. As we and our cohabitants in the world become more interdependent, the information required for decision making and action becomes more crucial for survival. The costs of conflict cancel the possibility of survival and require humans to discard the terrorism of the violence mythos as a relic of the passing industrial age and to learn the ways of cooperation.

The information delivery transformation from paper to pixels in the digital economy is like riding in a car after using a horse and buggy. It is more convenient, faster, and more interesting, yet with less real feel. There is a rise in Internet online services, including financial, retail, news, educational, and medical applications to name a few. World Wide Web pages intrigue the senses with multimedia (audio, text, video, graphics). The information glut is becoming less cumbersome with the advent of smart technologies such as knowbots and intelligent agents, or specialized software tools that are employed to perform tasks for users in virtual reality.[93] Online social interaction is facilitated by virtual communities, newsgroups, and MUDs (multiuser dungeons).[94] Interactive videoconferencing and interactive television trials inch us toward a cyber simulation of social interaction in the "real world" that has become increasingly intolerable and unsafe.

It is not solely a retreat to the so-called home fortress/prison that drives the push toward digital delivery systems. Humans base our behaviors on decisions derived from associative, expectant interpretations of our experience. Decisions require information, whether time critical or recreational. Access to information is crucial, for once we have it, we can assess our options and manage our responses to our environment, time phased as we deem appropriate. Instantaneous information delivery may serve to aid the decision-making process if ubiquitously and consciously accessible. To this end, high-speed communications networks such as the National Information Infrastructure in the United States will include applications for managing distributed databases and electronic libraries, distance education and lifelong learning, telemedicine, multimedia tutorials for environmental assessment, and more.[95] Overwhelming in quantity, instantaneous information may not necessarily be disempowering. It may require that we make more conscious decisions about information use, privacy, availability, responsibilities, priorities, and boundaries that were previously taken for granted.

The ubiquitous computing designs from Xerox PARC foresee a time when computers become invisible and nonintrusive, enabling us to use them without thinking and focus beyond them on new goals.[96] These computer-augmented environments merge distributed electronic systems into the physical world, instead of using computers to position people in an artificial world, as does virtual reality. See-through displays and projectors allow everyday objects to take on electronic properties without losing their familiar physical properties.[97] For example, an electronic whiteboard is an electronic surface that looks like a whiteboard. However, it uses an electronic stylus to input information like a scripting touchscreen, as well as a keyboard. Graphic and video images may be imported to the display. Data then may be captured electronically for distribution as a file or printed as hard copy.

It is these types of technology applications that may enhance our lives, that fly in the face of technology naysayers shrouded in the shadow of the tradition of ominous military technologies created in the exploitive imbalance of the violence mythos. We need to monitor appropriately and guide technologies of vicarious and direct traumatization while developing technologies of interdependence and global sustenance. We need technologies to fit the multidimensionality of our complex postmodern linguistic and somatic interchanges in our world. Fond as I am of playing in muddy clay on the wheel or up to my happy elbows in charcoal after a life drawing session, I experience equally a thrill at keyframing an animation sequence and viewing the playback that zips the image across the screen. The same goes for the beauty of David Rokeby's interactive *Very Nervous System* when I arc my arm and sway in an open space, creating music through movement that is recorded and translated into sound by a sophisticated system of behind-the-scenes videocameras, synthesizers, computers, and other electronic equipment. Technology has wonder in it too.

There has been some speculation that instead of trailing behind industrialized nations, emerging countries are in a unique position to leapfrog over some of the industrialized world by deploying inexpensive wireless network technologies without having to dismantle and upgrade cumbersome existing systems characteristic of many firms in developed countries. Nicholas Negroponte sees the openness of the Net as an opportunity for emerging nations to participate in the global economy of ideas. They "can no longer pretend they are too poor to reciprocate with basic, bold, and new ideas."[98] Research previously published in journals months after submission can become instantaneously available globally on the Net. The claim that "a developing nation can only draw from the inventory of ideas that comes from wealthy countries" is "rubbish." The digital world should do away with debtor nations. "In the new balance of trade of ideas, very small players can contribute very big ideas."[99] If the digital economy contributes to the actual dismantling of the victimized state of postcolonial countries and the actual retraction of the dominance of industrial nations over them, then these may be worthy objectives. The virtual playing field must be a fair playing field, not an aphasiac battlefield.

Virtually and physically, humans may learn to enjoy the friendship and company of their fellow humans and share in the sometime tranquillity of the sage under the bo tree. Edward Feigenbaum and Pamela McCorduck ponder Yoneiji Masuda's vision where "our knowledge-rich future will coax us away from a preoccupation with material concerns and toward a preoccupation with the nonmaterial."[100] This would take the form of freedom for individual self-actualization and a possible worldwide religious renaissance, not storied by belief in a transcendent god, but rather by "awe and humility in the presence of the collective human spirit and its wisdom, humanity living in a symbolic tranquillity with the planet we have found ourselves upon, regulated by a new set of global ethics."[101] A sensitivity to and respect for cultural differences needs to be heeded as we address the humanization of computing and the issues of privacy, accessibility, and network access equity, as well as the applications of biotechnology, such as the Human Genome Project.[102]

A Synoptic Glance

The purpose of this text has been to rethink the context of and the assumptions about violence in Western culture. The result has been to reconfigure violence as an effect of transgenerational trauma transference that obscures the valuation of the body, trust, and technologies in relationships of interdependent respect. The task has also been to question the direct legitimization of violent behavior of the hero and the indirect acceptance of perpetrator practices of social divisiveness and blaming the victim. The underside of the acceptance of the violence of mistrust is the devaluation of the trust triad, the constricted interpretation and expression of anger and emotion, and misplaced ascription of violence to technology.

Symbolic discourse has been used as a key phenomenon, in its function as a type of communal memory chip, that allows the urgent stories for a community to be compressed into coded information and transmitted between generations with little effort to ensure a culture's understanding of itself and hence survive. History functions as a comprehensive purveyor of vicarious learning, replacing trillions of decisions that one would have to make on one's own at great risk of survival, with compressed information that has had survival value for a community, from which decisions have been made and with which decisions will be made about one's place, behaviors, and expectations in relationship with others and the world. As such, history is a tale of ties. In the West, this has meant learning much about attempting to control perpetual trauma and less about understanding and preventing it.

The purpose has been to probe a larger perspective of the culture in which most of the presented materials developed, while acknowledging the silent stories of the voiceless victims of violence. The inquiry into indirect acceptance of norms and values of the legitimacy of violence has questioned what David Tracy calls "our all-too-canny illusions of rationality and humanity."[103] Cultural interpretation has required an emphasis upon the historical and symbolic nature of discourse and praxis. This in turn allows for the analysis of beliefs arising from experience and the role of consent in authority and tradition, ideology, and alternatives in the transmission and the possibility of changing those beliefs.

Within the violence mythos, the discourses of the two approaches to violence, innate and acquired behavior, were elaborated through the texts of the human sciences and types of violence, namely war, murder, rape, assault. These concrete considerations shifted to the mythic history and development of the hero mythology. The theoretical perspectives of Freud, Ricoeur, Girard, and Derrida exposed the dynamics of the trust triad and the trauma triad in linguistic and somatic interchange and the cultural imagination.

In the interdependent mythos, restoration of trust included exploring Gadamer's play in tradition and the trust process upon which it depends. The continuance of culture rests upon the success of trust and respect in human relations in order to continue to risk in the life process in the somatic interchange of attachment. Technology was presented as an extension of human experience in the tradition of vicarious and direct trauma, with possibilities for enhancement of trust.

I have sought to open avenues for discourse on reinterpretations of what Western culture has sanctioned as legitimate violence, from its explicit conscious expressions in militarism to its quiet indirect acceptance and endorsement of innate male violence, against men themselves, women, and children in the model for masculinity as hero/ perpetrator. The tentacles of the violence mythos are varied discourses that radiate from a central cultural belief in innate violence that masks unresolved trauma. Integrating trauma traces in a dimensional identity without the center of violence, the tentacles transform into schools of interdependent agents.

The text has consistently emphasized the relational aspect of violence and hence opted for a mutual responsibility for violence between those who commit acts of violence and the society in which we live. It is not a binary logic of either/or, it is the wholistic logic of both/and. We need to have measures that consider the both/and when we redress traumatic violence. This text also has emphasized the lacuna in our language for trauma talk about anger, emotion, and vulnerability, a lacuna that stems from the long association and devaluation of body, emotion, women, and animality. Thus, the broader discourse of Western culture has not expressed these aspects of human existence in complexity or sophistication, or validation, as they have been devalued and marginalized in the discourse of the violence mythos. We need a richer, broader lexicon to accommodate the language of somatic interchange in the trust triad and its postmodern dimensions.

We need cultural trauma detoxification with transgenerational traditions, practices, attitudes, and understanding. We need to be able to process pain, to understand it, and to develop a social sensibility of interdependency. Withdrawal from the hero/perpetrator mythology will not be easy for men or for women. Trust takes time, something of which the trauma technostructure is intolerant. Time is the realm of feeling, and our emotional processing does not abide by the rules of hi-tech, hi-speed compression. We have surpassed the pace of our organic biorhythms with digital technology. We cannot keep up with the pace of technological change, nor should we; it should be made to conform to our collective needs. We have taken the wrong bait in ascribing an inherent value to technical advance as culturally enhancing, as better. Just because it is possible does not mean it is necessary. Like the addiction to violence, there is an addiction to technology, the simulation hero. It is the fifty-seven channels and nothing on syndrome. Well, nothing except more trauma that is arché-ic and by now, boring. The Hollywood training manual on 999,000 ways to blow up *anything* is out of date. We need to clean up the toxic trauma waste/traces that have devastated our somatic interchanges of self, other, and world with alienation, suspicion, and exploitation. We need to refocus our attention on what we need to live and sustain healthy, satisfactory lives as interdependent humans.

The shift from violence to respect requires a comprehensive revaluation of relationship within culture. Violence is a learned and habituated behavioral response—through tradition, symbolic modeling, and experience. It has been culturally sanctioned for centuries and reinforced in the symbolic discourse and action of trauma transference. Prevention and accountability for violent behavior thus require a reinterpretation of cultural symbolization and institutions as well as the meaning of responsible human behavior. This includes a reintegration between mind and body, where we learn to trust and to care for our bodies and listen to what our bodies tell us about the health of our lifestyles.

A revaluation of masculinity as heroic brutality with the "strength"/isolation to tolerate physical and emotional pain includes acknowledging the validity of fear, vulnerability, empathy, and attachment needs. The acceptance of the hero myth has developed through indirect acquiescence, or the willingness to engage in a given social practice or tradition, to social agreements made through repetition and reinforcement in childhood and socialization, and enforced through social acceptance or ostracism based on hero imitation and hero worship. The acceptance of the perpetrator role as hero double/antagonist has developed through the indirect acquiescence to social agreements about innate violence and male aggressiveness, leaving a boundaryless shadow world of complete freedom to exploit. If violence is innate, or predetermined, the perpetrator cannot be held responsible for what is "natural." In this context, brutality is to be accepted and feared and requires overwhelming by heroic effort, making the hero indispensable to cultural survival and trauma legitimate. The symbolic associations of the perpetrator include the body, emotion, private life, creativity, change, nature, and invisibility, the devalued counterparts to the hero. The hero's world is controlled, visible, and scanned with the suspicious gaze/mind: one cannot fight what one cannot see/understand. The true counterpart of the perpetrator is the victim, who is rendered invisible to the point of nonexistence, as the hero/perpetrator dualism replaces the true trauma dynamic of perpetrator/victim/rescuer in culture. The victim is placed outside of the moral order determined by the hero/perpetrator, in a silent secrecy dominated by the perpetrator, invisible to detection by the heroic gaze.

The culture implicitly and explicitly accepts this heroic order of things. In order to sustain the false façade of invulnerability it depends upon for survival, it requires the hero and the hero's foe, the perpetrator. Caught in the compulsive replication of a fantastic dualism, the culture preoccupies itself with death in order to survive. Life and its ordinary cycles of birth, growth, adulthood, partnering, reproduction, and death are overshadowed, overwhelmed by the repetitive dualing Banquos. The victim is a reality threat to this maladaptive coping mechanism. To allow the victim equal position would restore the essentially triadic nature of things and would risk revealing that the hero has no armor, only skin, and the perpetrator no shadow, only a face, and the victim no violence, only a need to live.

The culture thus collapses the trauma triad and renders the trust triad unintelligible in the unassimilated memory traces maladapted into a repeating dualism. It constructs direct assumptions that elaborate symbolic associations, attitudes, beliefs, and behaviors centered around compulsive innate violence and its need for control and the corresponding perpetrator and hero roles in the violence mythos. Its indirect assumptions disintegrate the trust triad of self, other, and world and deny the victim, and hence vulnerable, bounded, interdependent life.

Problems in communities—be they internecine warfare, drugs, youth alienation/neglect, the wounded frustration of men, the safety of women and children, or the loneliness of the elderly—cannot find effective solutions if they are hidden behind walls of denial and lost in unresolved trauma traces. Solutions can be found in the openness of active dialogue, participation, and the willingness to work together by community members and business and government agencies to promote mutual confidence and commitment.

The addiction to violence and the paranoid rationality tied to technology have withdrawal symptoms. Prisoners released from long-term confinement are disoriented and recoil from freedom foreign to them. So too the culture of the violence mythos will need to learn to tolerate a decrease in hyperarousal and anxiety to learn to expect responsible behavior from themselves and others based upon respect, equity, and participation. The decades of restive disillusionment of the 1960s, 1970s, and 1980s showed the results of centuries-old resistance and social upheaval toward colonialism, racism, sexism, and domestic and child abuse that left us confused and disoriented. The 1990s have roused resentment, mistrust, and beleaguered hope that our multidimensional world can somehow be understood enough to survive. We are war weary. Instead of trauma reenactments, it is time to rejuvenate, reintegrate, and reschematize our understandings of our selves and our worlds, this time with an understanding of traumatology that has bound us in a cycle of transgenerational exploitation.

It is time to let the trauma triad roles rest in peace and listen to each other as humans. The hero/rescuer has had the weight of centuries of civilization on all-too-human shoulders for too long. The perpetrator has been trapped in mistrust and exploitation to the point of asocial isolation. The victim has been trammeled by trauma traces for generations. We can celebrate our local heros in our collective ties that connect and heal our sometime perpetrators in our collective pain that understands interdependent responsibility. Most of all, we can empower our silent victims in our reciprocal relations of ordinary lives that affirm and sustain us in the cyclical continuity of generations. We can release ourselves from the trauma triad when we give trust a try. "There are many things in life that you cannot get by a brutal approach. You must invite them."[104]

In a study of thirty thousand American centenarians, researchers found a common denominator of primary factors in their longevity.[105] In reverse order of priority, these were successfully coping with loss, keeping busy, and maintaining a positive attitude. "Success or failure, the truth of a life really has little to do with its quality. The quality of life is in proportion, always, to the capacity for delight. The capacity for delight is the gift of paying attention."[106] And attention takes time, for ourselves, others, and the world. Priscilla Presley remembers a time with Elvis at their Circle G ranch in Mississippi: "There was always a lot of jamming. Elvis, Lamar Fike, and Charlie Hodge would get together in the middle of the room, harmonizing a favorite song. When they were really going good Elvis would yell, 'Whew! Hot damn! One more time!' He'd sometimes spend an hour just on an ending because it had 'the *feel*—the ingredients of a masterpiece.' "[107]

Some memories we want to forget, some memories we can, if we heal properly. Some memories we cannot, but we need not constantly remember. In learning how to let go, we learn how to get. In learning how to get, we learn how to give. Some times we get memories we want to keep. Some times, if we pay attention, we get—the *feel*—of life. One more time . . .

NOTES

Introduction

1. The distinction between myth and mythos is brought to bear here. Myth, as a narrative of events that are said to have happened, or, conversely, certainly not what happened, differs from mythos in that mythos depicts a movement in time up to and followed by an act of understanding. Northrop Frye gives the example of a joke, where someone may say, "Stop me if you've heard this one," because if we "see" the joke, the joke is all over, and what is considered is the afterimage of its structure. In this respect, myth is the "joke," and mythos is the "seeing" of the "joke." And so, in telling the discourses of the myths of violence, seeing their interconnectedness is seeing the violence mythos. See Northrop Frye, *Myth and Metaphor: Selected Essays, 1974–1988* (Charlottesville: University Press of Virginia, 1990), 6.

2. The idea of the use of tautological legitimations to uphold social structures is not new. Theorists such as Marx and Gramsci have used it to critique the ideological link between individualism and capitalism. For violence and culture, as Elisabeth Bronfen points out, in his study of Freud, Ricoeur analyzed culture as making life prevail against death. See Elisabeth Bronfen, "The Jew as Woman's Symptom: Kathlyn Bigelow's Conflictive Representation of Feminine Power," in *Violence and Mediation in Contemporary Culture* (Albany: State University of New York Press, 1996), ed. Ronald Bogue and Marcel Cornis-Pope, 77. For Ricoeur, culture's "supreme weapon is to employ internalized violence against externalized violence; its supreme ruse is to make death work against death." See Paul Ricoeur, *Freud and Philosophy: An Essay on Interpretation* (New Haven: Yale University Press, 1970), trans. Denis Savage, 309.

3. Marc Luyckx, "Religions Confronted with Science and Technology: Churches and Ethics after Prometheus," Report for Forecasting and Assessment in Science and Technology (Brussels: Commission of the European Communities, August 1992), 35.

4. Ibid., 36.

5. Judith Lewis Herman, *Trauma and Recovery: The Aftermath of Violence-from Domestic Abuse to Political Terror* (New York: Basic Books, 1992), 32.

6. Lynn White, Jr., "The Historical Roots of Our Ecological Crisis," in *Western Man and Environmental Ethics* (Reading, MA: Addison-Wesley, 1973), ed. Ian G. Barbour, 24.

7. L. S. Stavrianos, *Global Rift: The Third World Comes of Age* (New York: William Morrow and Company, 1981), 173.

8. See Max Horkheimer and Theodor W. Adorno, *Dialectic of Enlightenment* (New York: Seabury Press, 1944); Max Horkheimer, *Critique of Instrumental Reason* (New York: Continuum, 1974); and Herbert Marcuse, *One-Dimensional Man* (Boston: Beacon Press, 1964).

9. Stavrianos, *Global Rift*, 42.

10. Calvin O. Schrag, *Communicative Praxis and the Space of Subjectivity* (Bloomington: Indiana University Press, 1986), 157.

11. Manfred Stanley, *The Technological Conscience: Survival and Dignity in an Age of Expertise* (Chicago: The University of Chicago Press, 1978), 102.

12. Ibid., 103.

13. Ibid.

14. Clifford Geertz, *The Interpretation of Cultures* (New York: Basic Books, Inc., 1973), 241.

15. Paul Ricoeur, *Interpretation Theory: Discourse and the Surplus of Meaning* (Fort Worth: The Texas Christian University Press, 1976), 19.

16. Mgr. Paul Poupard avec une Déclaration de Jean-Paul II, *Galileo Galilei: 350 ans d'histoire 1633–1983* (Tournai: Desclée International, 1983).

17. Martin Van Creveld, *Technology and War: From 2000 B.C. to the Present* (New York: The Free Press, 1989), 314.

18. Ursula Franklin, *The Real World of Technology* (Toronto: CBC Enterprises, 1990), 78.

19. Rosemary Radford Ruether, *Sexism and God-Talk: Toward a Feminist Theology* (Boston: Beacon Press, 1983), 54.

20. Ibid.

21. Gerda Lerner, *The Creation of Patriarchy* (New York: Oxford University Press, 1986), 52.

22. Michel Foucault, *The History of Sexuality: Volume I: An Introduction* (New York: Vintage Books, 1980), 68.

23. Ibid., 69.

24. Lerner, *The Creation of Patriarchy*, 52–53.

25. Jacques Ellul, *The Technological Society* (New York: Alfred Knopf, 1964); and *The Technological System* (New York: Continuum, 1980).

26. Marshal McLuhan, *Understanding Media: The Extensions of Man* (New York: Mentor, 1964).

1. The Violence Question: What Is It?

1. Antoine de Saint Exupéry, *The Little Prince* (New York: Harcourt Brace Jovanovich, 1943), 87.

2. Northrop Frye, "The Cultural Development of Canada," Address to the Social Sciences and Humanities Research Council of Canada (Hart House, University of Toronto, October 17, 1990), 2.

3. Ibid.

4. Northrop Frye, *Myth and Metaphor: Selected Essays*, 1974–1988 (Charlottesville: University Press of Virginia, 1990), 5.

5. Ibid.

6. José Miguez Bonino, *Toward a Christian Political Ethics* (Philadelphia: Fortress Press, 1983), 50.

7. Ibid.

8. Edward S. Herman and Noam Chomsky, *Manufacturing Consent: The Political Economy of the Mass Media* (New York: Pantheon Books, 1988).

9. See Susan Thistlethwaite, *Sex, Race and God: Christian Feminism in Black and White* (New York: Crossroad, 1989); and Sharon Welch, *A Feminist Ethic of Risk* (Minneapolis: Fortress Press, 1990).

10. Robert McAfee Brown, *Religion and Violence* (Philadelphia: The Westminster Press, 1987), 2nd ed., 7.

11. Ibid.

12. Ibid., 8.

13. Ibid., 73.

14. Ibid., 97.

15. Paul Ricoeur, *The Rule of Metaphor* (Toronto: University of Toronto Press, 1977), 285.

16. David E. Klemm, *The Hermeneutical Theory of Paul Ricoeur: A Constructive Analysis* (Lewisburg: Bucknell University Press, 1983), 109.

17. Leonard Lawlor, *Imagination and Chance: The Difference between the Thought of Ricoeur and Derrida* (Albany: State University of New York Press, 1992), 1.

18. Hans-Georg Gadamer, *Truth and Method* (New York: Crossroad, 1975), 357.

19. Stanley, *The Technological Conscience*, 108.

20. Ibid.

21. Ibid.

22. Ibid., 109.

23. M. F. Ashley Montagu, "The New Litany of 'Innate Depravity,' or Original Sin Revisited," in *Man and Aggression* (New York: Oxford University Press, 1968), ed. M. F. Ashley Montagu, 3.

24. Ibid., 5.

25. Dale Purves, *Body and Brain: A Trophic Theory of Neural Connections* (Cambridge: Harvard University Press, 1988), 172.

26. Friedrich von Bernhardi, as cited in Montagu, *Man and Aggression*, 10.

27. Albert Bandura, "Psychological Mechanisms of Aggression," in *Aggression: Theoretical and Empirical Reviews* (New York: Academic Press, 1983), vol. 1, ed. Russell G. Geen and Edward I. Donnerstein, 2.

28. Robin M. Williams, Jr., "The Legitimate and Illegitimate Uses of Violence: A Review of Ideas and Evidence," in *Violence and the Politics of Research* (New York: Plenum Press, 1981), ed. Willard Gaylin, Ruth Macklin, and Tabitha M. Powledge, 26.

29. Connie Guberman and Margie Wolfe, eds., *No Safe Place: Violence against Women and Children* (Toronto: The Women's Press, 1985), 12.

30. T. Tedeschi, "Social Influence Theory and Aggression," in *Aggression: Theoretical and Empirical Reviews* (New York: Academic Press, 1983), vol. 1, ed. Russell G. Geen and Edward I. Donnerstein, 154–55.

31. Robin M. Williams, Jr., "The Legitimate and Illegitimate Uses of Violence," 26.

32. Sigmund Freud, *Civilization and Its Discontents* (New York: W. W. Norton & Company, 1961), trans. James Strachey, 42.

33. Ibid., 58.

34. Anatol Rapoport, *The Origins of Violence: Approaches to the Study of Conflict* (New York: Paragon House, 1989), 10.

35. Alfie Kohn, *The Brighter Side of Human Nature: Altruism and Empathy in Everyday Life* (New York: Basic Books, Inc., 1990), 46.

36. Ibid.

37. Lorenz claims that the human has "in his heart the aggression drive inherited from his anthropoid ancestors, which this same intelligence cannot control." Konrad Lorenz, *On Aggression* (London: Methuen & Co. Ltd., 1963), trans. Marjorie Latzke, 40–42.

38. Montagu, *Man and Aggression*, 11.

39. Ibid., 14.

40. Purves, *Body and Brain*, 16.

41. Ibid., 42.

42. Ibid., 165.

43. Ibid., 172.

44. Ibid.

45. Ibid.

46. Montagu, *Man and Aggression*, 16.

47. Roland Littlewood and Maurice Lipsedge, *Aliens and Alienists: Ethnic Minorities and Psychiatry* (London: Unwin Hyman, 1989), 2d ed., 223.

48. Dana Crowley Jack, *Silencing the Self: Women and Depression* (Cambridge: Harvard University Press, 1991), 122.

49. Albert Bandura, "Psychological Mechanisms of Aggression," 4.

50. Ibid.

51. Larsen, *Aggression*, 48.

52. Ibid.

53. Vernon Mark and Frank Ervin, *Violence and the Brain* (New York: Harper and Row, 1970), 6.

54. Ibid., 156.

55. Ibid., 132.

56. Luigi Valzelli, *Psychobiology of Aggression and Violence* (New York: Raven Press, 1981), 73.

57. Elliot Valenstein, *Great and Desperate Cures* (New York: Basic Books Inc., 1965), 337.

58. Ibid., 339.

59. Ibid., 338.

60. Ibid.

61. Ibid., 339.

62. Allan M. Brandt, *No Magic Bullet: A Social History of Venereal Disease in the United States since 1880* (New York: Oxford University Press, 1987), 203. Brandt's discussion of the social consruction of AIDS is helpful in pointing out the difficult task of separating deeply irrational fears from scientific understanding in the social construction of disease and a disease's close association with violation of the moral code. The "violent individual" has this dual association of disease, or dysfunction, and moral violation (as injurious to others).

63. Larsen, *Aggression: Myths and Models*, 48.

64. Ibid.

65. Kohn, *The Brighter Side of Human Nature*, 49.

66. S. L. A. Marshall, *Men against Fire*, as quoted in Kohn, 50.

67. Al Santoli, *Everything We Had: An Oral History of the Vietnam War by Thirty-three American Soldiers Who Fought It* (New York: Ballantine Books, 1981), 64.

68. Larsen, *Aggression: Myths and Models*, 49.

69. Ibid., 50.

70. Bandura, "Psychological Mechanisms of Aggression," 12.

71. Ibid., 13.

72. Larsen, *Aggression: Myths and Models*, 50.

73. Larry Baron and Murray A. Straus, *Four Theories of Rape in American Society: A State-Level Analysis* (New Haven: Yale University Press, 1989), 151.

74. Ibid.

75. Bandura, "Psychological Mechanisms of Aggression," 13.

76. Ibid., 12.

77. Larsen, *Aggression: Myths and Models*, 4.

78. K. E. Moyer, *Violence and Aggression: A Physiological Perspective* (New York: Paragon House Publishers, 1987), 100.

79. Bandura, "Psychological Mechanisms of Aggression," 12.

80. Ibid.

81. Leonard Berkowitz, "The Experience of Anger as a Parallel Process," in *Aggression: Theoretical and Empirical Reviews* (New York: Academic Press, 1983), vol. 1, ed. Russell G. Geen and Edward I. Donnerstein, 112.

82. Roger Trigg, *Pain and Emotion* (Oxford: Clarendon Press, 1970), 8.

83. Alice Miller, *For Your Own Good: Hidden Cruelty in Child-Rearing and the Roots of Violence* (New York: Farrar, Straus and Giroux, 1983), trans. Hildegarde and Hunter Hannum, 261.

84. Ibid., 262.

85. Cheshire Calhoun and Robert C. Solomon, *What Is an Emotion? Classical Readings in Philosophical Psychology* (New York: Oxford University Press, 1984), 4.

86. Ibid., 13.

87. Ibid., 26.

88. Ibid., 22.

89. Ibid., 31.

90. Bandura, "Psychological Mechanisms of Aggression," 11.

91. Ibid.

92. Ibid.

93. Ibid., 12.

94. Ibid., 4.

95. Ibid.

96. *The Opposite Sex: Program 3 Sex and Emotion*, videocassette (Hunter's Hill, N.S.W. Australia: Robin Hughes and Associates, 1993), segment feature: Dr. Leslie Rogers, University of New England.

97. Paul Ekman, ed., *Emotion in the Human Face* (Cambridge: Cambridge University Press, 1982), 1, 141–42.

98. Herman, *Trauma and Recovery*, 38.

99. Eric Erikson, *Identity: Youth and Crisis* (New York: W. W. Norton & Company, 1968), 82.

100. *The Opposite Sex: Program 3 Sex and Emotion*, videocassette (Hunter's Hill, N.S.W. Australia: Robin Hughes and Associates, 1993), segment feature: Dr. Barbara Hort, University of Oregon.

101. Aaron Kipnis, *Knights without Armor: A Practical Guide for Men in Quest of Masculine Soul* (Los Angeles: Jeremy Tarcher, 1991), 20.

102. Ibid. Kipnis cites Ashley Montagu's book *Touching: The Human Significance of Skin* for these studies.

103. Kipnis, *Knights without Armor*, 24.

104. Ibid.

105. Ibid., 21.

106. Ibid.

107. Ibid.

108. Ibid., 22.

109. Ibid., 23.

110. Ibid.

111. Ibid.

112. Bandura, "Psychological Mechanisms of Aggression," 6.

113. Ibid.

114. Ibid.

115. Ibid., 7.

116. Les Sussman and Sally Bordwell, *The Rapist File* (New York: Chelsea House, 1981), 119.

117. Bandura, "Psychological Mechanisms of Aggression," 7.

118. Peggy Reeves Sanday, as quoted in Timothey Beneke, *Men on Rape* (New York: St. Martin's Press, 1982), 10.

119. Bandura, "Psychological Mechanisms of Aggression," 7.

120. Larsen, *Aggression: Myths and Models*, 59.

121. Berkowitz, "The Experience of Anger as a Parallel Process," 112.

122. Ibid.

123. John H. Krystal, "Animal Models for Posttraumatic Stress Disorder," in *Biological Assessment and Treatment of Posttraumatic Stress Disorder* (Washington, D.C.: American Psychiatric Press, Inc., 1990), ed. Earl L. Giller, Jr., 3.

124. Bruce D. Perry, Steven M. Southwick, Rachel Yehuda, and Earl L. Giller, Jr., "Adrenergic Receptor Regulation in Posttraumatic Stress Disorder," in *Biological Assessment and Treatment of Posttraumatic Stress Disorder*, 89.

125. Herman, *Trauma and Recovery*, 51.

126. Ibid.

127. Ibid., 53.

128. Edward K. Rynearson, "The Homicide of a Child," in *Post-Traumatic Therapy and Victims of Violence* (New York: Brunner/Mazel, 1988), ed. Frank M. Ochberg, 217.

129. Krystal, "Animal Models for Posttraumatic Stress Disorder," 7.

130. Ibid., 10.

131. M. Michele Murberg, Miles E. McFall, and Richard C. Veith, "Catecholamines, Stress, and Posttraumatic Stress Disorder," in *Biological Assessment and Treatment of Posttraumatic Stress Disorder*, 47.

132. Scott Orr, "Psychophysiological Studies of Posttraumatic Stress Disorder," in *Biological Assessment and Treatment of Posttraumatic Stress Disorder*, 149.

133. Herman, *Trauma and Recovery* , 136.

134. Ibid., 137.

135. Ibid., 140.

136. Ibid.

137. James F. Monroe, Jonathan Shay, Lisa Fisher, Christine Makary, Katheryn Rapperport, and Rose Zimering, "Preventing Compassion Fatigue: A Team Treatment Model," in *Compassion Fatigue: Coping with Secondary Traumatic Stress Disorder in Those Who Treat the Traumatized* (New York: Brunner/Mazel, 1995), ed. Charles R. Figley, 210.

138. Laurie Leydie Harkness, "Transgenerational Transmission of War-Related Trauma," in *International Handbook of Traumatic Stress Syndromes* (New York: Plenum Press, 1993), ed. John Wilson and Beverley Raphael, 635.

139. Herman, *Trauma and Recovery*, 141.

140. Ibid.

141. Ibid., 139.

142. Ibid., 144.

143. Ibid., 145.

144. Ibid.

145. Daniel van Kammen and Patricia Ver Ellen, "Afterword," in *Biological Assessment and Treatment of Posttraumatic Stress Disorder*, 242.

146. Wilson, "Understanding the Vietnam Veteran," 243.

147. Harkness, "Transgenerational Transmission of War-Related Trauma," 635.

148. Akbar Zargar, Bahman Najarian, and Derek Roger, "Settlement Reconstruction and Psychological Recovery in Iran," in *International Handbook of Traumatic Stress Syndromes*, 980.

149. Wilson, "Understanding the Vietnam Veteran," 243.

150. Ibid.

151. Ibid.

152. Ibid., 244.

153. Ibid.

154. Ibid., 245.

155. Jack, *Silencing the Self*, 53.

156. Carol Gilligan, *In a Different Voice: Psychological Theory and Women's Development* (Cambridge: Harvard University Press, 1982), 43.

157. Yael Danieli, "Treating Survivors and Children of Survivors of the Nazi Holocaust," in *Post-Traumatic Therapy and Victims of Violence*, 290.

158. Jack, *Silencing the Self*, 135.

159. Andrea Dworkin, *Our Blood* (New York: Harper & Row, 1976), 85–86.

160. Ibid., 85.

161. Evan Stark and Anne Flitcraft, "Personal Power and Institutional Victimization: Treating the Dual Trauma of Woman Battering," in *Post-Traumatic Therapy and Victims of Violence*, 127.

162. Miller, *For Your Own Good*, 139.

163. Ibid., 75.

164. Ibid., 140.

2. Violence and Legitimation

1. Tedeschi, "Social Influence Theory and Aggression," in *Aggression: Theoretical and Empirical Reviews*, 159.

2. Ibid.

3. Ibid.

4. Ibid., 158.

5. John Bradshaw, *Bradshaw On: The Family: A Revolutionary Way of Self Discovery* (Deerfield Beach, FL: Health Communications, Inc., 1988), 130: R. L. Light, *The Harvard Review* (November) 1973.

6. Tedeschi, "Social Influence Theory and Aggression," 159.

7. Freud, *Civilization and Its Discontents*, 59.

8. Williams, "Legitimate and Illegitimate Uses of Violence," 24.

9. Ibid.

10. Ibid.

11. Ibid., 32.

12. Tedeschi, "Social Influence Theory and Aggression," 156.

13. Williams, "Legitimate and Illegitimate Uses of Violence," 33.

14. Howard Zehr, *Death as a Penalty: A Moral, Practical and Theological Discussion* (Elkhart, Indiana: MCC U.S. Office of Criminal Justice, c. 1986), 11.

15. Tedeschi, "Social Influence Theory and Aggression," 157.

16. Littlewood and Lipsedge, *Aliens and Alienists*, 2d ed., 27.

17. Tedeschi, "Social Influence Theory and Aggression," 157.

18. Ibid.

19. Littlewood and Lipsedge, *Aliens and Alienists*, 27.

20. Williams, "Legitimate and Illegitimate Uses of Violence," 37.

21. Ibid., 39.

22. Michael Ondaatje, *The English Patient* (Toronto: McClelland & Stewart, 1992).

23. Bandura, "Psychological Mechanisms of Aggression," 2.

24. Stark and Flitcraft, "Personal Power and Institutional Victimization: Treating the Dual Trauma of Woman Battering," 124.

25. Ibid., 121.

26. The Taskforce Report to General Synod 1986 of the Anglican Church of Canada, *Violence against Women: Abuse in Society and Church and Proposals for Change* (Toronto: Anglican Book Centre, 1987), 30.

27. Ibid.

28. Ibid.

29. Ibid., 31.

30. Herman, *Trauma and Recovery*, 78.

31. Maria Roy, ed., *The Abusive Partner: An Analysis of Domestic Battering* (New York: Van Nostrand Reinhold, 1982).

32. Karen Rodgers, "Wife Assault in Canada," *Statistics Canada-Catalogue 11–008E: Canadian Social Trends*, Autumn 1994, 3.

33. Affidavit of victim; name held in confidence by the author.

34. Testimony of a wife abuser from James Ptacek, "Why Do Men Batter Their Wives?" in *Feminist Perspectives on Wife Abuse* (Beverly Hills: Sage, 1988), ed. K. Yllo and M. Bograd, as quoted in Melanie Randall, *The Politics of Woman Abuse: Understanding the Issues* (Toronto: Education Wife Assault, 1989), 5.

35. Ibid.

36. Ibid.

37. Ibid.

38. Ibid., 6.

39. Ibid.

40. Ibid.

41. Stark and Flitcraft, "Personal Power and Institutional Victimization: Treating the Dual Trauma of Woman Battering," 121.

42. Littlewood and Lipsedge, *Aliens and Alienists*, 198.

43. Susan Brownmiller, *Against Our Will: Men, Women and Rape* (New York: Simon and Schuster, 1975), 369.

44. Littlewood and Lipsedge, *Aliens and Alienists*, 164.

45. Ibid., 29.

46. Ibid.

47. Ibid., 28.

48. Ibid.

49. Ibid., 52.

50. Baron and Straus, *Four Theories of Rape in American Society: A State-Level Analysis*, 185. The authors analyze the concept of the 'status of women'

into gender attainment and gender equality. The status of women is perceived as a multidimensional phenomenon that includes the *absolute* as well as the *relative* degree to which women have attained valued social characteristics. Gender attainment refers to the extent to which members of a particular gender have achieved socially valued statuses such as education, economic resources, and physical and mental health. Gender equality refers to the position women have as a group, compared with men as a group, in different fields of society, including gender *in*equality that is institutionalized in social institutions such as family, religious, political, legal, and educational institutions. The authors focus upon "the extent to which equality between men and women is associated with the absolute level of gender attainment and other indicators of social and psychological well-being" (63).

51. Ibid.

52. Elly Danica, *Don't: A Woman's Word* (Charlottetown, P.E.I.: Gynergy Books, 1988), 51–59.

53. The perception of madness as a challenge to dominant beliefs is shown in the concept of 'insanity as sin' in medieval Europe, which then became a failure of self-sufficiency, and later an affront to "man's basic rationality." See Littlewood and Lipsedge, *Aliens and Alienists*, 198; Michel Foucault, *Madness and Civilization: A History of Insanity in the Age of Reason* (New York: Vintage Books, 1965), trans. Richard Howard.

54. Sussman and Bordwell, *The Rapist File*, 5.

55. Beneke, *Men on Rape*, 30.

56. Sussman and Bordwell, *The Rapist File*, 179.

57. Ibid., 180.

58. Ibid., 187.

59. Ibid., 121.

60. Ibid., 63.

61. Beneke, *Men on Rape*, 31.

62. Mary Douglas, *Purity and Danger: An Analysis of the Concepts of Pollution and Taboo* (London: Routledge & Kegan Paul, 1966), 128.

63. Williams, "Legitimate and Illegitimate Uses of Violence," 44.

64. Marie Fortune, as quoted in the Taskforce Report to General Synod 1986 of the Anglican Church of Canada, *Violence Against Women: Abuse in Society and Church and Proposals for Change*, 19.

65. Michel Foucault, *Discipline and Punish: The Birth of the Prison* (New York: Vintage Books, 1979), 138.

66. Ibid., 141.

67. Bennett G. Braun, "Multiple Personality Disorder and Posttraumatic Stress Disorder: Similarities and Differences," in *International Handbook of Traumatic Stress Syndromes* 42.

68. Paul Ricoeur, "Ideology and Utopia as Cultural Imagination," in *Being Human in a Technological Age* (Athens: Ohio University Press, 1979), ed. D. Borchert and D. Stewart, 107.

69. Ibid., 108.

70. Ibid., 109.

71. Ibid., 113.

72. Ibid.

73. Ibid., 114.

74. Ibid.

75. Hannah Arendt, *On Violence* (New York: Harcourt Brace Jovanovich, Publishers, 1969), 44.

76. Ibid., 71.

77. Ibid., 49.

78. Ricoeur, "Ideology and Utopia as Cultural Imagination," 117.

79. Ibid., 119.

80. Ibid., 120.

3. Myth and War

1. Hans-Georg Gadamer, *Philosophical Hermeneutics* (Berkeley: University of California Press, 1976), 33.

2. Gadamer, *Truth and Method*, 249.

3. Ibid.

4. Williams, "Legitimate and Illegitimate Uses of Violece: A Review of Ideas and Evidence," 24.

5. Northrop Frye, *Myth and Metaphor: Selected Essays, 1974–1988* (Charlottesville: University Press of Virginia, 1990), 3.

6. Ibid., 4.

7. Ibid., 5.

8. Ibid.

9. Lee W. Gibbs, "Myth and Mystery of the Future," in *Myth and the Crisis of Historical Consciousness* (Missoula: Scholars Press, 1975), ed. Lee Gibbs and W. Taylor Stevenson, 29.

10. W. Taylor Stevenson, "Myth and the Crisis of Historical Consciousness," in *Myth and the Crisis of Historical Consciousness*, 2.

11. Ibid., 3.

12. Ibid., 5.

13. David Little and Sumner B. Twiss, *Comparative Ethics* (San Francisco: Harper & Row, Publishers, 1978), 67.

14. Ibid., 66.

15. Robert Nozick, *Anarchy, State and Utopia* (New York: Basic Books, Inc., 1974), 92.

16. See Albert Weinberg, *Manifest Destiny* (Baltimore: The Johns Hopkins Press, 1935); Winthrop Talbot, *Americanization* (New York: H. W. Wilson Co., 1917).

17. Mircea Eliade, *The Myth of the Eternal Return or, Cosmos and History* (Princeton: Princeton University Press, 1954), trans. Willard R. Trask, 21.

18. Ibid., 37.

19. H. Munro and N. K. Chadwick, as cited in Eliade, *The Myth of the Eternal Return*, 43.

20. Ibid.

21. Ibid.

22. Ibid., 44.

23. Lorna V. Williams, "From Dusky Venus to Mater Dolorosa: The Female Protagonist in the Cuban Antislavery Novel," in *Woman as Myth and Metaphor in Latin American Literature* (Columbia: University of Missouri Press, 1985), ed. C. Virgillo and N. Lindstrom, 122.

24. G. W. F. Hegel, *The Phenomenology of Spirit* (Oxford: Oxford University Press, 1977), 347.

25. Mark C. Taylor, *Erring: A Postmodern A/theology* (Chicago: The University of Chicago Press, 1984), 23.

26. Ibid.

27. Ibid.

28. Ibid., 24.

29. Ibid.

30. Hegel, *The Phenomenology of Spirit*, 114.

31. Ibid.

32. Taylor, *Erring*, 30.

33. Ibid., 33.

34. Hegel, *Phenomenology of Spirit*, 289.

35. Karl Löwith, *From Hegel to Nietzsche: The Revolution in Nineteenth-Century Thought* (New York: Garland Publishing, Inc., 1984), trans. David E. Green, 40.

36. Ibid., 34.

37. Ibid., 35.

38. Norman F. Cantor, *Medieval History: The Life and Death of a Civilization* (New York: Macmillan Publishing Co., Inc., 1969), 2nd. ed., 223.

39. Ibid.

40. Weinberg, *Manifest Destiny*, 308.

41. Cantor, *Medieval History*, 111.

42. Ibid., 108.

43. Michael Alexander, trans., *Beowulf* (Middlesex: Penguin Books, 1973), 31.

44. Cantor, *Medieval History*, 76.

45. Carolyn Merchant, *The Death of Nature: Women, Ecology and the Scientific Revolution* (New York: Harper & Row, 1980), 68.

46. Ibid., 2.

47. White, "The Historical Roots of Our Ecological Crisis," 24.

48. Ibid.

49. Ibid.

50. Ibid., p. 27.

51. George Piero Ferzoco, *Bernard of Clairvaux and Early Christian Cistercian Thought regarding the Salvific Role of Violence in Twelfth-Century Christian Society* (Master's Thesis, Trent University, 1985), 4.

52. Ibid., 54.

53. John Lambert, "St. Bernard of Clairvaux: the Historical Background," in *Bernard of Clairvaux: Nine Hundred Years* (Pretoria: University of South Africa, 1990), ed. Leonie Viljoen, 16.

54. Ibid.

55. Jeffrey Burton Russell, *Witchcraft in the Middle Ages* (Ithaca: Cornell University Press, 1972), p.42.

56. Jacob Grimm, *Teutonic Mythology* (London: George Bell and Sons, 1883), trans. James S. Stallybrass, 369.

57. J. J. Bachofen, *Myth, Religion and Mother Right* (Princeton: Princeton University Press, 1967), trans. Ralph Manheim, 80.

58. Williams, *Woman as Myth and Metaphor in Latin American Literature*, 123.

59. Ibid.

60. Roland H. Bainton, *Christian Attitudes toward War and Peace: A Historical Survey and Critical Re-evalution* (Nashville: Abingdon Press, 1960), 102.

61. Alasdair MacIntyre, *After Virtue: A Study in Moral Theory* (Notre Dame: University of Notre Dame Press, 1984), 166.

62. George Boas, "Warfare in the Cosmos," in *Violence and Aggression in the History of Ideas* (New Brunswick, N.J.: Rutgers University Press, 1974), ed. Philip P. Wiener and John Fisher, 9.

63. Barbara Tuchman, *A Distant Mirror: The Calamitous Fourteenth Century* (New York: Balantine Books, 1978), 135.

64. Ibid.

65. Boas, "War in the Cosmos," 10.

66. Ibid., 11.

67. Ibid., 12.

68. Alexander, *Beowulf*, 33.

69. Richmond Lattimore, trans., *The Iliad of Homer* (Chicago: The Univeristy of Chicago Press, 1951), 165.

70. Joseph Campbell, *The Hero with a Thousand Faces* (Princeton: Princeton University Press, 1973), 16.

71. Ibid., 17.

72. Hegel as quoted in Löwith, *From Hegel to Nietzsche*, 40.

73. Aristotle, *The Physics, vol. I*, (Cambridge: Harvard University Press, 1929), 235.

74. Bainton, *Christian Attitudes toward War and Peace*, 28.

75. Douglas, *Purity and Danger*, 164.

76. Bainton, *Christian Attitudes toward War and Peace*, 17.

77. Ibid., 18.

78. Ibid., 20.

79. Bachofen, *Myth, Religion and Mother Right*, 110.

80. Lerner, *The Creation of Patriarchy*, 144.

81. Ibid.

82. Bachofen, *Myth, Religion and Mother Right*, 111.

83. Kipnis, *Knights without Armor*, 151.

84. Ibid., 118.

85. Ibid., 221.

86. Lerner, *The Creation of Patriarchy*, 26.

87. Susan Brownmiller, *Against Our Will*, 64.

88. Merchant, *The Death of Nature*, 143.

89. Elizabeth Schüssler Fiorenza, *In Memory of Her: A Feminist Theological Reconstruction of Christian Origins* (New York: Crossroad, 1983), 42.

90. Merchant, *The Death of Nature*, 143.

91. Littlewood and Lipsedge, *Aliens and Alienists*, 54.

92. Ibid., 222.

93. Bainton, *Christian Attitudes toward War and Peace*, 95.

94. Ibid.

95. L. S. Stavrianos, *Global Rift*, 814.

96. Jean-François Lyotard, *The Postmodern Condition: A Report on Knowledge* (Minneapolis: University of Minnesota Press, 1984), 63.

97. Naomi Wolf, *The Beauty Myth: How Images of Beauty are Used against Women* (New York: Random House, 1991).

4. Freud and the Aggressive Impulse

1. Bruno Bettelheim, *Freud and Man's Soul* (New York: Alfred A. Knopf, 1983), 104.

2. Ibid.

3. Ibid., 106.

4. Ibid., 107.

5. Ibid.

6. Alice Miller, *The Drama of the Gifted Child: The Search for the True Self* (New York: Basic Books, Inc., 1981), 5.

7. Ibid., 6.

8. Ibid., 7.

9. Anatol Rapoport, *The Origins of Violence*, 7.

10. Freud, *Civilization and Its Discontents*, 59.

11. Calvin S. Hall, *A Primer of Freudian Psychology* (New York: Harper & Row, Publishers Inc., 1982), 54.

12. Sigmund Freud, "Beyond the Pleasure Principle," in *On Metapsychology* (London: Penguin Books, 1984), 325.

13. Ibid., 326.

14. Ibid.

15. Sebastian Gardner, "The Unconscious," in *The Cambridge Companion to Freud* (Cambridge: Cambridge University Press, 1991), ed. Jerome Neu, 137.

16. Freud, "Instincts and Their Vicissitudes," in *On Metapsychology: The Theory of Psychoanalysis*, 116, standard ed., 14, 109–40.

17. Ibid., "Beyond the Pleasure Principle," 275.

18. Ibid., "Repression," 145.

19. Ibid., 147.

20. Ibid., "Instincts and Their Vicissitudes," 116.

21. Ibid., 117.

22. Robert A. Paul, "Freud's Anthropology: A Reading of the 'Cultural Books'," in *The Cambridge Companion to Freud*, 279.

23. Ibid.

24. Ibid.

25. Freud, "Beyond the Pleasure Principle," 316.

26. Ibid., 330.

27. Freud, "The Ego and the Id," 381.

28. Ibid., 395.

29. Ibid.

30. Ibid., 398.

31. Ibid., "The Economic Problem of Masochism," 425.

32. Ibid.

33. Paul, "Freud's Anthropology: A Reading of the 'Cultural Books'," 279.

34. Ibid., 293.

35. Ibid., 301.

36. Ibid., 272.

37. Freud, *Civilization and Its Discontents*, 36.

38. Ibid., 58.

39. Ibid.

40. Ibid., 59.

41. Ibid.

42. Ibid.

43. Ibid., 67.

44. Ibid.

45. Ibid.

46. Ibid., 69.

47. Paul Ricoeur, *Freud and Philosophy: An Essay on Interpretation* (New York: Yale University Press, 1970), 119.

48. Ibid., 109.

49. Ibid., 135.

50. Ibid., 75n.

51. Ibid.

52. Ibid.

53. Ibid., 92.

54. Ibid., 97.

55. Ibid., 380.

56. Ibid., 382.

57. Ibid., 386.

58. Ibid., 61.

59. Ibid., 178.

60. Ibid.

61. Paul Ricoeur, *Time and Narrative,* volume 1 (Chicago: University of Chicago Press, 1984), trans. Kathleen McLaughlin and David Pellauer, 57.

62. Ricoeur, *Freud and Philosophy,* 179.

63. Ibid., 181.

64. Ibid., 213.

65. Ibid., 363.

66. Ibid., 365.

67. Ibid., 372.

68. Ibid.

69. Ibid., 408.

70. Ibid., 479.

71. Ibid., 388.

72. Ibid., 467.

73. Ibid.

74. Ibid., 314.

75. Ibid., 483.

76. Ibid., 472.

77. Ibid., 500.

78. Erikson, *Identity: Youth and Crisis*, 82–83.

79. Herman, *Trauma and Recovery*, 41.

80. Ibid., 39.

81. Ibid.

82. Ibid.

83. Ibid., 183.

84. Ibid.

85. Ibid., 158.

86. Ibid., 200.

87. Ibid.

88. Edith Wyschogrod, *Spirit in Ashes: Hegel, Heidegger, and Man-Made Mass Death* (New Haven: Yale University Press, 1985), 215.

89. Ibid., 206.

90. Ibid.

91. Don Ihde, *Hermeneutic Phenomenology: The Philosophy of Paul Ricoeur* (Evanston: Northwestern University Press, 1971), 112.

92. Ibid., 113.

93. Ibid., 129.

94. Ibid.

95. Ricoeur, *Political and Social Essays* (Athens: Ohio State University Press, 1974), 94.

96. Ibid.

97. Ibid., 95.

98. Ricoeur, *The Rule of Metaphor*, 205.

99. Ibid., 48. For Ricoeur, the duality of rhetoric and poetics reflects the duality in the use of speech as well as the situations of speaking. Oratory, the art of defence, of deliberation, and poetry, the art of emotive expression, are two types of discourse. Metaphor has "a foot in each domain." With respect to structure, it consists in the transfer of the meanings of words, and with respect to function, "it follows the divergent destinies of oratory and tragedy." Metaphor thus has one unique structure and two functions: a rhetorical function and a poetic function (12).

100. Ricoeur, *Political and Social Essays*, 95.

101. Klemm, *The Hermeneutical Theory of Paul Ricoeur*, 53.

102. Riceour, *Political and Social Essays*, 89.

103. Ricoeur, *Interpretation Theory*, 21.

104. Ricoeur, *Political and Social Essays*, 97.

105. Ibid., 96.

106. Ricoeur, *Freud and Philosophy*, 483.

107. Freud, *Civilization and Its Discontents*, 59.

108. Ibid., 58, n. 3. "Man is a wolf to man." Derived from Plautus, *Asinaria* II, iv, 88.

109. Michel Foucault, *Power/Knowledge: Selected Interviews and Other Writings 1972–1977* (New York: Pantheon Books, 1980), 114.

5. Girard and the Trauma Victim

1. Paul Dumouchel, "Introduction," in *Violence and Truth: On the Work of René Girard* (London: The Athlone Press, 1985), ed. Paul Dumouchel, 3.

2. René Girard, *Deceit, Desire, and the Novel* (Baltimore: The Johns Hopkins Press, 1961), trans. Yvonne Freccero, 106.

3. Ibid.

4. Dumouchel, "Introduction," 7.

5. Ibid., 8.

6. Ibid., 9.

7. Ibid.

8. Ibid., 13.

9. Ibid., 15.

10. Jean-Marie Domenach, "The End of the Sciences of Man," in *Violence and Truth*, 156.

11. Ibid., 157.

12. Andrew McKenna, *Violence and Difference: Girard, Derrida, and Deconstruction* (Urbana: University of Illinois Press, 1992), 14.

13. Paisley Livingston, "Demystification and History in Girard and Durkheim," in *Violence and Truth*, 131.

14. McKenna, *Violence and Difference*, 14.

15. Ibid., 167.

16. Ibid.

17. Ibid., 198.

18. Ibid.

19. René Girard, *Things Hidden since the Foundation of the World* (Stanford: Stanford University Press, 1987), trans. Stephen Baum and Michael Metteer, 85.

20. Ibid., 86.

21. Ibid., 87.

22. René Girard, *Violence and the Sacred* (Baltimore: The Johns Hopkins University Press, 1972), trans. Patrick Gregory, 146.

23. Ibid.

24. Kipnis, *Knights without Armor*, 22.

25. Erikson, *Identity: Youth and Crisis*, 99.

26. Ibid.

27. Ibid.

28. Ibid., 82.

29. Ibid.

30. Girard, *Violence and the Sacred*, 146.

31. Ibid., 148.

32. Ibid.

33. Erikson, *Identity: Youth and Crisis*, 82.

34. Ibid.

35. Ibid., 97.

36. Herman, *Trauma and Recovery*, 138.

37. Girard, *Violence and the Sacred*, 203.

38. Kathleen Noble, *The Sound of the Silver Horn: Reclaiming the Heroism in Contemporary Women's Lives* (New York: Fawcett Columbine, 1994), 138.

39. Braun, "Multiple Personality Disorder and Posttraumatic Stress Disorder: Similarities and Differences," 42.

40. Ibid.

41. Girard, *Violence and the Sacred*, 161.

42. Ibid.

43. Girard, *Things Hidden since the Foundation of the World*, 312.

44. Ibid., 33.

45. Ibid., 26.

46. Ibid., 32.

47. Girard, *Violence and the Sacred*, 203.

48. Girard, *Things Hidden since the Foundation of the World*, 260.

49. Herman, *Trauma and Recovery*, 136.

50. Ibid., 137.

51. Ibid.

52. Ibid., 139.

53. Ibid., 140.

54. Ibid.

55. James F. Monroe, et al., "Preventing Compassion Fatigue: A Team Treatment Model," 210.

56. Harkness, "Transgenerational Transmission of War-Related Trauma," 635.

57. Ibid., 144.

58. Ibid., 145.

59. Girard, *Violence and the Sacred*, p. 203.

60. Girard, *Things Hidden since the Foundation of the World*, 260.

61. Girard, *Violence and the Sacred*, 218.

62. Ibid., 221.

63. Girard, *Things Hidden since the Foundation of the World*, 32.

64. René Girard, "Generative Scapegoating," in *Violent Origins: Walter Burkert, René Girard and Jonathan Z. Smith on Ritual Killing and Cultural Formation* (Stanford: Stanford University Press, 1987), ed. Robert G. Hammerton-Kelly, 127.

65. Girard, *Things Hidden since the Foundation of the World*, 203.

66. Mihai Spariosu, *The Wreath of Wild Olive: Play, Liminality, and the Study of Literature* (Albany: State University of New York Press, forthcoming), 13.

67. Ibid.

68. Girard, *Things Hidden since the Foundation of the World*, 203.

69. Herman, *Trauma and Recovery*, 42.

70. Elisabeth Bronfen, "The Jew as Woman's Symptom: Kathlyn Bigelow's Conflictive Representation of Feminine Power," in *Violence and Mediation in Contemporary Culture* (Albany: State University of New York Press, 1996), ed. Ronald Bogue and Marcel Cornis-Pope, 77.

71. Ibid.

72. Ricoeur, *Freud and Philosophy*, 319.

73. Herman, *Trauma and Recovery*, 92.

74. Braun, "Multiple Personality Disorder and Posttraumatic Stress Disorder: Similarities and Differences," 40.

75. Herman, *Trauma and Recovery*, 38.

76. Ibid., 93.

77. Ibid., 145.

78. Erikson, *Identity: Youth and Crisis* , 83.

79. Ibid.

80. Frank Gervasi, *The Violent Decade* (New York: W. W. Norton & Company, 1989), 269.

81. This also could characterize Hegel's master/slave dialectic of figures, for it too repeats transgenerationally to a "resolution" in the positing of the idealized rescuer in the divinity of self-sufficient spirit.

82. Priscilla Beaulieu Presley, *Elvis and Me* (New York: G. P. Putnam's Sons, 1985), with Sandra Harmon, 317.

83. Ibid., 256.

84. Ibid., 320.

85. Kipnis, *Knights without Armor*, 83.

86. Ibid., 83.

87. As quoted in Elizabeth Stanko, *Everyday Violence: How Women and Men Experience Sexual and Physical Danger* (London: Pandora Press, 1990), 110.

88. Erma Bombeck, *Family: The Ties That Bind . . . and Gag!* (New York: MacGraw-Hill Book Company, 1987), 110.

89. Rodgers, "Wife Assault in Canada," 7.

90. Herman, *Trauma and Recovery*, 72.

91. Ibid.

92. Ibid., 32.

93. Ibid.

94. Ibid., 61.

95. David F. Noble, *The Forces of Production: A Social History of Industrial Automation* (New York: Alfred A. Knopf, Inc., 1984), 23.

96. Norman Hearst, Thomas B. Newman, and Stephen B. Hulley, "Delayed Effects of the Military Draft on Mortality," in *The New England Journal of Medicine* 314 (1986): 620–24.

97. Koerus, Julius, alias Elmo Karm. (1945) "To the West," (unpublished manuscript), 34.

98. Hans Zinsser, as quoted in Arnold J. Levine, *Viruses* (New York: Scientific American Library, 1992), 131.

99. Peter Goodchild, *J. Robert Oppenheimer: Shatterer of Worlds* (Boston: Houghton Mifflin Company, 1981), 167.

100. Vannevar Bush, "As We May Think," in *Interactions* 111.2 (March 1996): 44–46. Originally printed in *The Atlantic Monthly*, July 1945.

101. Akbar Zargar, et al., "Settlement Reconstruction and Psychological Recovery in Iran," 980.

102. Ibid.

103. Kipnis, *Knights without Armor*, 83.

104. Girard, *Violence and the Sacred*, 151.

105. Girard, *Things Hidden since the Foundation of the World*, 415.

106. Monroe, et al., "Preventing Compassion Fatigue: A Team Treatment Model," 211.

107. Ibid.

108. John P. Wilson, "Treating the Vietnam Veteran," in *Post-Traumatic Therapy and Victims of Violence*, 262.

109. Ibid.

110. The estimated fifty thousand suicides of Vietnam veterans has been debated, yet studies have shown Vietnam veterans were more likely to commit suicide than their peers after the war. See Jacob Lindy, *Vietnam: A Casebook* (New York: Brunner/Mazel, 1988), 33.

111. Paula Gunn Allen, "The Sacred Hoop: A Contemporary Indian Perspective on American Indian Literature," in *Literature of the American Indians: Views and Interpretations* (New York: Meridian, 1975), ed. Abraham Chapman, 130.

112. John P. Wilson, "Treating the Vietnam Veteran," 262.

113. Herman, *Trauma and Recovery*, 41.

114. Ibid., 39.

115. John P. Wilson, "Understanding the Vietnam Veteran," 233.

116. Ibid.

117. John P. Wilson, "Treating the Vietnam Veteran," 263.

118. Herman, *Trauma and Recovery*, 155.

119. John Wilson, "Treating the Vietnam Veteran," 269.

120. Herman, *Trauma and Recovery*, 22.

121. Ibid., 27.

122. In Aaron Kipnis, *Knights without Armor*, 69.

123. Girard, *Things Hidden since the Foundation of the World*, 414.

6. Derrida and the Heroic Arché

1. Carl Mydans and Shelley Mydans, *The Violent Peace* (New York: Atheneum, 1968), 166.

2. Stavrianos, *Global Rift*, 666.

3. Ibid.

4. Mydans and Mydans, *The Violent Peace*, 167.

5. Harkness, "Transgenerational Transmission of War-Related Trauma," 635. A thirty-nine-year-old Vietnam survior repeats his unforgettable rules learned in war: "Kill or be killed," "Don't grieve," "Survive at all costs," "Be unpredictable—it's safer," and "Shut off feelings."

6. Akbar Zargar, et al., "Settlement Reconstruction and Psychological Recovery in Iran," 980.

7. Jacques Derrida, *Positions* (Chicago: The University of Chicago Press, 1981), 29.

8. Ibid., 28.

9. Ibid., 26.

10. Ibid., 29.

11. Ibid., 33.

12. Ibid., 45.

13. Ibid., 9.

14. Ibid., 7.

15. Jacques Derrida, *Writing and Difference* (Chicago: The University of Chicago Press, 1978), 79.

16. Ibid., 116.

17. Ibid.

18. Husserl constructs a descriptive egology as intentionality that accepts the possible meaning *of* objects for consciousness in contrast to the Cartesian ego that derives knowledge from sense data which is then categorized according to principles innate to the ego and hence gives meaning *to* objects. The same act of presentation (a perceiving, imagining, or representing intention toward it) of an object to consciousness is the same act of apperception (an apprehension, interpretation) of sensations belonging to the act. The act that recognizes the relation of consciousness with the object, or the interpretation of the object, is a transcendent move which makes consciousness aware that it is itself not one object amongst objects, but a conscious unity of apperceptions in relation to an object or a world separate from itself. Hence, objects carry the dual constitution of sense and reference. Consciousness is aware of a single point of reference which transcends its own subjective experiences. This objectivating act transcends subjectivity and is a theoretical act that acts as the basis for rationality and for judgment that as theoretical is free

from the influence of history and tradition. See Edmund Husserl, *Cartesian Meditations* (The Hague: Martinus Nijoff, 1960); and Robert Sokolowski, *The Formation of Husserl's Concept of Constitution* (The Hague: Martinus Nijoff, 1964).

19. Edmund Husserl, *Ideas: General Introduction to Pure Phenomenology* (New York: Collier Books, 1962), trans. W. R. Boyce Gibson, 46.

20. Ibid.

21. Alfred Schutz, *Collected Papers III: Studies in Phenomenological Philosophy* (The Hague: Martinus Nijoff, 1975), 52.

22. Derrida, *Writing and Difference*, 124.

23. Ibid. Derrida refers to Husserl's analogical appresentation necessary for the empathic intuition of the other in order to establish the theoretical grounds for objectivity.

24. Ibid.

25. Ibid., 125.

26. Ibid., 116.

27. Ibid., 125. In Heideggerian terms, facticity is the problem of the interrelatedness of Dasein with all that it encounters in its own world. As existing in a world, Dasein defines this existence as a fact, of being bound up in its destiny with other entitites in the world. A hermeneutics of facticity is a continual interpretation of the relations of Dasein (human there-being) with other entities of being. It is an interpretation of the events, or situations which Dasein finds itself and through which it comes to understand itself. Derrida's claim is that this facticity is always already violent.

28. Ibid.

29. Ibid.

30. Ibid., 117.

31. Ibid., 119.

32. Ibid., 129.

33. Husserl, *Ideas*, 46.

34. As quoted in Sherry Turkle, *Life on the Screen: Identity in the Age of the Internet* (New York: Simon & Schuster, 1995), 103.

35. Friedrich Nietzsche, *On the Advantage and Disadvantages of History for Life* (Indianapolis: Hackett Publishing Company, Inc., 1980), trans. Peter Preuss, 16.

36. Derrida, *Positions*, 6.

37. Herman, *Trauma and Recovery*, 136.

38. Ibid., 137.

39. Ibid.

40. Ibid.

41. Ibid.

42. Monroe, et al., "Preventing Compassion Fatigue: A Team Treatment Model," 211.

43. Ibid.

44. Spariosu, *The Wreath of Wild Olive*, 7.

45. Derrida, *Positions*, 49.

46. Braun, "Multiple Personality Disorder and Posttraumatic Stress Disorder: Similarities and Differences," 38.

47. Ibid.

48. Ibid., 41.

49. Ibid.

50. Ibid.

51. Ibid., 43.

52. Ibid.

53. Turkle, *Life on the Screen*, 259.

54. Ibid.

55. Arthur Cohen, *The Tremendum: A Theological Interpretation of the Holocaust* (New York: Crossroad, 1981), 45.

56. Foucault, *Power/Knowledge*, 114.

57. Turkle, *Life on the Screen*, 265.

58. Ibid.

59. Peter H. Lindsay and Donald A. Norman, *Human Information Processing: An Introduction to Psychology* (New York: Academic Press, 1972), 431.

60. Ibid.

61. Bush, "As We May Think," 43.

62. Ibid.

63. Taylor, *Erring*, 29.

64. Ibid., 53.

65. Herman, *Trauma and Recovery*, 36.

66. Ibid.

67. Ibid., 168.

68. Ricoeur, *The Rule of Metaphor*, 285.

69. Turkle, *Life on the Screen*, 268. See also Mihai Spariosu, *The Wreath of Wild Olive*.

70. Monroe, "Preventing Compassion Fatigue," 211.

71. Herman, *Trauma and Recovery*, 154.

72. Ibid.

7. Restoration and Trust

1. Vine Deloria, Jr., "Indian Humor," in *Literature of the American Indians: Views and Interpretations*, 154.

2. Stavrianos, *Global Rift*, 75–76.

3. Denise Ackermann, "Women, Violence and Theology," in *Theology and Violence: The South African Debate* (Grand Rapids: William B. Eerdmans Publishing Company, 1988), ed. Charles Villa-Vicencio, 266.

4. Ibid.

5. Ibid.

6. Kipnis, *Knights without Armor*, 179.

7. Ibid.

8. Ibid.

9. Herman, *Trauma and Recovery*, 156.

10. Munroe, et al., "Preventing Compassion Fatigue: A Team Treatment Model," 219.

11. Ibid., 222.

12. Ibid.

13. Herman, *Trauma and Recovery*, 172.

14. Ibid., 116. From G. T. Hotaling and D. G. Sugarman, "An Analysis of Risk Markers in Husband-to-Wife Violence: The Current State of Knowledge," in *Violence and Victims*, (1986): 101–24.

15. Herman, *Trauma and Recovery*, 133.

16. Ibid., 134.

17. Harkness, "Transgenerational Transmission of War-Related Trauma," 635.

18. Ibid., 636.

19. Ibid.

20. Ibid., 641.

21. Ibid., 637.

22. Herman, *Trauma and Recovery*, 155.

23. Wilson, "Treating the Vietnam Veteran," 269.

24. Ibid.

25. Wilson, "Understanding the Vietnam Veteran," 232.

26. Ibid.

27. Ibid.

28. Ibid., 233.

29. Ibid.

30. Ibid., 276.

31. Ibid., 215.

32. Kipnis, *Knights without Armor*, 23.

33. Gustavo Gutierrez, *A Theology of Liberation: History, Politics and Salvation* (Maryknoll: Orbis Books, 1973), 22.

34. Gadamer, *Truth and Method*, 238.

35. Ibid., 245.

36. Ibid., 249.

37. Ibid.

38. Ibid.

39. Ibid., 250.

40. Ibid.

41. Ibid., 255.

42. Ibid., 260.

43. Ibid., 92.

44. Ibid., 93.

45. Ibid., 95.

46. Ibid., 97.

47. Ibid., 267.

48. Herman, *Trauma and Recovery*, 214.

49. Ibid.

50. Robert L. Swinth, "The Establishment of the Trust Relationship," *Journal of Conflict Resolution*, vol. 11 no. 3 (1967): 335.

51. Ibid.

52. Conditions of trust affect the percentage of trust and include payoff matrices, personality, strategy of the other player, possibilities for communication, number of trials, magnitude of reward, and sex (Swinth, 335 n. 2).

53. W. Bennis, E. Schein, D. Berlew, and F. Steele, *Interpersonal Dynamics: Essays and Reading on Human Interaction* (Homewood, Ill: Dorsely, 1964), 217, as quoted in R. L. Swinth.

54. Swinth, "The Establishment of the Trust Relationship," 336.

55. Ibid., 343.

56. Ibid.

57. Niklas Luhmann, *Trust and Power* (New York: John Wiley & Sons, 1979), trans. Howard Davis, John Raffan, and Kathryn Rooney, 43.

58. Gadamer, *Truth and Method*, 273.

59. Ibid., 338.

60. Ibid., 341.

61. Gadamer, *Philosophical Hermeneutics*, 32.

62. Ibid.

63. Ibid., 34.

64. Margaret Visser, *The Rituals of Dinner: The Origins, Evolution and Eccentricities and Meaning of Table Manners* (Toronto: Harper Perennial, 1991).

8. Attachment and Actualization

1. Munroe, et al., "Preventing Compassion Fatigue: A Team Treatment Model," 211.

2. Ibid.

3. Erikson, *Identity: Youth and Crisis*, 82.

4. Ibid.

5. John Bowlby, "Psychoanalysis as a Natural Science," in *Psychoanalytic Psychology* vol. 1, n. 1 (1984): 9.

6. Dorothy Dinnerstein, *The Mermaid and the Minotaur: Sexual Arrangements and Human Malaise* (New York: Harper Collins Publishers, 1976), 166–67.

7. Ibid., 2.

8. Ibid., 238.

9. Erikson, *Identity: Youth and Crisis*, 82.

10. Kipnis, *Knights without Armor*, 160.

11. Ibid.

12. Ibid.

13. Ibid., 54.

14. Bruce Perry, et al., "Adrenergic Receptor Regulation in Posttraumatic Stress Disorder," 106.

15. Ibid.

16. Bowlby, "Psychoanalysis as a Natural Science, " 13.

17. Ibid., 16.

18. Ibid., 17.

19. Jack, *Silencing the Self*, 109.

20. Ibid., 119.

21. Ibid., 7.

22. Fred R. Dallmayr, *Twilight of Subjectivity: Contributions to a Post-Individualist Theory of Politics* (Amherst: University of Massachusetts Press, 1981), 2.

23. Ibid., 295 n. 3.

24. Ibid., 2.

25. Jack, *Silencing the Self*, 7.

26. Ibid.

27. Ibid., 8.

28. Ibid., 9.

29. Ibid.

30. Ibid., 10.

31. Ibid.

32. Ibid., 11.

33. J. Bowlby, as quoted in Jack, *Silencing the Self*, 11.

34. Gilligan, *In a Different Voice*, 8.

35. Ibid.

36. Jack, *Silencing the Self*, 13.

37. Ibid., 123.

38. Foucault, *Discipline and Punish*, 198.

39. Ibid., 194.

40. Jack, *Silencing the Self*, 124.

41. Ibid., 41.

42. Ibid., 53.

43. Ibid., 41.

44. Ibid., 180.

45. Ibid.

9. Technology and Interactivity

1. Joyce Nelson, *The Perfect Machine: TV in the Nuclear Age* (Toronto: Between the Lines, 1987), 69.

2. Ibid.

3. Ibid., 70.

4. Ibid.

5. Ibid.

6. Ibid., 71.

7. Ibid.

8. Ibid., 72.

9. Ibid.

10. Ibid.

11. Ibid., 73.

12. Carroll W. Pursell, Jr., and Melvin Kranzberg, "Epilogue," in *Technology in Western Civilization: The Emergence of Modern Industrial Society: Earliest Times to 1900* vol. 1 (New York: Oxford University Press, 1967), ed. Melvin Kranzberg and Carroll W. Pursell, Jr., 742.

13. Nelson, *The Perfect Machine*, 75.

14. Herman, *Trauma and Recovery*, 38.

15. Lindsay and Norman, *Human Information Processing*, 634. Lindsay and Norman describe emotional states as manipulable by the combination of three factors: cognitive processes (expectations), physiological states, and environmental influences.

16. Bandura, "Psychological Mechanisms of Aggression," in *Aggression: Theoretical and Empirical Reviews*, 7.

17. Joe Chidley, "Toxic TV: Is TV Violence Contributing to Aggression in Kids?" in *Maclean's*, June 17, 1996, quoting Doug Hallstead of Winnipeg, 37.

18. Ibid., 38.

19. Bandura, "Psychological Mechanisms of Aggression," 7.

20. Quoted from Dr. Edward Donnerstein, "The Researcher's View," in *Reclaiming Childhood: Responsible Solutions to TV Violence & Our Children (Conference Report)* (Toronto: C. M. Hincks Institute, February 1993), 13.

21. Dr. Edward Donnerstein, "The Researcher's View," 14.

22. Ibid.

23. Ibid., 15.

24. Ibid.

25. Chidley, "Toxic TV: Is TV Violence Contributing to Aggression in Kids?", 37.

26. Les Levidow, "The Gulf Massacre as Paranoid Rationality," in *Culture on the Brink: Ideologies of Technology* (Seattle: Bay Press, 1994), ed. G. Bender and T. Druckrey, 322.

27. Michael Shnayerson, "Natural Born Opponents," in *Vanity Fair*, July 1996, 98–144.

28. Kipnis, *Knights without Armor*, 220.

29. Ibid., 73.

30. Donnerstein, "The Researcher's View," 16–17.

31. Stanko, *Everyday Violence*, 100.

32. Donnerstein, "The Researcher's View," 17.

33. Ibid.

34. Ibid.

35. Ibid., 21.

36. Kipnis, *Knights without Armor*, 57.

37. Ibid., 56.

38. See the *Journal of the American Medical Association,* and Statistics Canada reports on violence against women, 1993.

39. Howard Rheingold, *The Virtual Community: Homesteading on the Electronic Frontier* (New York: HarperPerennial, 1993), 147.

40. Kevin Robins, "The Haunted Screen," in *Culture on the Brink: Ideologies of Technology*, 310.

41. Ibid., 311.

42. Ibid., 312.

43. C. P. Snow, *The Two Cultures and a Second Look* (Cambridge: Cambridge University Press, 1991), 2.

44. O. B. Hardison, Jr., *Disappearing through the Skylight: Culture and Technology in the Twentieth Century* (New York: Penguin Books, 1989), xiii.

45. Rheingold, *The Virtual Community*, 147.

46. Ibid., 292.

47. Ibid., 5, 335.

48. Emily Martin, "Body Narratives, Body Boundaries," in *Cultural Studies* (New York: Routledge,1992), ed. L. Grossberg, C. Nelson, P. Treichler, 410.

49. Ibid., 411.

50. Ibid.

51. John Fiske, "The Culture of Everyday Life," in *Cultural Studies*, 162.

52. Sherry Turkle, as quoted in Rheingold, *The Virtual Community*, 153.

53. Ibid.

54. Ibid., 174.

55. Ibid., 286.

56. *NeXT WebObjects* seminar brochure (Redwood City, CA: NeXT Software, Inc., 1996), 6.

57. See Jeffrey Moussaieff Masson, *When Elephants Weep: The Emotional Lives of Animals* (New York: Delacorte, 1995).

58. Frank Thomas and Ollie Johnston, *The Illusion of Life: Disney Animation* (New York: Hyperion, 1981), 542.

59. Faith Popcorn, *The Popcorn Report* (New York: HarperBusiness, 1992), 4.

60. Ricoeur, *Freud and Philosophy*, 181.

61. Gadamer, *Truth and Method*, 351–52.

62. Jay Dark, Karl Ederle, Christine Winkel, *Nordstrom: A Paradigm Shift*, from Nordstrom Business Policy/Marketing 590, Winter 1994, 3.

63. See Jacques Ellul, *The Technological Society;* Ellul, *The Technological System.*

64. Neil Postman, *Technopoly: The Surrender of Culture to Technology* (New York: Vintage Books, 1993), 182.

65. Ibid., 179.

66. Martin Heidegger, *The Question concerning Technology and Other Essays* (New York: Harper & Row, 1977), trans. William Lovitt, 33.

67. Ibid., 13.

68. Ibid., 34.

69. McLuhan, *Understanding Media: The Extensions of Man*, 73.

70. Franklin, *The Real World of Technology*, 17.

71. Ibid.

72. Ibid., 18.

73. Ibid., 23.

74. Ibid., 25.

75. Ibid., 30.

76. Cecil Helman, *Body Myths* (London: Chatto & Windus, 1991), 106.

77. Ibid.

78. *Sun-tzu the Art of Warfare: The First English Translation Incorporating the Recently Discovered Yin-ch 'üeh-shan Texts* (New York: Ballantine Books, 1993), trans. with an introduction and commentary by Roger T. Ames, 108.

79. Van Creveld, *Technology and War: From 2000 B.C. to the Present*, 10.

80. Daniel R. Headrick, *The Invisible Weapon: Telecommunications and International Politics 1851–1945* (Oxford: Oxford University Press, 1991), v.

81. Ibid.

82. Ibid., 273.

83. Ibid., 274.

84. Ibid.

85. *Sun-tzu: The Art of Warfare*, 104.

86. Ibid., 166.

87. Alvin Toffler, *Powershift: Knowledge, Wealth, and Violence at the Edge of the Twenty First Century* (Toronto: Bantam Books, 1990), 379.

88. Ibid., 368.

89. Alvin and Heidi Toffler, *War and Anti-War: Survival at the Dawn of Twenty-first Century* (Toronto: Little, Brown and Company, 1993), 133.

90. Marshall McLuhan and Quintin Fiore, *War and Peace in the Global Village* (Toronto: Touchstone, 1968), 179.

91. Ithiel de Sola Pool, *Technologies without Boundaries: On Telecommunications in a Global Age* (Cambridge: Harvard University Press, 1990), ed. Eli M. Noam, 241.

92. Kenneth Kraemer, "Strategic Computing and Administrative Reform," in *Computerization and Controversy: Value Conflicts and Social Choices* (Boston: Academic Press, 1991), ed. Charles Dunlop and Rob Kling, 167.

93. Sams, *On the Cutting Edge of Technology* (Carmel: Sams Publishing, 1993), 16.

94. Rheingold, *The Virtual Community*.

95. *High Performance Computing and Communications: Toward a National Information Infrastructure*, A Report by the Committee on Physical, Mathematical and Engineering Sciences; Federal Coordinating Council for Science, Engineering and Technology; Office of Science and Technology Policy, Washington, D.C., 1994.

96. Mark Weiser, "The Computer for the Twenty First Century," in *Scientific American: The Computer in the Twenty First Century Special Issue*, 1995, 78.

97. Pierre Wellner, Wendy Mackay, and Rich Gold, "Computer-Augmented Environments: Back to the Real World," in *Communications of the ACM*, vol. 36, no. 7 (July 1993): 26.

98. Nicholas Negroponte, "The Balance of Trade of Ideas," in *Wired* (April 1995) 188.

99. Ibid.

100. Edward Feigenbaum and Pamela McCorduck, "Excerpts from *The Fifth Generation: Artificial Intelligence and Japan's Computer Challenge to the World*," in *Computerization and Controversy: Value Conflicts and Social Choices*, 54.

101. Ibid.

102. Nanotechnology suggests the manipulation of micro composites of matter and the eventual development of computers small enough to alter DNA. See Toffler, *Powershift*, 397. The Human Genome Project is a $3 billion federally funded American research program which intends to map all human genes and enable scientists to explain and alter human variations, i.e., susceptibility to disease. See Stephen Manes, and Paul Andrews, *Gates: How Microsoft's Mogul Reinvented an Industry—and Made Himself the Richest Man in America* (New York: Touchstone, 1994), 417.

103. David Tracy, *The Analogical Imagination: Christian Theology and the Culture of Pluralism* (New York: Crossroad, 1981), 362.

104. Kimon Nicolaides, *The Natural Way to Draw: A Working Plan for Art Study* (Boston: Houghton Mifflin Company, 1969), 17.

105. Nicholas Negroponte, "Being Decimal," in *Wired*, vol. 3, no. 11, (November 1995): 252.

106. Julia Cameron, *The Artist's Way: A Spiritual Path to Higher Creativity* (New York: Jeremy P. Tarcher/Perigree Books, 1992), 53.

107. Presley, *Elvis and Me*, 227.

BIBLIOGRAPHY

Ademran, T., and Y. Alexander. (1983). *International Violence*. New York: Praeger.

Alexander, Michael trans. (1973). *Beowulf*. Middlesex: Penguin Books.

Altizer, Thomas. J. J., Mark C. Taylor, Robert P. Scharlemann, Carl Raschke, Charles E. Winquist, and Max Myers. (1982). *Deconstruction and Theology*. New York: Crossroad.

Ames, Roger, trans. (1993). *Sun-tzu the Art of Warfare: The First English Translation Incorporating the Recently Discovered Yin-ch'üeh-shan Texts*. New York: Ballantine Books.

Anglican Church of Canada, The Task Force Report to the General Synod 1986. (1987). *Violence against Women: Abuse in Society and Church and Proposals for Change*. Toronto: Anglican Book Centre.

Arendt, Hannah. (1958). *The Human Condition*. Chicago: The University of Chicago Press.

———. (1970). *On Violence*. New York: Harcourt, Brace & World.

Aristotle. (1929). *The Physics Volume I*. Cambridge: Harvard University Press.

———. (1929). *The Physics Volume II*. Cambridge: Harvard University Press.

———. (1934). *Nicomachean Ethics*. Cambridge: Harvard University Press.

Bachofen, J. J. (1967). *Myth, Religion and Mother Right*. Princeton: Princeton University Press.

Bainton, Roland. (1960). *Christian Attitudes toward War and Peace: A Historical Survey and Critical Re-evaluation*. Nashville: Abingdon Press.

Barbé, Dominic. (1989). *A Theology of Conflict and Other Writings on Nonviolence*. Maryknoll: Orbis Books.

Barbour, Ian G., ed. (1973). *Western Man and Environmental Ethics*. Reading, MA: Addison-Wesley.

Baron, Larry and Murray Straus. (1989). *Four Theories of Rape in American Society: A State-Level Analysis*. New Haven: Yale University Press.

Bender, Gretchen, and Timothy Druckrey. (1994). *Culture on the Brink: Ideologies of Technology*. Seattle: Bay Press.

Beneke, Timothy. (1982). *Men on Rape*. New York: St. Martin's Press.

Bettelheim, Bruno. (1983). *Freud and Man's Soul*. New York: Alfred A. Knopf.

Bogue, Ronald, and Marcel Cornis-Pope, eds. (1996). *Violence and Mediation in Contemporary Culture*. Albany: State University of New York Press.

Bombeck, Erma. (1987). *Family: The Ties That Bind . . . and Gag!* New York: MacGraw-Hill Book Company.

Bonino, José Miguez. (1983). *Toward a Christian Political Ethics*. Philadelphia: Fortress Press.

Borchert, David, and Donald Stewart, eds. (1979). *Being Human in a Technological Age*. Athens: Ohio University Press.

Bowlby, John. (1984). "Psychoanalysis as a Natural Science," in *Psychoanalytic Psychology* 1 (1).

Bradshaw, John. (1988). *Bradshaw On: The Family, a Revolutionary Way of Self Discovery*. Deerfield Beach, FL: Health Communications, Inc.

Brandt, Allan. (1987). *No Magic Bullet*. New York: Oxford University Press.

Brown, Robert M. (1987). *Religion and Violence*. Philadelphia: The Westminister Press.

Brownmiller, Susan. (1975). *Against Our Will*. New York: Simon and Schuster.

Bush, Vannevar. (1996). "As We May Think," in *Interactions*, March, Volume 111.2. Originally printed in *The Atlantic Monthly*, July 1945.

Butterfield, Herbert. (1957). *The Origins of Modern Science: 1300–1800*. London: G. Bell and Sons, Ltd.

Calhoun, Cheshire, and Robert C. Solomon. (1984). *What Is an Emotion? Classical Readings in Philosophical Psychology*. New York: Oxford University Press.

Cameron, Julia. (1992). *The Artist's Way: A Spiritual Path to Higher Creativity*. New York: Jeremy P. Tarcher/Perigree Books.

Campbell, Joseph. (1973). *The Hero with a Thousand Faces*. Princeton: Princeton University Press.

Cantor, Norman. (1969). *Medieval History: The Life and Death of a Civilization*. New York: Macmillan Publishing Co., Inc.

Chapman, Abraham, ed. (1975). *Literature of the American Indians: Views and Interpretations*. New York: Meridian.

Chidley, Joe. (1996). "Toxic TV: Is TV Violence Contributing to Aggression in Kids?" in *Maclean's*, June 17.

Clagett, M. (1955). *Greek Science in Antiquity*. New York: Abelard-Schuman.

Cohen, Alfred. (1981). *The Tremendum.* New York: Crossroad.

Dallmayr, Fred. (1981). *Twilight of Subjectivity: Contributions to a Post-Individualist Theory of Politics.* Amherst: The University of Massachusetts Press.

Danica, Elly. (1988). *Don't: A Woman's Word.* Charlottetown: Gynergy Books.

Dark, Jay, Karl Ederle, Christine Winkel. (1994). *Nordstrom: A Paradigm Shift.* Seattle: Nordstrom Business Policy/Marketing 590, Winter Report.

Dean, William. (1988). *History: The New Historicism in American Religious Thought.* New York: State University of New York Press.

Derrida, Jacques. (1978). *Writing and Difference.* Chicago: The University of Chicago Press.

———. (1981). *Positions.* Chicago: The University of Chicago Press.

DiCenso, James. (1990). *Hermeneutics and the Disclosure of Truth: A Study in the Work of Heidegger, Gadamer, and Ricoeur.* Charlottesville: University Press of Virginia.

Dinnerstein, Dorothy. (1976). *The Mermaid and the Minotaur: Sexual Arrangements and Human Malaise.* New York: HarperCollins Publishers.

Douglas, Mary. (1966). *Purity and Danger.* London: Routledge & Kegan Paul.

Dumouchel, Paul. (1987). *Violence and Truth: On the Work of René Girard.* London: The Athlone Press.

Dunlop, Charles, and Rob Kling, eds. (1991). *Computerization and Controversy: Value Conflicts and Social Choices.* Boston: Academic Press.

Dworkin, Andrea. (1976). *Our Blood.* New York: Harper & Row.

Ekman, Paul, ed. (1982). *Emotion in the Human Face.* Cambridge: Cambridge University Press.

Eliade, Mircea. (1954). *The Myth of the Eternal Return or, Cosmos and History.* Princeton: Princeton University Press.

Ellul, Jacques. (1964). *The Technological Society.* New York: Alfred Knopf.

———. (1980). *The Technological System.* New York: Continuum.

Elshtain, Jean B. (1981). *Public Man, Private Woman: Women in Social and Political Thought.* Princeton: Princeton University Press.

Erikson, Erik. (1968). *Identity: Youth and Crisis.* New York: W. W. Norton & Company.

Ferzoco, G. P. (1985). *Bernard of Clairvaux and Early Cistercian Thought regarding the Salvific Role of Violence in Twelfth-Century Christian Society.* Master's Thesis, Trent University.

Figley, Charles, ed. (1995). *Compassion Fatigue: Coping with Secondary Traumatic Stress Disorder in Those Who Treat the Traumatized.* New York: Brunner/Mazel.

Fingarette, Herbert. (1972). *Confucius: The Secular as Sacred.* New York: Harper & Row, Publishers.

Fiorenza, Elizabeth Schüssler. (1983). *In Memory of Her: A Feminist Theological Reconstruction of Christian Origins.* New York: Crossroad.

Flax, Jane. (1990). *Thinking Fragments: Psychoanalysis, Feminism, and Postmodernism in the Contemporary West.* Berkeley: University of California Press.

Foucault, Michel. (1965). *Madness and Civilization.* New York: Vintage Books.

———. (1979). *Discipline and Punish: The Birth of the Prison.* New York: Vintage Books.

———. (1980). *The History of Sexuality, Volume I: An Introduction.* New York: Vintage Books.

———. (1980). *Power/Knowledge: Selected Interviews and Other Writings 1972–1977.* New York: Pantheon.

Franklin, Ursula. (1990). *The Real World of Technology.* Toronto: CBC Enterprises.

Fraser, Nancy. (1989). *Unruly Practices: Power, Discourse and Gender in Contemporary Social Theory.* Minneapolis: University of Minnesota Press.

Freud, Sigmund. (1961). *Beyond the Pleasure Principle.* London: The Hogarth Press.

———. (1961). *Civilization and Its Discontents.* New York: W. W. Norton & Company. Trans. James Strachey.

———. (1984). *On Metapsychology: The Theory of Psychoanalysis (Beyond the Pleasure Principle, The Ego and the Id and other works).* New York: Penguin Books. Trans. James Strachey.

Frye, Northrop. (1990). *The Cultural Development of Canada.* An Address Delivered to the Social Sciences and Humanities Research Council of Canada and Associated Scholars at Hart House, University of Toronto, October 17, 1990.

———. (1990). *Myth and Metaphor: Selected Essays 1974–1988.* Charlottesville: University Press of Virginia.

Gadamer, Hans Georg. (1975). *Truth and Method.* New York: Crossroad.

———. (1976). *Philosophical Hermeneutics.* Berkeley: University of California Press.

Gaylin, Willard, Ruth Macklin, and Tabitha Powledge. (1981). *Violence and the Politics of Research.* New York: Plenum Press.

Geen, Russell, and Edward Donnerstein, eds. (1983). *Aggression: Theoretical and Empirical Reviews.* New York: Academic Press.

Geertz, Clifford. (1973). *The Interpretation of Cultures.* New York: Basic Books.

Georges, R. (1968). *Studies on Mythology.* Homewood: The Dorsey Press.

Gervasi, Frank. (1989). *The Violent Decade.* New York: W. W. Norton & Company.

Gibbs, Lee, and W. Taylor Stevenson, eds. (1975). *Myth and the Crisis of Histori-cal Consciousness.* Missoula: Scholars Press.

Giller, Earl, Jr., ed. (1990) *Biological Assessment and Treatment of Posttraumatic Stress Disorder.* Washington, D.C.: American Psychiatric Press, Inc.

Gilligan, Carol. (1982). *In a Different Voice: Psychological Theory and Women's Development.* Cambridge: Harvard University Press.

Girard, René. (1961). *Deceit, Desire, and the Novel.* Baltimore: The Johns Hopkins Press. Trans. Yvonne Freccero.

————. (1972). *Violence and the Sacred.* Baltimore: The Johns Hopkins University Press.

————. (1986). *The Scapegoat.* Baltimore: The Johns Hopkins University Press.

————. (1987). *Things Hidden since the Foundation of the World.* Stanford: Stanford University Press.

Goodchild, Paul. (1981). *J. Robert Oppenheimer: Shatterer of Worlds.* Boston: Houghton Mifflin Company.

Graham, H. D. (1971). *Violence: The Crisis of American Confidence.* Baltimore: The Johns Hopkins Press.

Grimm, Jacob. (1883). *Teutonic Mythology.* London: George Bell and Sons.

Groebel, J., and R. Hinde. (1989). *Aggression and War.* Cambridge: Cambridge University Press.

Grossberg, L., C. Nelson, and P. Treichler. (1992). *Cultural Studies.* New York: Routledge.

Guberman, Connie, and M. Wolfe. (1985). *No Safe Place: Violence against Women and Children.* Toronto: The Women's Press.

Gutierrez, Gustavo. (1973). *A Theology of Liberation: History, Politics and Salva-tion.* Maryknoll: Orbis Books.

Habermas, Jürgen. (1968). *Knowledge and Human Interests.* Boston: Beacon Press.

————. (1988). *On the Logic of the Social Sciences.* Cambridge: Polity Press. Trans. Shierry Weber Nicholsen and Jerry A. Stark.

Hacking, Ian, ed. (1981). *Scientific Revolutions.* Oxford: Oxford University Press.

Hall, Calvin. (1982). *A Primer of Freudian Psychology.* New York: Mentor Books.

Hammerton-Kelly, Robert, ed. (1987). *Violent Origins: Walter Burkert, René Girard and Jonathan Z. Smith on Ritual Killing and Cultural Formation.* Stanford: Stanford University Press.

Hardison, O. B., Jr. (1989). *Disappearing through the Skylight: Culture and Technology in the Twentieth Century.* New York: Penguin Books.

Hawking, Stephen W. (1988). *A Brief History of Time: From the Big Bang to Black Holes.* Toronto: Bantam Books.

Headrick, Daniel. (1991). *The Invisible Weapon: Telecommunications and International Politics 1851–1945.* Oxford: Oxford University Press.

Hearst, Norman, Thomas B. Newman, and Stephen B. Hulley. (1986). "Delayed Effects of the Military Draft on Mortality," in *The New England Journal of Medicine,* 314: 620–24.

Hegel, G. W. F. (1956). *The Philosophy of History.* New York: Dover Publications.

———. (1977). *The Phenomenology of Spirit.* Oxford: Oxford University Press.

Heidegger, Martin. (1962). *Being and Time.* New York: Harper & Row. Trans. J. Macquarrie and E. Robinson.

———. (1977). *The Question concerning Technology and Other Essays.* San Francisco: Harper & Row. Trans. W. Lovitt.

Helman, Cecil. (1991). *Body Myths.* London: Chatto & Windus.

Herman, Edward, and Noam Chomsky. (1988). *Manufacturing Consent: The Political Economy of the Mass Media.* New York: Pantheon.

Herman, Judith Lewis. (1992). *Trauma and Recovery: The Aftermath of Violence- From Domestic Abuse to Political Terror.* New York: Basic Books.

High Performance Computing and Communications: Toward a National Information Infrastructure, A Report by the Committee on Physical, Mathematical and Engineering Sciences; Federal Coordinating Council for Science, Engineering and Technology; Office of Science and Technology Policy, Washington, D.C., 1994.

Hincks Institute. (1993). *Reclaiming Childhood: Responsible Solutions to TV Violence and Our Children (Conference Report).* Toronto: C. M. Hincks Institute.

Hofstadter, R., and M. Wallace. (1970). *American Violence: A Documentary History.* New York: Alfred A. Knopf.

Horkheimer, Max. (1974). *Critique of Instrumental Reason.* New York: Continuum.

Horkheimer, Max, and Theodor Adorno. (1944). *Dialectic of Enlightenment.* New York: Seabury Press.

Husserl, Edmund. (1960). *Cartesian Meditations.* The Hague: Martinus Nijoff.

———. (1962). *Ideas: General Introduction to Pure Phenomenology.* New York: Collier Books.

Hutcheon, Linda. (1988). *A Poetics of Postmodernism: History, Theory, Fiction.* New York: Routledge.

Ihde, Don. (1971). *Hermeneutic Phenomenology: The Philosophy of Paul Ricoeur.* Evanston: Northwestern University Press.

Jack, Dana Crowley. (1991). *Silencing the Self: Women and Depression.* Cambridge: Harvard University Press.

Jaggar, A., and S. R. Bordo. (1989). *Gender/Body/Knowledge: Feminist Reconstructions of Being and Knowing.* New Brunswick: Rutgers University Press.

Jameson, Frederic. (1981). *The Political Unconscious.* Ithaca: Cornell University Press.

Johansen, Robert. (1991). "Teams for Tomorrow," plenary speech in the *Proceedings of the Twenty-Fourth Hawaii International Conference on Systems Science.* January 8–11.

Jonas, Hans. (1984). *The Imperative of Responsibility: In Search of an Ethics for a Technological Age.* Chicago: The University of Chicago Press.

Kamenka, E. (1983). *The Portable Karl Marx.* Middlesex: Penguin Books.

Kemp, T. P., and D. Rasmussen. (1988). *The Narrative Path: The Later Works of Paul Ricoeur.* Cambridge: The MIT Press.

Keohane, N., M. Rosaldo, and B. C. Gelpi. (1982). *Feminist Theory: A Critique of Ideology.* Chicago: The University of Chicago Press.

Kesey, Ken. (1962). *One Flew over the Cuckoo's Nest: A Novel.* New York: Viking Press.

Kipnis, Aaron. (1991). *Knights without Armor: A Practical Guide for Men in Quest of Masculine Soul.* Los Angeles: Jeremy Tarcher.

Klemm, David. (1983). *The Hermeneutical Theory of Paul Ricoeur: A Constructive Analysis.* Lewisburg: Bucknell University Press.

Klenig, J. (1985). *Ethical Issues in Psychosurgery.* London: George Allen and Unwin.

Koerus, Julian, alias Elmo Karm. (1945). "To the West." Unpublished manuscript.

Kohn, Alfie. (1990). *The Brighter Side of Human Nature: Altruism and Empathy in Everyday Life.* New York: Basic Books.

Kranzberg, Melvin, and Carroll W. Pursell, Jr., eds. (1967). *Technology in Western Civilization: The Emergence of Modern Industrial Society Earliest Times to 1900: Volume I and II.* New York: Oxford University Press.

Larsen, Knud. (1976). *Aggression: Myths and Models.* Chicago: Nelson-Hall.

Lattimore, Richard, trans. (1951). *The Iliad of Homer.* Chicago: The University of Chicago Press.

Lawlor, Leonard (1992). *Imagination and Chance: the Difference between the Thought of Ricoeur and Derrida.* Albany: State University of New York Press.

Lerner, Gerda. (1986). *The Creation of Patriarchy.* New York: Oxford University Press.

Levinas, Emmanuel. (1969). *Totality and Infinity.* Pittsburgh: Duquesne University Press.

Levine, Arnold J. (1992). *Viruses.* New York: Scientific American Library.

Lindsay, Paul, and Donald Norman. (1972). *Human Information Processing: An Introduction to Psychology.* New York: Academic Press.

Lindy, Jacob. (1988). *Vietnam: A Casebook.* New York: Brunner /Mazel.

Little, David, and Sumner Twiss. (1978). *Comparative Ethics.* San Francisco: Harper & Row, Publishers.

Littlewood, Roland, and Maurice Lipsedge. (1989). *Aliens and Alienists: Ethnic Minorities and Psychiatry.* London: Unwin Hyman. Second Edition.

Lorenz, Konrad. (1963). *On Aggression.* London: Methuen & Co. Ltd.

Löwith, Karl. (1964). *From Hegel to Nietzsche: The Revolution in Nineteenth-Century Thought.* New York: Holt, Rinehart, and Winston.

Luhmann, Niklas. (1979). *Trust and Power.* New York: John Wiley & Sons.

Luyckx, Marc. (1992). "Religions Confronted with Science and Technology: Churches and Ethics after Prometheus," exploratory Report, Forecasting and Assessment in Science and Technology. Brussels: Commission of the European Communities.

Lyotard, Jean Francois. (1988). *The Postmodern Condition: A Report on Knowledge.* Minneapolis: University of Minnesota Press.

MacIntyre, Alasdair. (1984). *After Virtue.* Notre Dame: University of Notre Dame Press.

Manes, Stephen, and Paul Andrews. (1994). *Gates: How Microsoft's Mogul Reinvented an Industry and Made Himself the Richest Man in America.* New York: Touchstone.

Marcuse, Herbert. (1955). *Eros and Civilization: A Philosophical Inquiry into Freud.* Boston: Beacon Press.

———. (1964). *One-Dimensional Man.* Boston: Beacon Press.

Mark, Vernon, and Frank Ervin. (1970). *Violence and the Brain.* New York: Harper & Row.

Masson, Jeffrey Moussaeiff. (1995). *When Elephants Weep: The Emotional Lives of Animals.* New York: Delacorte.

May, H., and B. Metzger, eds. (1977). *The New Oxford Annotated Bible with the Apocryphia.* New York: Oxford University Press.

McKenna, Andrew. (1992). *Violence and Difference: Girard, Derrida, and Deconstruction.* Urbana: University of Illinois Press.

McLuhan, Marshall. (1964). *Understanding Media: The Extensions of Man.* New York: Mentor.

McLuhan, Marshall, and Quintin Fiore. (1968). *War and Peace in the Global Village.* Toronto: Touchstone.

McMurtry, John. (1978). *The Structure of Marx's World-View.* Princeton: Princeton University Press.

Merchant, Carolyn. (1980). *The Death of Nature: Women, Ecology and the Scientific Revolution.* New York: Harper & Row.

Miller, Alice. (1981). *The Drama of the Gifted Child: The Search for the True Self.* New York: Basic Books.

————. (1984). *For Your Own Good: Hidden Cruelty in Child-Rearing and the Roots of Violence.* New York: Farrar-Strauss-Giroux.

————. (1990). *The Untouched Key: Tracing Childhood Trauma in Creativity and Destructiveness.* London: Virago Press.

Montagu, Ashley, ed. (1968). *Man and Aggression.* New York: Oxford University Press.

Moraga, C., and G. Anzaldúa. (1983). *This Bridge Called My Back: Writings by Radical Women of Color.* New York: Kitchen Table/Women of Color Press.

Moyer, K. E. (1987). *Violence and Aggression: A Physiological Perspective.* New York: Paragon House.

Mydans, Carl, and Shelley Mydans. (1968). *The Violent Peace.* New York: Atheneum.

Negroponte, Nicholas. (1995). *Being Digital.* New York: Alfred A. Knopf.

————. (1995). "The Balance of Trade of Ideas," in *Wired,* April.

————. (1995). "Being Decimal," in *Wired,* November.

Nelson, Joyce. (1987). *The Perfect Machine: TV in the Nuclear Age.* Toronto: Between the Lines.

Neu, Jerome, ed. (1991). *The Cambridge Companion to Freud*. Cambridge: Cambridge University Press.

NeXT WebObjects. (1996) Redwood City, CA: NeXT Software, Inc.

Nicolaides, Kimon. (1969). *The Natural Way to Draw: A Working Plan for Art Study*. Boston: Houghton Mifflin Company.

Nietzsche, Friederich. (1980). *On the Advantage and Disadvantages of History for Life*. Indianapolis: Hackett Publishing Co.

Noble, David. (1984). *The Forces of Production: A Social History of Industrial Automation*. New York: Alfred A. Knopf, Inc.

Noble, Kathleen. (1994). *The Sound of the Silver Horn: Reclaiming the Heroism in Contemporary Women's Lives*. New York: Fawcett Columbine.

Nozick, Richard. (1974). *Anarchy, State and Utopia*. New York: Basic Books, Inc.

Ochberg, Frank. (1988). *Post-Traumatic Therapy and Victims of Violence*. New York: Brunner/Mazel.

Ondaatje, Michael. (1992). *The English Patient*. Toronto: McClelland & Stewart.

Opposite Sex, The. (1993). Videocassette. Hunter's Hill, N.S.W. Australia: Robin Hughes and Associates.

Orwell, George. (1961). *1984*. New York: Signet.

Pelczynski, Z. A. (1971). *Hegel's Political Philosophy: Problems and Perspectives*. Cambridge: Cambridge University Press.

Pool, Ithiel de Sola. (1990). *Technologies without Boundaries: On Telecommunications in a Global Age*. Cambridge: Harvard University Press. Ed. E. Noam.

Popcorn, Faith. (1992). *The Popcorn Report*. New York: HarperBusiness.

Postman, Neil. (1992). *Technopoly: The Surrender of Culture to Technology*. New York: Vintage Books.

Poupard, Paul avec une Déclaration de Jean-Paul II. (1983). *Galilei: 350 ans d'historie 1633–1983*. Tournai: Desclée International.

Presley, Priscilla Beaulieu. (1985). *Elvis and Me*. New York: G. P. Putnam's Sons. With Sandra Harmon.

Puhvel, M. (1979). *Beowulf and Celtic Tradition*. Waterloo: Wilfred Laurier University Press.

Purves, Dale. (1988). *Body and Brain: A Trophic Theory of Neural Connections*. Cambridge: Harvard University Press.

Randall, Melanie. (1989). *The Politics of Woman Abuse: Understanding the Issues*. Toronto: Education Wife Assault.

Rapoport, Anatol. (1974). *Conflict in Man-Made Environment*. Baltimore: Penguin Books.

———. (1989). *The Origins of Violence: Approaches to the Study of Conflict*. New York: Paragon House.

Reagan, Charles E., and David Stewart. (1978). *The Philosophy of Paul Ricoeur: An Anthology of His Work*. Boston: Beacon Press.

Rheingold, Howard. (1993). *The Virtual Community: Homesteading on the Electronic Frontier*. New York: HarperPerrenial.

Rice, D., and J. Stambaugh. (1979). *Sources for the Study of Greek Religion*. Missoula: Scholars Press.

Ricoeur, Paul. (1967). *The Symbolism of Evil*. Boston: Beacon Press.

———. (1970). *Freud and Philosophy: An Essay on Interpretation*. New Haven: Yale University Press.

———. (1974). *Political and Social Essays*. Athens: Ohio University Press. Ed. D. Stewart and J. Bien.

———. (1976). *Interpretation Theory: Discourse and the Surplus of Meaning*. Fort Worth: The Texas Christian University Press.

———. (1977). *The Rule of Metaphor: Multi-disciplinary Studies of the Creation of Meaning in Language*. Toronto: University of Toronto Press.

———. (1984). *Time and Narrative, Volume I*. Chicago: University of Chicago Press. Trans. Kathleen McLaughlin and David Pellauer.

———. (1986). *Lectures on Ideology and Utopia*. New York: Columbia University Press.

Rodgers, Karen. (1994). "Wife Assault in Canada," *Statistics Canada-Catalogue 11–008C: Canadian Social Trends*. Autumn 1994.

Ropp, Theodore. (1962). *War in the Modern World*. New York: Collier Books.

Roy, Maria, ed. (1982). *The Abusive Partner: An Analysis of Domestic Battering*. New York: Van Nostrand Reinhold.

Ruether, Rosemary Radford. (1983). *Sexism and God Talk: Toward a Feminist Theology*. Boston: Beacon Press.

Russell, Jeffrey Burton. (1972). *Witchcraft in the Middle Ages*. Ithaca: Cornell University Press.

Saint Exupéry, Antoine. (1943). *The Little Prince*. New York: Harcourt Brace Jovanovich.

Sams Publishing, (1993). *On the Cutting Edge of Technology*. Carmel: Sams Publishing. 1993.

Sanday, Peggy Reeves. (1981). "The Socio-cultural Context of Rape," *Journal of Social Issues*, 37.

Santoli, Al. (1981). *Everything We Had: An Oral History of the Vietnam War by Thirty-three American Soldiers Who Fought It.* New York: Ballantine Books.

Schrag, Calvin O. (1986). *Communicative Praxis and the Space of Subjectivity.* Bloomington: Indiana University Press.

Schutz, Alfred. (1975). *Collected Papers III: Studies in Phenomenological Philosophy.* The Hague: Martinus Nijoff.

Shnayerson, Michael. (1996). "Natural Born Opponents." *Vanity Fair.* July.

Snow, C. P. (1964). *The Two Cultures and a Second Look.* Cambridge: Cambridge University Press.

Sokolowski, Robert. (1964). *The Formation of Husserl's Concept of Constitution.* The Hague: Martinus Nijoff.

Spariosu, Mihai. (Forthcoming). *The Wreath of Wild Olive: Play, Liminality, and the Study of Literature.* Albany: State University of New York Press.

Stanko, Elizabeth. (1990). *Everyday Violence: How Women and Men Experience Sexual and Physical Danger.* London: Pandora Press.

Stanley, Manfred. (1978). *The Technological Conscience: Survival and Dignity in an Age of Expertise.* Chicago: The University of Chicago Press.

Stavrianos, L. S. (1981). *Global Rift: The Third World Comes of Age.* New York: William Morrow and Company.

Sussman, Les, and Sally Bordwell. (1981). *The Rapist File.* New York: Chelsea House.

Swinth, Robert L. (1967). "The Establishment of the Trust Relationship," *Journal of Conflict Resolution* (11) 3:335.

Talbot, Winthrop. (1917). *Americanization.* New York: H. W. Wilson Co.

Taylor, Mark C. (1984). *Erring: A Postmodern A/Theology.* Chicago: The University of Chicago Press.

Thistlethwaite, Susan. (1989). *Sex, Race and God: Christian Feminism in Black and White.* New York: Crossroad.

Thomas, Frank, and Ollie Johnston. (1981). *The Illusion of Life: Disney Animation.* New York: Hyperion.

Toffler, Alvin. (1990). *Powershift: Knowledge, Wealth, and Violence at the Edge of the Twenty First Century.* Toronto: Bantam Books.

Toffler, Alvin, and Heidi. (1993). *War and Anti-War: Survival at the Dawn of the Twenty First Century.* Toronto: Little, Brown and Company.

Tracy, David. (1975). *Blessed Rage for Order*. Minneapolis: Seabury Press.

———. (1981). *The Analogical Imagination*. New York: Crossroad.

———. (1987). *Plurality and Ambiguity: Hermeneutics, Religion, and Hope*. San Francisco: Harper & Row.

Trigg, Roger. (1970). *Pain and Emotion*. Oxford: Clarendon Press.

Tuchman, Barbara. (1978). *A Distant Mirror: The Calamitous Fourteenth Century*. New York: Ballantine Books.

Tucker, R., ed. (1978). *The Marx-Engels Reader*. New York: W. W. Norton and Company.

Turkle, Sherry. (1984). *The Second Self: Computers and the Human Spirit*. New York: Simon & Schuster.

———. (1995). *Life on the Screen: Identity in the Age of the Internet*. New York: Simon & Schuster.

Twain, Mark. (1971). *The War Prayer*. New York: Harper & Row.

Valenstein, Elliot. (1965). *Great and Desperate Cures*. New York: Basic Books.

———. (1980). *The Psychosurgery Debate*. San Francisco: W. H. Freeman and Company.

Valzelli, Luigi. (1981). *Psychobiology of Agression and Violence*. New York: Raven Press.

Van Creveld, Martin. (1991). *Technology and War: From 2000 B.C. to the Present*. New York: The Free Press.

Van den Brande, Liev. (1993). "R & D on Telematic Systems in the European Community: The Case of Flexible and Distance Learning," in *Proceedings of Multimedia Communications '93 Conference*, Banff, Alberta, April 13–16. Amsterdam: IOS Press.

Villa-Vecencio, Charles. (1988). *Theology and Violence: The South African Debate*. Grand Rapids: William B. Eerdmans Publishing Co.

Viljoen, L. (1990). *Bernard of Clairvaux: Nine Hundred Years*. Pretoria: University of South Africa.

Virgillo, C., and N. Lindstrom. (1985). *Woman as Myth and Metaphor in Latin American Literature*. Columbia: University of Missouri Press.

Visser, Margaret. (1991). *The Rituals of Dinner: The Origins, Evolution and Eccentricities and Meaning of Table Manners*. Toronto: HarperPerennial.

Webster's New Collegiate Dictionary. Springfield: G. & C. Merriam Company. 1981.

Weinberg, Albert. (1935). *Manifest Destiny.* Baltimore: The Johns Hopkins Press.

Weiser, Mark. (1995). "The Computer for the 21st Century," in *Scientific American: The Computer in the 21st Century Special Issue.*

Welch, Sharon. (1990). *A Feminist Ethic of Risk.* Minneapolis: Fortress Press.

Wellner, Pierre, Wendy Mackay, and Ron Gold. (1993). "Computer-Augmented Environments: Back to the Real World," in *Communications of the ACM,* July, Vol. 36, No. 7.

Wiener, Philip P., and John Fisher. (1974). *Violence and Aggression in the History of Ideas.* New Brunswick: Rutgers University Press.

Wilson, John P., and Beverley Raphael, eds. (1993). *International Handbook of Traumatic Stress Syndromes.* New York: Plenum Press.

Wolf, Naomi. (1991). *The Beauty Myth: How Images of Beauty Are Used against Women.* New York: Random House.

Wyschogrod, Edith. (1985). *Spirit in Ashes.* New Haven: Yale University Press.

Yllo, K., and M. Bograd, eds. (1989). *The Politics of Woman Abuse: Understanding the Issues.* Beverley Hills: Sage.

Zehr, Howard. (1986). *Death as a Penalty: A Moral, Practical, and Theological Discussion.* Elkhart, Indiana: MCC U.S. Office of Criminal Justice.

INDEX